The integrated Rule-Oriented Data System (iRODS 4.0) Microservice Workbook

Arcot Rajasekar
Terrell Russell
Jason Coposky
Antoine de Torcy
Hao Xu
Michael Wan
Reagan W. Moore
Wayne Schroeder
Sheau-Yen Chen
Mike Conway
Jewel H. Ward

The integrated Rule-Oriented Data System (iRODS 4.0) Microservice Workbook
by Arcot Rajasekar, Terrell Russell, Jason Coposky, Antoine de Torcy, Hao Xu, Michael Wan, Reagan W. Moore, Wayne Schroeder, Sheau-Yen Chen, Mike Conway, and Jewel H. Ward

Published by the Renaissance Computing Institute, 100 Europa Drive, Suite 540, Chapel Hill, North Carolina, 27517 USA.

May 2015

ISBN-10: 1511732776
ISBN-13: 978-1511732772

ABSTRACT

The Integrated Rule-Oriented Data System (iRODS) is open source data management software used by research organizations and government agencies worldwide. iRODS is released as a production-level distribution aimed at deployment in mission critical environments. It virtualizes data storage resources, so users can take control of their data, regardless of where and on what device the data is stored. As data volumes grow and data services become more complex, iRODS is increasingly important in data management. The development infrastructure supports exhaustive testing on supported platforms; plug-in support for microservices, storage resources, drivers, and databases; and extensive documentation, training and support services.

This book is a microservice workbook, with descriptions of the input and output parameters and usage examples for each of the available microservices. Together with the iRODS Primer, a community may use this book to assemble a data management infrastructure that reliably enforces their management policies, automates administrative tasks, and validates assessment criteria. The microservices referenced in this book are supported by iRODS version 4.0, an open source release from the iRODS Consortium, http://irods.org/consortium.

TABLE OF CONTENTS

TABLE OF FIGURES

PREFACE

Technologies for the management of distributed collections have evolved significantly over the last twenty years. The original data grid software, the Storage Resource Broker (SRB), focused on the consistent management of the properties of a collection across all operations performed upon collection contents. This meant that all policies were hard coded within the software framework to ensure that consistency guarantees could be met as files were moved between storage systems or were modified. While the SRB has been highly successful software that has managed petabytes of data distributed around the world, each new application and corresponding set of policies has required changes to the software framework.

The new generation of data grids, represented by the integrated Rule-Oriented Data System (iRODS), extracts policies from the software framework and manages them as computer actionable rules that are enforced by a distributed Rule Engine. At the place where a consistency constraint was present in the Storage Resource Broker, the iRODS data grid places a policy enforcement point. When an action causes the traversal of a policy enforcement point, a rule base is accessed to determine whether a policy has been defined and should be applied. A distributed rule engine then executes the associated computer actionable rule. This makes it possible to manage multiple sets of policies within a distributed collection, with local policies taking precedence. By extracting the policies from the data management framework, it became possible to build generic infrastructure that supports all phases of the data life cycle. Policies appropriate for controlling each stage can be added as the driving purpose behind the management of the collection evolves.

The development of the iRODS data grid has been strongly driven by requirements from multiple user communities. In particular, the application of iRODS in data grids, digital libraries, processing pipelines, and persistent archives has ensured that generic software has been created that can enforce the data management goals of each community. This has resulted in a software framework that is highly extensible, that can be integrated with a wide variety of user interfaces, and that can manage data stored in a wide variety of repositories. It is expected that the use of policy-based data management systems will lead to self-consistent systems that are capable of verifying their internal properties and recovering from any detected problems. Such a system should be able to enforce community specific policies, automate administrative functions, and periodically validate assessment criteria for verifying compliance with the desired policies.

In This Workbook and Reference Manual

The description of policy-based data management systems has been broken down into three separate topic areas.

- A general description of policy-based data management is available in the book: iRODS Primer: integrated Rule-Oriented Data System. The iRODS Primer describes the rule language and collection properties and provides examples of policies for iRODS version 2.5 and earlier. While a list of basic functions (microservices) is provided, no information is given on the input and output variables generated by each microservice.

- A detailed description of each basic function (microservice) provided by iRODS version 3.0 is available in The integrated Rule-Oriented Data System (iRODS 3.0) Micro-service Workbook. The basic functions can be chained together to create procedures that enforce a specific policy. Since there are a variety of desired policies, from automated replication to metadata extraction to creation of derived data products to the validation of assessment criteria, there are many categories of microservices. For each category, a description of the uses of the microservices is provided. For each microservice, a description of the input and output parameters is provided along with an example of the use of the microservice within a rule.

- This book describes advances in the rule language, and lists rule examples for the microservices available in version 4.0 of iRODS. Since version 4.0 supports pluggable microservices, it is possible to easily add new microservices and control functions beyond those listed in this book.

- A description of the policies that are composed from microservices that are in use in production data management environments will be available through the Research Data Alliance. Examples of iRODS policies will be provided to serve as a convenient guide for choosing policies to implement within a new data grid or digital library or preservation environment. The policies are intended to serve as a starter kit for creating community-specific policy sets.

In this iRODS microservices workbook and reference manual, **Part I** provides an introduction to the concept of policy-based data management. Actions requested by clients are trapped at policy enforcement points within the iRODS middleware. At each policy enforcement point, a rule base is consulted to determine which policy to apply. Each policy controls remote procedures that are executed at an iRODS server by the distributed rule engine. A remote procedure is composed by chaining together microservices. State information generated by the procedures are saved in the iCAT metadata catalog. Example procedures include workflows that can query the metadata catalog, retrieve a list of files, and then loop over the file list to implement a desired policy. A more detailed explanation of rule-based data management is available in the iRODS Primer.

Part II describes the rule language syntax that is supported in iRODS versions 3.0-4.0. Extensions to the rule language for iRODS version 4.0 are listed, including support for automating loops over all rows returned by a query, and a dot operator for simplified reference to attributes in key-value pairs.

Part III lists the categories of microservices and the conventions used to name parameters, session variables, and persistent state information. It also describes how to write a new microservice, and discusses the policy enforcement points and persistent state variables available in version 4.0. Not all state information can be queried. There are additional state information attributes used by the data grid. Lists of the policy enforcement points and persistent state variables are provided in the Appendices.

Part IV describes the microservices that are used to implement a procedure that can be run at a remote storage location. The microservices are organized into categories related to core iRODS capabilities and modules that require integration with additional software systems. The core microservices manage collections, manipulate database objects, manipulate data objects, provide support functions, manage the rule engine, manipulate strings, provide workflow functions, support the messaging system, support the iRODS framework, support metadata catalog queries (iCAT), send e-mail, process key-value pairs, support user functions, and support remote database access. Properties about users, collections, files, resources, and rules can be managed. General queries can be issued against the metadata catalog to extract sets of files for further processing. General framework support microservices include setting the number of parallel I/O streams, number of execution threads, and choice of default storage locations for file storage and replication.

The iRODS system uses in-memory structures to manage the exchange of information between micro services. The in-memory structures can be serialized (through packing instructions) for transfer over a network. Specification of the in-memory structures is contained in the
"iRODS/lib/core/include/rodsPackTable.hpp" file
and the
"iRODS/lib/core/include/msParam.hpp" file.
Utility functions that manipulate the structures are defined in
"iRODS/lib/core/src/msParam.cpp".
Packing instructions are defined in
"iRODS/lib/core/include/packStruct.hpp".

Also included in this workbook are the **Authors' Biographies**.

Platform Notes

The microservices that are described can be executed within an iRODS data grid version 4.0 or higher, as of the printing of this book. Note that the structures used to exchange information between microservices continue to evolve. The in-memory structures used by the listed microservices are specified in **Part IV**. The structures required by microservices in future releases of the iRODS software may be more sophisticated and require use of the newer version of iRODS.

Typesetting

The following conventions are used in this book.

1. iRODS Commands in examples and in text are in italics.

    Example 1:
    > mycommandline% *ils*
    > **/tempZone/home/rods/t1:**
    > **file1**
    > **file2**

    Example 2: *icd* "modules/MODNAME"

2. Microservices in text and output from an i-command are in bold.

    Example 1: "FindObjectType" microservice: **msiGetObjType**.

    Example 2:
    > mycommandline% *ils*
    > **/tempZone/home/rods/t1:**
    > **file1**
    > **file2**

3. Filenames and directory paths in text are in straight quotes, "".

    Example 1: The "info.txt" file in a module's top-level directory describes the module.

    Example 2: For instance, those in the "server/re/src" directory are part of the Rule Engine, whereas those in the "clients/icommands/src" directory are command-line tools.

4. Rule examples are indented.
    rulemsiXsltApply(*xsltObjPath, *origObjPath, *BUF)
    {
         msiDataObjCreate(*xmlObjPath, "null", *DEST_FD);
         msiDataObjWrite(*DEST _FD,*BUF,*Written);
         msiDataObjClose(*DEST_FD,*junk);
         msiLoadMetadataFromXml(*origObjPath, *xmlObjPath);
    }
    INPUT *origObjPath="orig.xml", *xmlObjPath="formatted.xml", *xsltObjPath="format_xml.xsl"
    OUTPUT ruleExecOut

Note that all input parameters for a rule are assumed to be entered on a single line. Code examples may appear to be on a new line, when in fact, the line has wrapped due to physical space limitations of this text.

Other Books

The syntax used to express iRODS policies supports invocation of well defined functions called microservices. More information about the syntax can be found at the iRODS wiki at http://wiki.irods.org.

Finally, while this book may serve as a microservice workbook and reference manual for both new and experienced users of iRODS, all levels of users are encouraged to review the first iRODS book, the iRODS Primer. The iRODS Primer covers the following areas in greater depth than this book: *iRODS*; the *iRODS Architecture*; *Rule-Oriented Programming*; the *iRODS Rule System*; *Example Rules*; *Extending iRODS*; *iRODS Shell Commands*; *RuleGen Grammar*; and, *Exercises*.

You may acquire the iRODS Primer from Morgan Claypool:

iRODS Primer: Integrated Rule-Oriented Data System. Morgan & Claypool, 2010. 143 pages, (doi:10.2200/S00233ED1V01Y200912ICR012). Available: http://www.morganclaypool.com/doi/abs/10.2200/S00233ED1V01Y200912ICR012?journalCode=icr

Online Resources: the iRODS Wiki and Doxygen

This microservice reference book covers microservices in more depth than the iRODS Primer. The reference material is current for iRODS version 4.0. The microservice documentation is also available in the iRODS code and online (https://wiki.irods.org/doxygen/). While the content of this workbook is current with the in-code documentation contained in the iRODS 4.0 release, additions and changes may be made to the documentation at each iRODS release. Readers are encouraged to review the microservice documentation in the iRODS code or via the Doxygen output online for the latest versions.

Readers may also want to consider examining the iRODS wiki (http://wiki.irods.org) and the iRODS support mailing list (http://groups.google.com/group/iROD-Chat/) for other iRODS-related information.

How to Contact Us

We have verified the information in this book to the best of our ability. If you find any errors, or have any suggestions for future editions, you may reach us on the iRODS mailing list or via US mail at:

The iRODS Consortium
100 Europa Center, Suite 540
University of North Carolina at Chapel Hill
Chapel Hill, North Carolina 27517
(919) 962-9548

Acknowledgements

This research was supported by:

NSF ITR 0427196, Constraint-Based Knowledge Systems for Grids, Digital Libraries, and Persistent Archives (2004–2007).

NARA supplement to NSF SCI 0438741, Cyberinfrastructure; From Vision to Reality— Developing Scalable Data Management Infrastructure in a Data Grid-Enabled Digital Library System (2005–2006).

NARA supplement to NSF SCI 0438741, Cyberinfrastructure; From Vision to Reality— Research Prototype Persistent Archive Extension (2006–2007).

NSF SDCI 0910431, SDCI Data Improvement: Data Grids for Community Driven Applications (2007–2010).

NSF/NARA OCI 0848296, NARA Transcontinental Persistent Archive Prototype (2008–2010).

NSF OCI 1032732, SDCI Data Improvement: Improvement and Sustainability of iRODS Data Grid Software for Multi-Disciplinary Community Driven Applications (2010-2012).

NSF OCI 0940841, DataNet Federation Consortium (2011-2013).

The views and conclusions contained in this document are those of the authors and should not be interpreted as representing the official policies, either expressed or implied, of the National Archives and Records Administration (NARA), the National Science Foundation (NSF), or the U.S. Government.

The derivation of metadata attributes associated with each rule was supported by Shane Pusz, University of North Carolina at Chapel Hill.

PART I A BRIEF INTRODUCTION TO iRODS

In this chapter:
Microservices Overview
Data Grid Overview
iRODS Overview
Policy-based Data Management Overview
The Rule engine
The In-memory Rule Base
Summary

Policy-based data management systems provide the essential capabilities required to automate administrative tasks, validate assessment criteria, and enforce institutional procedures. The integrated Rule-Oriented Data System (iRODS) represents the state-of-the-art in policy-based distributed data management infrastructure in 2015. The concepts driving the implementation of the iRODS data grid can be categorized as follows:

- There is a driving purpose for the formation of a sharable collection that spans institutions and administrative domains. The purpose represents a community consensus on the reason for assembling the collection.
- The driving purpose determines the set of properties that are possessed by digital objects within the collection. The properties represent a community consensus on appropriate contents for the collection.
- The desired properties are enforced through the specification of policies that are implemented as computer actionable rules. The policies represent a community consensus on how the collection should be managed.
- The policies control the execution of procedures that enforce the desired properties. The procedures are composed by chaining together basic functions (microservices) to assemble a computer executable workflow. The workflow may be executed across the distributed environment.
- The procedures generate state information that tracks the results of the application of all actions on the collection. The state information maintains all consistency information, as well as environment variables used to manage the system.
- The state information can be queried through periodic assessment policies to verify that the desired properties have been preserved. Assessment policies can also manipulate audit trails for tracking compliance over time, or execute procedures to verify integrity of the state information.

This provides an end-to-end environment for building a community consensus, enforcing the consensus, automating administrative functions, and verifying the enforcement of management policies.

The iRODS data grid maps policies to machine actionable rules. Each rule controls the execution of a procedure that either applies an administrative task, or validates a property of a collection, or enforces a required property. The procedures are composed from basic operations that are chained together into workflows. Each basic operation is encapsulated within a C language function called a microservice. The application of the microservice generates state information that is managed by iRODS in a metadata catalog (iCAT). Validation of the properties of the collection is accomplished either through queries on the metadata catalog or through parsing of audit trails. By selecting the appropriate microservices, any desired computer executable procedure can be implemented. By developing the appropriate rules, any computer actionable policy can be enforced. Through use of the distributed data management capabilities of the iRODS data grid, the policies and procedures can be applied to data stored at multiple institutions across a wide variety of storage systems.

This book describes the set of microservices that are provided with release 4.0 of the iRODS data grid. The iRODS software is distributed under an open source BSD license, and is available at http://irods.org. The listed microservices are used in production applications of the iRODS software to support digital libraries, preservation environments, and data grids.

Figure 1 illustrates the concepts behind policy-based data management and the implementation within iRODS. The default iRODS version 4.0 installation provides 11 standard policies related to management of distributed data within a collaboration environment. A standard procedure is provided for each policy. A total of 205 microservices are available for composing new procedures, and a total of 338 persistent state information attributes can be queried. The policies and procedures can be designed to support applications such as archives, data grids, project collections, digital libraries, and processing pipelines.

Each client action is trapped at one or more of the 70 policy enforcement points. A policy is selected from the rule base, the associated procedure is executed, and the persistent state information is updated and stored as an attribute on one of the 7 name spaces managed by iRODS (Users, Files, Collections, Storage systems, Metadata, Rules, and Microservices).

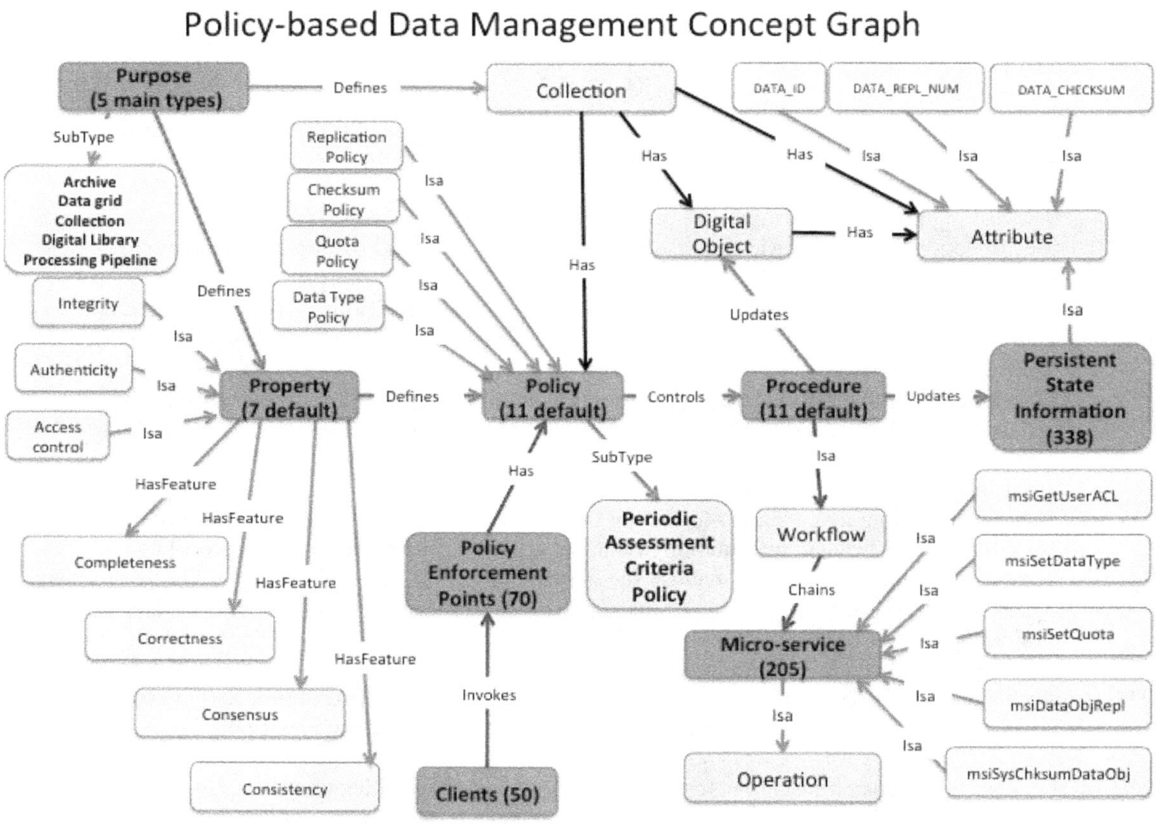

Policy-based Data Management Concept Graph

Figure 1. Implementation of Policy-based Data Management within iRODS

1.1   Microservices Overview

The term "microservice" refers to a C procedure that performs a simple task as part of a distributed workflow system. Each microservice is small and well defined. Application programmers, systems administrators, and system programmers can use existing microservices, but can also write and compile new microservices into server code within the integrated Rule-Oriented Data System (iRODS). This system is a community-driven, open source, middleware data grid that enables researchers, archivists and other managers to share, organize, preserve, and protect sets of digital files. The size of these data sets may range from a few dozen files to hundreds of millions of files, and from a few megabytes in size to petabytes.

The iRODS framework is based upon 16 years of experience with the deployment and production use of the Storage Resource Broker (SRB) data grid technology. The iRODS system combines ideas and technologies from the data grid, digital library, and archives domains to create the core concepts behind policy-based data management. Additional concepts and theories from within computer science include workflows, business rule systems, service-oriented architecture, active databases, transactional systems, constraint-management systems, logic programming, and program verification. The resulting system – iRODS – may be applied as: a digital library for publishing data; a persistent archive for preserving data; a system for large-scale data analysis; a system that gathers collections of real-time sensor data; and a collaboration environment for sharing data.

Microservices are the building blocks upon which procedures and management policies are implemented at the machine-level, regardless of the purpose of the particular iRODS instance. The microservices can be reused by each new application through appropriate chaining into a procedure required by the new application domain policies. Thus, microservices comprise the fundamental building blocks on which a policy-based data management system is built.

1.2   Data Grid Overview

A generic data grid is a system that virtualizes data collections. Data grids manage the properties of a data collection independently of the choice of storage system or database. One implication is that they can organize distributed data into a sharable collection. Another implication is that the data grid can enforce management policies across administrative domains.

A generic data grid has three main characteristics. First, a data grid manages data distributed across multiple storage systems, such as tape archives, file systems, cloud storage, and institutional repositories. Second, it manages collection attributes such as system state information, descriptive metadata, and provenance information. Third, a data grid provides the interoperability mechanisms needed to manage technology evolution, so that when software and hardware become obsolete, newer technology can be integrated with minimal effort.

If a data grid is to act as a digital library, or a persistent archive, or a workflow system for data analysis, or a real-time sensor system, the architecture must also have the ability to meet the diverse requirements of each environment. A digital library publishes data, and the system must support browsing and discovery. A persistent archive preserves data, and the system must be able to manage technology evolution while enforcing authenticity, integrity, chain of custody, and original arrangement. A workflow system provides the ability to analyze data, and the system must be able to integrate data management procedures with data analysis procedures. A real-time sensor system federates sensor data, and the system must be able to manage data within a sensor stream.

The architecture of a data grid that can meet all of the above requirements provides infrastructure independence, enforces management policies, manipulates structured information across distributed resources, is highly modular and extensible, provides scalability mechanisms, and enables community standards. In a production data grid, each community is able to implement different management policies that are specific to a collection or user group or storage resource or file type. Based on the management policies and preservation objectives, assertions about properties of the shared collection can be validated and shown to hold over time. The iRODS data grid provides all of these capabilities.

A collection can have an associated life cycle, with each stage of the life cycle corresponding to a different motivating purpose. Thus a collection may start as a way to organize data within a project. Researchers might build a hierarchical collection that sorts observational data into one directory, sorts analysis results into a second directory, and publications into a third directory. The policies used to manage the collection may assume strong tacit knowledge by the researchers on allowed data formats, descriptive metadata, and provenance metadata. If the collection is shared with researchers at another institution through creation of a data grid, the tacit knowledge should be made explicit. This can be done by creating policies that automate recording of provenance information, manage distribution between the institutions, and manage access controls. The original collection policies are modified to handle the new data sharing environment policies. Similarly, when data are formally published for access by members of a science land engineering discipline, new policies will be needed to enforce application of domain standards for descriptive metadata and data formats. When a processing pipeline is created to generate derived data products, additional policies are needed to control the analysis services. When the data are archived, policies will be needed to manage authenticity, chain of custody, integrity, and original arrangement. Each stage of the collection life cycle requires a modified set of policies for effective management. Since the policies in iRODS are managed in a rule base, it is possible to add new policies over time as the collection purpose changes. As such, iRODS is capable of virtualizing the collection life cycle through evolution of the policies and procedures that are used to manage the data collection.

A policy-based data management system can capture domain knowledge. There are typically three types of knowledge needed to build national-scale cyberinfrastructure: 1) mechanisms that encapsulate the knowledge needed to interact with an existing data repository or information catalog or web service; 2) workflows that orchestrate the processing steps used in data-driven research; and 3) management policies that control assertions about the research products. The iRODS data grid provides three types of mechanisms to encapsulate domain knowledge: 1) microservices that can execute the protocol needed to interact with a remote system, 2) drivers that support execution of iRODS operations on remote data, and 3) policies that implement computer actionable rules. These mechanisms form the basis for generic data management infrastructure.

1.3   iRODS Overview

The iRODS architecture belongs to the Adaptive Middleware Architecture (AMA) class. Middleware is generally designed as a black box that does not allow programmatic changes to the workflow, except for a few predetermined configuration options. Adaptive middleware provides a "glass box" such that users can examine the system processes, understand how they work, and adjust them to meet each users' unique needs. The approach used to implement the AMA within iRODS is Rule-Oriented Programming (ROP). ROP provides the means for a user to customize data management functions by coding the processes that are being performed in iRODS as "rules". When an action is invoked by a particular task, these rules explicitly control the operations (microservices) that are being performed. The execution of rules may be prioritized within the system so that one type of rule is executed prior to another type of rule. Similarly, users may modify the flow of tasks by adding, deleting, or modifying the microservice(s) used within a rule; or by re-writing and recompiling, or deprecating the microservice code itself.

The iRODS adaptive middleware architecture has three major features. First, the iRODS data grid architecture is based on a client-server model that manages the interactions among and between distributed compute and storage resources. The iRODS server maps from the action requested by a client to the protocol required by the local storage system. Second, a metadata catalog, called the iCAT, maintains persistent state and data attributes generated by remote operations in a database of your choice. Third, a distributed Rule Engine controls the execution and enforcement of the Rules (Figure 2). Actions requested by clients are trapped at policy enforcement points, the rule engine is invoked, and the rule base is examined for an appropriate rule to execute. The policy enforcement points are listed in Appendix A along with example policies. Each enforcement point is given a unique name. The rule engine selects the first actionable rule from the rule base for a given policy enforcement point.

The iRODS Server software and the distributed Rule Engine are installed on each storage system. Thus, the elements of the iRODS system include: a Rule Engine and data grid server installed at each storage location; a Rule Base at each storage location that contains the available rules; a central iCAT Metadata Catalog; and multiple clients for accessing the data grid. The iCAT stores the persistent state information as attributes on users, attributes on collections, attributes on files, attributes on resources, and attributes on rules (Figure 2). iRODS uses 338 attributes to manage information about each file, each collection, each storage resource, each user, and each rule. Examples of these stored attributes include the filename, owner, location, checksum, and data expiration date, among others. The attributes are listed in Appendix B, with a short explanation of their meaning. The persistent state attributes can be retrieved from the iCAT catalog, used within rules to determine required processing steps, and updated through invocation of appropriate microservices. The metadata catalog contains all of the information needed to manage the distributed collection, including versions of rules, versions of metadata attributes, system variables, load information, quota information, access controls, queues of deferred operations, and the structure of the data grid itself.

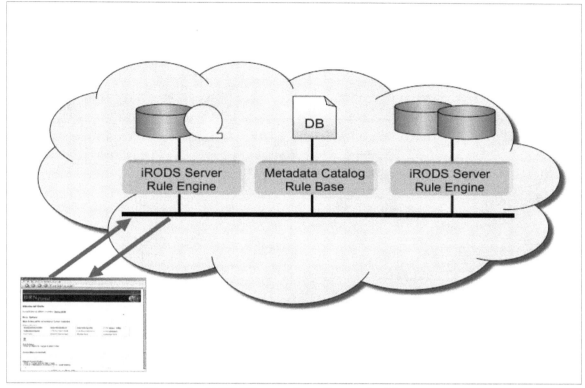

Figure 2 - iRODS Peer-to-Peer Server Architecture

An iCommand (unix shell command) can be executed to list all of the persistent state variables.
    iquest attrs

A rule in the iRODS/clients/icommands/test/rules4.0 directory can be executed to list the policy enforcement points.
    irule –F ruleshowCore.r

In order to access an iRODS server, a user must be authenticated by the iCAT via information exchanged between the client, the iCAT catalog, and the iRODS server. The user may then proceed to invoke the desired procedures on that server. The Rule Engine at the server location applies additional constraints, controls the procedure execution, and passes the output of the operations back to the user's client. The iRODS catalog stores any generated state information.

Session variables are used to capture information about the interaction. Depending upon the type of user action, session variables are available for identification of the user, or of files that are being manipulated, or of storage systems that are being accessed. A list of session variables is provided in Appendix C. Note that not all session variables are available at each policy enforcement point. A table is provided in Appendix C to list which session variables may be used interactively or applied in a policy.

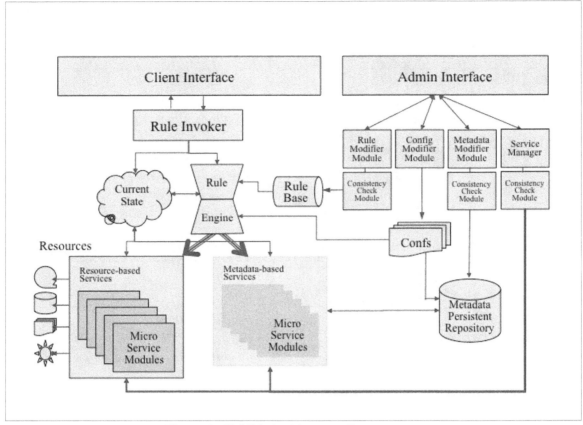

Figure 3 - iRODS Architecture Components

1.4   Policy-based Data Management Overview

iRODS automates the application of data management policies for pre- and post-processing, metadata extraction, loading, replication, distribution, retention, and disposition. The system also automates policies for services such as authentication, auditing, accounting, authorization, and administration. iRODS provides the ability to characterize the management policies required to enforce chain of custody, access restrictions, data placement, data presentation, integrity, and authenticity.

The simple core concepts driving the iRODS design are that every collection is created for a purpose, that every collection has management policies that enforce the collection purpose, and that every policy is implemented through a procedure (composed from microservices). These fundamental concepts are implemented within iRODS technically by breaking them down into four distinguishing characteristics: *workflow virtualization, management policy virtualization, service virtualization,* and *rule virtualization.*

1.   **Workflow virtualization**

The iRODS middleware enables the remote administration of collections of tightly controlled digital objects that are stored across heterogeneous storage locations. The data grid manages distributed objects and related metadata by providing infrastructure-independent procedures that can be run on any type of operating system. Effectively, the microservices issue a standard API that is based on an extension of POSIX I/O. The standard I/O calls are mapped to the storage access protocols required by each type of operating system. Thus, the same procedures are able to run on any computer. Microservices are installed with each iRODS instance at each storage location. iRODS administrators and users "chain" the microservices together to implement macro-level functions, called Actions. An iRODS administrator may control exactly which functions are executed at each storage location.

These procedures may be executed remotely or locally. An administrator may implement a function multiple ways by creating multiple chains of microservices for a particular Action. He or she may then set up the system to "choose" the best microservice by setting up priorities and validation conditions that are evaluated at runtime. Note that an Action corresponds to one of the Policy Enforcement Points.

2. Management policy virtualization

One way to think of priorities and validation conditions is that they are machine-level implementations of management procedures. These individual procedures are expressed in iRODS as management policies in the form of rules. The administrator controls the execution of a chain of one or more microservices via these rules. For example, if the policy of a particular repository is to keep a log of all checksums associated with all files in directory "foo", an administrator would create a list of all checksums associated with the files by chaining together a series of microservices in the form of a "rule" that would create a written log of the checksum values. Specifically, depending on the administrator's requirements, the rule might contain a microservice that gets the checksum value for each file in directory "foo", a microservice that finds the name of each associated file, a microservice that finds the name of the associated directory (e.g., "collection"), and a microservice that writes these values to a log file. The administrator is in control of the data grid, ensuring that even in a distributed environment, all files within a shared collection can be managed under the same policies.

3. Service virtualization

Rule-based data management is operationalized through microservices. The concept behind the design of microservices is that they have well-defined input-output properties, that policies are designed to support consistency verification, and that policies provide error recovery in the form of roll-back procedures. The compositional framework that microservices provide is realized at run-time. One key capability of the iRODS design is that a user does not have to change any management policies during a microservice upgrade. iRODS uses a logical name space for microservices that provides the ability to organize and name them to ensure proper execution independent of any upgrades. The policies can be changed dynamically by modifying the rule base. It is possible to build an environment in which an original collection is managed by an original set of policies and procedures; a new collection can be defined that is controlled by new policies and procedures; and a policy can be written that manages the migration of files from the original collection to the new collection.

4. Rule virtualization

A logical name space for rules provides the ability to version, name, and organize rules in sets that allow for the evolution of the rules themselves. Since 3.0, iRODS supports the management of policies within the iCAT metadata catalog, supports the publication of policies to a remote storage location for inclusion within the local rule base, and supports versioning of policies. The rules control the execution of procedures that are operating system independent. The same procedures can be executed on Windows, or Mac, or Linux computers. This means that the rules can be applied across arbitrary choices of infrastructure. Through use of a distributed rule engine, the policies can be enforced across administrative domains.

1.5   The Rule Engine

The rule engine is the interpreter of rules in the iRODS system. The rule engine can be invoked by any server-side procedure call, including the rule engine itself, using the rule engine application programming interface (API). The rule engine API supports execution of single actions and sequences of actions. An action usually consists of an action name and a list of arguments. Depending on the action name, executing the action may involve calling a microservice or applying a rule.

Policy enforcement points are embedded in the iRODS data grid framework. When an action requested by a client traverses a policy enforcement point, the associated policy is invoked. The iRODS "core.re" file (local rule base) contains policies for each of the policy enforcement points. By convention, a standard set of policy names are used within the "core.re" file. Additional policies can be added to the rule base that can be invoked by explicit execution of a rule through the "irule" command.

An argument to an action may correspond to: an input parameter, whose value is passed from the calling routine to the rule engine; an output parameter, whose value is passed from the rule engine back to the calling routine; or a parameter that is both an input parameter and an output parameter. Figure 4, below, shows the workflow performed by the rule engine when a server-side procedure executes an action through the rule engine API.

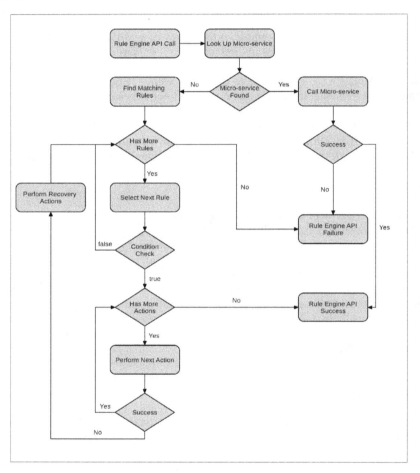

Figure 4 - iRODS Rule Engine Workflow

First, the rule engine tries to look up a rule whose rule name is the same as the action name. If a rule is found, it may cause multiple microservices to be executed. If a microservice succeeds, the microservice should return a success status to the calling routine. If it fails, the microservices can use the rule execution context provided by the rule engine to pass a failure status and error messages back to the calling routine. If the microservice **applyAllRules** is invoked, the rule engine selects all the rules whose rule names are the same as the action name that is passed in through the rule engine API.

The rules selected are prioritized based on how they are read into the rule base of the rule engine. The first rule in the list is checked for validation of its condition. If the condition fails, then the next rule is tried. If no more rules are available, then the action fails and a failure status (negative number) is returned to the calling routine. The rule engine performs optimizations to improve rule lookup efficiency when it loads rules into the rule base, but the optimization does not change the rule lookup semantics.

If the rule condition succeeds, then the microservices in the rule are executed one after the other in the order they are given in the rule. For each action, the rule engine repeats the process described here recursively. If all of the microservices in the rule succeed, then the rule execution is considered a success and a success status (usually 0) is returned to the calling routine. In such a case, the arguments that correspond to output parameters will hold any output values returned by the rule execution and the data structures holding the rule execution context will reflect any modifications that are made by the rule execution.

If one of the microservices fails while executing the chain of actions, the rule engine starts a recovery procedure. For each microservice that is executed, it applies the corresponding recovery microservice defined in the rule. The recovery action for the failed action is performed first, followed by the recovery actions of all the previously successful actions in reverse order. The recovery actions can be defined so that they rollback any side-effects and restore the system to the initial state right before the rule execution.

1.6   The In-memory Rule Base

The In-memory Rule Base is a structure managed in memory that contains the rules that are used in a session. The rules are automatically loaded into memory from a local "core.re" file on initiation of the session. In addition, **msiAdmAddAppRuleStruct** can be called to load additional rules for the session into the memory structure.

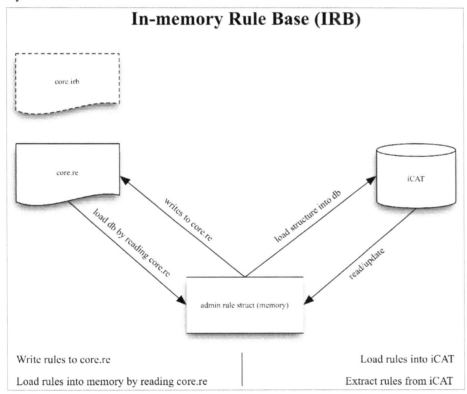

Figure 5 - iRODS In-memory Rule Base

The persistent rules and rule versions are maintained in the iCAT catalog. To load rules into the iCAT, they must first be listed in a ".re" file. This file is loaded into memory using **msiAdmReadRulesFromFileIntoStruct**. The rules are then moved from memory into the iCAT catalog using **msiAdmInsertRulesFromStructIntoDB**. Rules that are loaded into the iCAT catalog cannot be removed. Instead, versions are created for each rule change to enable persistent governance of the data collection. The rule tables in the iCAT catalog comprise a persistent rule base.

The iRODS data grid manages distribution of rules from the persistent rule base into local "core.re" files. Each distributed rule engine reads a local "core.re" file to improve performance, and enable application of local rules. The process for creating a "core.re" file is the inverse of the process for loading rules into the iCAT catalog. **msiAdmRetrieveRulesFromDBIntoStruct** writes rules from the iCAT catalog into the In-memory Rule Base. **msiAdmWriteRulesFromStructIntoFile** can then be used to write a local rule (".re") file.

The In-memory Rule Base manages three types of rules:
1. Rules that are automatically loaded for the session from the local "core.re" file. These rules are indexed to improve rule engine performance.
2. Rules that are session-dependent that are loaded from an ancillary rule file using **msiAdmAddAppRuleStruct**.
3. Rules that are dynamically specified within an irule command.

A "core.re" file is provided with iRODS release 4.0 for use by the rule engine. The iCAT stores all persistent rules and all versions of rules. Once a rule is checked into the iCAT, it can never be deleted.

1.7   Summary

The iRODS system of microservice-based rules provides an extensible set of data management procedures targeted at programmers, users, and systems administrators who desire a variety of data management applications. iRODS is generic software "middleware" infrastructure that can be adapted to the needs of individual data repositories, whether the need is for a collaborative data sharing environment, a digital library that publishes image, text and audio files, or a dark archive that must preserve and retain data for the indefinite long-term.

PART II A BRIEF INTRODUCTION TO THE iRODS RULE LANGUAGE

In this chapter:
> *Comments and Directives*
> *Variables*
> *Data types*
> *Functions*
> *Rules*
> *Control Structures*
> *Types*
> *Microservices*
> *Rule Indexing*
> *Backward Compatibility*

The iRODS Rule Language is used by iRODS to define policies and procedures. A policy defines when a procedure can be executed. Actions are policies that are automatically applied by the data grid, and are listed in the core.re file. A rule corresponds to the implementation of a policy in the iRODS rule language. The iRODS Rule Language is tightly integrated with other components of iRODS. Many frequently used policies and actions can be configured easily by writing simple rules, yet the language is flexible enough to allow complex policies or actions to be defined.

A typical rule written in the iRODS rule language looks like this:

```
acPostProcForPut {
    on($objPath like "*.txt") {
        msiDataObjCopy($objPath, "$objPath.copy");
    }
}
```

In this rule, the rule name "acPostProcForPut", meaning "post process for put", is a policy enforcement point (event hook) defined in iRODS. When the rule is included in the core.re file, iRODS automatically applies this rule when a file is "put" or uploaded into the system. The "on(...)" clause is a rule condition. The "{...}" block following the rule condition is a sequence of actions that is executed if the rule condition is true when the rule is applied. For another example, the customary hello world rule looks like this:

```
HelloWorld {
    writeLine("stdout", "Hello, world!");
}
```

For releases 4.0 of iRODS, a rule engine is included that comes with an array of features and improvements that takes care of some corner cases where the original rule engine was ambiguous, such as when parsing special characters in strings, by following the conventions of mainstream programming languages.

In the following sections, we go over some features of the rule engine, with a focus on changes and improvements over the original rule engine.

2.1   Comments and Directives

The rule engine parses characters between the "#" token and the end of the line as comments. Therefore, a comment does not have to occupy its own line. For example, the following comments are valid:

```
# comments
                # comments
*A=1;           # comments
```

Although the parser is able to parse comments starting with "##", it is not recommended to begin comments with "##", as "##" is also used in the backward compatible mode as the actions connector (the original rule engine syntax used "##" as a delimiter). It is recommended to begin comments with a single "#".

Directives can be used to provide the rule engine with compile-time instructions. For example, the "@include" directive allows including a different rule file into the current rule file, similar to "#include" in C. For example, if we have a rule base file "definitions.re" located in iRODS/server/config/reConfigs, then we can include it with the following directive:

    @include "definitions"

2.2   Variables

Variables in the iRODS Rule Language are prefixed with "*" or "$". The scope of variables prefixed with "*" is a single top-level rule application. A variable may have any identifier as its name. The scope of variables prefixed with "$" is a session (which may contain several top-level rule applications). These session variables are predefined by iRODS and cannot be created by a user. The session variables are listed in Appendix C. Note that session variables are associated with specific policy-enforcement points. Thus an action for adding a file to the data grid will set session variables related to the file name and path, but will not set session variables related to administrative actions such as adding a storage vault.

Variables can be assigned values using "=":

    *A=1;

They can also be used in expressions and actions:

    *A = *A+1;
    msi(*A);   # here msi is a microservice that takes *A as an argument.

Rule parameters are also variables, and they are prefixed with "*". A rule parameter may be: an input parameter, whose value is passed from the calling rule to the rule being called; an output parameter, whose value is passed from the rule being called back to the calling rule; or a parameter that is both an input parameter and an output parameter:

    div(*X, *Y, *Z) {
        *X = *Y / *Z;
    }

"*Y" and "*Z" are input parameters and "*X" is an output parameter.

2.3   Data Types

2.3.1   Boolean

There are two boolean literals: "true" and "false". Boolean operators include "!" (not), "&&" (and), "||" (or), and additionally in the original rule engine syntax "%%" (or):

    true && true
    false && true
    true || false
    false || false
    true %% false

false %% false
! true

2.3.2   Numeric

There are two primitive numeric data types: integer and double. The corresponding literals are integer literals and floating-point literals. An integral literal does not have a decimal, while a floating-point literal does:

```
1    # integer
1.0  # double
```

Arithmetic operators include, ordered by precedence from highest to lowest:

- - (negation)
- ^ (power)
- * (multiplication) / (division) % (modulo)
- - (subtraction) + (addition)
- > < >= <=
- == !=

Note for C, C++, and Java programmers: the iRODS rule language does not implement integer division as found in C, C++, and Java; division between integers is the same as division between doubles.

Arithmetic functions include:

- exp
- log
- abs
- floor
- ceiling
- average
- max
- min

For example:

```
exp(10)
log(10)
abs(-10)
floor(1.2)
ceiling(1.2)
average(1,2,3)
max(1,2,3)
min(1,2,3)
```

In the iRODS Rule Language, an integer can be converted to a double. The reverse is not always true. A double can be converted to an integer only if the fractional part is zero. The rule engine, however, provides two functions that can be used to truncate the fractional part of a double: "floor" and "ceiling". Also, the numeric values 0 and 1 can be converted to boolean using the "bool" function. "bool" converts 1 to true and 0 to false. Note that queries on the iCAT catalog will generate output values that are strings. In most cases, the output string will need to be converted to an integer for comparison operations.

2.3.3 String

One of the features in the rule language that differs from the old rule engine (version 2.5 and prior) is how it handles strings. The rule engine requires, by default, that every string literal is quoted. The quotation marks can be either matching single quotes:

'This is a string.'

or double quotes:

"This is a string."

Care must be taken when copying quoted strings from Microsoft word documents. Microsoft uses slanted/smart quotes instead of straight quotes. All strings in the rule language must be specified with straight quotes.

If a programmer needs to quote strings containing single (double) quotes using single (double) quotes, then the quotes in the strings should be escaped using a backslash "\" just as in C:

```
writeLine("stdout", "\"\"");   # output is ""
```

Single quotes inside double quotes are viewed as regular characters, and vice versa. They can be either escaped or not escaped:

```
writeLine("stdout", "'");      # output '
writeLine("stdout", "\'");     # output '
```

The rule engine also supports various other escaped characters:

```
\n          # new line
\r          # carriage return
\t          # horizontal tab
\\          # backslash
\'          # single quotation mark
\"          # double quotation mark
\$          # dollar sign
\*          # asterisk
```

An asterisk should always be escaped if it is a regular character and is followed by letters. Otherwise the sequence is interpreted as a variable.

The rule engine supports the string concatenation operator "++":

```
writeLine("stdout", "This "++" is "++" a string.");
# output This is a string.
```

the wildcard matching operator "like":

```
writeLine("stdout", "This is a string." like "This\*string.");
# output true
```

the regular expression matching operator "like regex":

```
writeLine("stdout", "This is a string." like regex "This.\*string[.]");
# output true
```

the substring function "substr":

```
writeLine("stdout", substr("This is a string.", 0, 4));
# output This
```

the length function "strlen":

```
writeLine("stdout", strlen("This is a string."));
# output 17
```

and the split function "split":

```
writeLine("stdout", split("This is a string.", " "));
# output [This,is,a,string.]
```

In a quoted string, an asterisk followed immediately by a variable name (without whitespace) makes an expansion of the variable:

```
"This is *x."
```

is equivalent to:

```
"This is "++str(*x)++"."
```

The "str" function converts a value of type boolean, integer, double, time, or string to string:

```
writeLine("stdout", str(123));
# output 123
```

A string can be converted to values of type boolean, integer, double, time, or string:

```
int("123")
double("123")
bool("true")
```

2.3.4   Rules for Quoting Action Arguments

A parameter to a microservice is of type string if the expected type is MS_STR_T. When a microservice expects a parameter of type string and the argument is a string constant, the argument has to be quoted. For example, writeLine("stdout", "This is a string."). When a microservice expects a parameter of type string and the argument is not of type string, a type error may be thrown:

```
*x = 123;
strlen(*x);
```

This error can be fixed by either using the "str" function:

    strlen(str(*x));

or by putting *x into quotes:

    strlen("*x");

Action names and keywords are not arguments. Therefore, they do not have to be quoted.

2.3.5   Wildcard and Regular Expressions

The rule engine supports both the wildcard matching operator "like" and a new regular expression matching operator "like regex" (it is an operator, not two separate keywords). Just as the old rule engine does, the rule engine supports the "*" wildcard:

    "abcd" like "ab*"

In case of ambiguity with variable expansion, the "*" must be escaped:

    "abcd" like "a*d"

because:

    "a*d"

is otherwise interpreted as:

    "a"++str(*d)++""

When a wildcard is not expressive enough, the regular expression matching operator can be used:

    "abcd" like regex "a.c."

A regular expression matches the whole string. It follows the syntax of the POSIX API.

2.3.6   Quoting Code

Sometimes when passing code or regular expressions into an action, escaping every special character in the string can be very tedious:

    "writeLine(\"stdout\", *A)"

or:

    *A like regex "a*c\\\\\\[\\]" # matches the regular expression a*c\\\[\]

In this case, matching sets of two back ticks ("``") can be used instead of the regular double quotes. The rule engine does not look any further for things to expand within strings between two "``"s. With "``", the examples above can be written as:

    ``writeLine("stdout", *A)``

and:

    *A like regex ``a*c\\\[\]``

2.3.7 Lists

The rule engine provides built-in support for lists. A list can be created using the "list" microservice:

    list("This", "is", "a", "list")

All elements of a list should have the same type. Elements of a list can be retrieved using the "elem" microservice. The index starts from 0:

    elem(list("This", "is", "a", "list"),1)   # evaluates to "is"

If the index is out of range it fails with an error code.

The "setelem" microservice takes three parameters, a list, an index, and a value, and returns a new list that is identical to the list given by the first parameter except that the element at the index given by the second parameter is replaced by the value given by the third parameter:

    setelem(list("This", "is", "a", "list"),1,"isn't") # evaluates to list("This", "isn't", "a", "list")

If the index is out of range it fails with an error code.

The "size" microservice takes one parameter, a list, and returns the size of the list:

    size(list("This", "is", "a", "list"))   # evaluates to 4

The "hd", or head, microservice returns the first element of a list and the "tl", or tail, microservice returns the remainder of the list. If the list is empty, then both fail with an error code.

    hd(list("This", "is", "a", "list"))   # evaluates to "This"
    tl(list("This", "is", "a", "list"))   # evaluates to list("is", "a", "list")

2.3.8 Interactions with Packing Instructions

Complex data types such as lists of lists can be constructed locally, but mapping from some complex data types to packing instructions are not yet supported. The supported list types that can be packed are integer lists and string lists. When remote execute or delay execution is called while there is a complex list in the current runtime environment's scope, an error will be generated.

For example, consider the following rule:

```
test {
    *A = list(list(1,2), list(3,4));
    *B = elem(*A, 1);
    delay("<PLUSET>1m</PLUSET>") {
        writeLine("serverLog", *B);
    }
}
```

Even though *A is not used in the delay execution block, the rule will still generate an error since *A was defined and is a complex list. One solution to this is to create a rule "loglater", which encapsulates the delay action and excludes the more complex list from its scope.

```
test {
    *A = list(list(1,2), list(3,4));
    *B = elem(*A, 1);
    loglater(*B);
}
loglater(*B) {
    delay("<PLUSET>1m</PLUSET>") {
        writeLine("serverLog", *B);
    }
}
```

2.3.9   Datetime variables

The current time can be found by using

```
time()
```

This returns the time in a datetime variable. A datetime variable is converted to a string when printed using the default format:

```
"%m %d %Y %H:%M:%S"
```

Note that the microservice:

datetimef(*str, *format) converts a string stored in *str to a datetime variable, according to the *format parameter.

datetime(*str) converts a string stored in *str to a datetime variable, according to the default format.

timestrf(*time, *format) converts a datetime variable stored in *time to a string, according to the *format parameter.

timestr(*time, *format) converts a datetime variable stored in *time to a string, according to the default format.

The format string can be defined according to the standard C library. For example,

```
datetime(*str)
datetimef(*str, "%Y %m %d %H:%M:%S")
timestr(*time)
timestrf(*time, "%Y %m %d %H:%M:%S")
```

2.3.10   Dot Expression

This feature was added after the 3.2 release
The dot operator provides a simple syntax for creating and accessing key value pairs. To write to a key value pair, use the dot operator on the left hand side:

```
*A.key = "val"
```

If the key is not a syntactically valid identifier, quotes can be used. Escape rules for strings also apply:

```
*A."not an identifier" = "val"
```

If the variable *A is undefined, a new key value pair data structure will be created.

To read from a key value pair, use the dot operator as a binary infix operation in any expression. Currently key value pairs only support the string type for values.

The str() function has been extended to support converting a key value pair data structure to an options format for use as arguments in microservices:

```
*A.a=A;
*A.b=B;
*A.c=C;
str(*A); # a=A++++b=B++++c=C
```

To loop over the key value pairs that are defined above, one can use:

```
foreach(*key in *A) {
  writeLine("stdout", *key ++ " : " ++ *A.*key);
}
```

2.3.11   Constant

This feature was added after the 3.2 release
A constant can be defined as a function that returns a constant. A constant definition has the following syntax:

```
<constant name> = <constant value>
```

where the constant value can be one of the following:

```
an integer
a double
a string (with no variable expansion in it)
a boolean
```

A constant name can be used in a pattern and is replaced by its value (whereas a non constant is treated as a constructor). For example, with

CONST = 1

the following expression

match CONST with
| CONST => "CONSTANT"
| *_ => "NOT CONSTANT"

returns "CONSTANT". With a non constant function definition such as

CONST = time()

it returns "NOT CONSTANT".

2.4   Control Structures

2.4.1   Actions

A rule consists of a sequence of actions. Each action can apply a rule or execute a microservice. For example, if there is a nullary microservice named "msi" and a binary rule named "rule", then the following actions apply the rule and execute the microservice:

rule(*A, *B);
msi;

There is a set of familiar workflow microservices, such as "assign", "if", and "foreach", that have special syntax support. For example:

if(*A==0) {*B=true;} else {*B=false;}

The iRODS rule engine has a unique concept of recovery action. Every action in a rule definition may have a recovery action. The recovery action is executed when the action preceding it fails. This allows iRODS rules to rollback some side effects and restore most of the system state to a known previous point. The rule engine supports a more general notion of an action recovery block. An action recovery block has the form:

{
    $A_1 ::: R_1$
    $A_2 ::: R_2$
    ...
    $A_n ::: R_n$
}

The basic semantics are that if A_x fails then R_x, R_{x-1}, ..., and R_1 will be executed. The programmer can use this mechanism to restore the system state to the point before this action recovery block began to be executed.

The rule engine makes the distinction between expressions and actions. An expression does not have a recovery action. Examples of expressions include the rule condition, and the conditional expressions in the "if", "while", and "for" actions. An action always has a recovery action. If a recovery action is not specified for an action, the rule engine will use "nop", or no operation, as the default recovery action:

```
{
    msi;
}
```

is equivalent to:

```
{
    msi ::: nop;
}
```

There is no intrinsic difference between an action and an expression. An expression becomes an action when it occurs at an action position in an action recovery block. An action recovery block, in turn, is an expression.

The principle is that a syntactical construct should only be used as an expression if it is side-effect free. If a syntactical construct has side-effects, it should only be used as an action. This property is not checked in the current version of the rule engine (v4.0). The programmer has to make sure that it holds for the rule base being executed.

2.4.2   "if"

The rule engine has a few useful extensions to the "if" keyword that makes programming in the rule language more convenient.

In addition to the traditional way of using "if" in the rule language, the rule engine supports a new way of using "if". The traditional way will be referred to as the "logical if", where "if" is used as an action which either succeeds, or fails with an error code. The new way will be referred to as the "functional if", where it may return a value of any type if it succeeds. The two different usages have slightly different syntaxes.

The "logical if" has the same syntax as before:

    if <expr> then { <actions> } else { <actions> }

The "functional if" has the following syntax:

    if <expr> then <expr> else <expr>

For example, the following is written as an older "logical if":

    if (*A==1) then { true; } else { false; }

And now the same written as a newer "functional if":

    if *A==1 then true else false

To make the syntax of "logical if" more concise, the rule engine allows the following abbreviations:

    if (...) { ... } else { ... }
    if (...) then { ... } else if (...) then {...} else {...}

Multiple abbreviations can be combined, for example:

```
if (*X==1) { *A = "Mon"; }
    else if (*X==2) {*A = "Tue"; }
    else if (*X==3) {*A = "Wed"; }  ...
```

2.4.3   "while"

The syntax for "while" is:

```
while(<expr>) { <actions> }
```

The semantics are similar to C. The actions are performed iteratively until the expression becomes false:

```
*X = 0;
*S = 0;
*N =5;
while(*X < *N) {
    *S = *S + *X;
    *X = *X + 1;
}
```

2.4.4   "for"

The syntax for "for" is:

```
for(<expr>;<expr>;<expr>) { <actions> }
```

Initially, the first expression is evaluated. The actions are performed iteratively, until the second expression becomes false. The third expression is evaluated after each iteration.

For example,

```
*S = 0;
*N = 5;
for(*X = 0;*X < *N; *X = *X + 1) {
    *S = *S + *X;
}
```

2.4.5   "foreach"

The syntax for "foreach" is:

```
foreach(<variable>) { <actions> }
```

The variable has to have a collection type such as the general query result type or a list type, something that can be iterated through by the foreach. The foreach action goes through all elements stored in the variable and performs the actions, during which the variable is bound to the current element.

The rule engine allows defining a different variable name for the iterator variable in the foreach action:

```
foreach(<variable> in <expr>) { <actions> }
```

For example:

```
foreach(*E in *C) {
    writeLine("stdout", *E);
}
```

This is equivalent to the earlier syntax:

```
foreach(*C) {
    writeLine("stdout", *C);
}
```

This new feature allows the collection to be a complex expression:

```
foreach(*E in list("This", "is", "a", "list")) {
    writeLine("stdout", *E);
}
```

This is equivalent to the earlier syntax:

```
*C = list("This", "is", "a", "list");
foreach(*C) {
    writeLine("stdout", *C);
}
```

The expression can also be a query on the iCAT catalog. For example:

```
*Query = select DATA_NAME where COLL_NAME = '*Coll';
foreach(*Row in *Query) {
    *File = *Row.DATA_NAME;
    writeLine(" stdout", "*File is in collection *Coll");
}
```

The foreach loop automatically loops over all values returned by the query. This is equivalent to the earlier syntax:

```
*ContInxOld = 1;
msiMakeGenQuery("DATA_NAME", "COLL_NAME = '*Coll'", *GenQInp);
msiExecGenQuery(*GenQInp, *GenQOut);
msiGetContInxFromGenQueryOut(*GenQOut,*ContInxNew);
while(*ContInxOld > 0) {
  foreach(*GenQOut) {
    msiGetValByKey(*GenQOut, "DATA_NAME", *File);
    writeLine("stdout", "*File is in collection *Coll");
  }
  *ContInxOld = *ContInxNew;
  if(*ContInxOld > 0) {msiGetMoreRows(*GenQInp,*GenQOut,*ContInxNew);}
}
```

2.4.6   "let"

The syntax for the let expression is:

    let <assignment> in <expr>

For example:

    quad(*n) = let *t = *n * *n in *t * *t

The variable on the left hand side of the assignment in the let expression is a let-bound variable. A let-bound variable should not be reassigned inside the let expression.

2.5   Functions

The rule engine allows defining functions. Functions can be thought of as microservices written in the rule language. The syntax of a function definition is:

    <name>(<param>, …, <param>) = <expr>

For example:

    square(*n) = *n * *n

Function names should be unique within the rule engine (no function-function or function-rule name conflicts).

Functions can be defined in a mutually exclusive manner:

    odd(*n) = if *n==0 then false else even(*n-1)
    even(*n) = if *n==0 then true else odd(*n-1)

To use a function, call it as if it was a microservice.

2.6   Rules

The syntax of a rule with a nontrivial rule condition is as follows:

    <name>(<param>, …, <param>) {
        on(<expr>) { <actions> }
    }

If the rule condition is trivial or unnecessary, the rule can be written in the simpler form:

    <name>(<param>, …, <param>) { <actions> }

Multiple rules with the same rule name and parameters list can be combined in a more concise syntax where each set of actions is enumerated for each set of conditions:

```
<name>(<param>, …, <param>) {
    on(<expr>) { <actions> }
    …
    on(<expr>) { <actions> }
}
```

2.6.1 Rule Name

In the rule engine, rule names have to be valid identifiers. Identifiers start with letters followed by letters or digits:

    ThisIsAValidRuleName

There should not be whitespace in the rule name:

    This Is Not A Valid Rule Name

2.6.2 Rule Condition

In the rule engine, rule conditions should be expressions of type boolean. The rule is executed only when the rule condition evaluates to true. This means that there are three failure conditions:

1. The rule condition evaluates to false.
2. An action in the rule condition fails which causes the evaluation of the entire rule condition to fail.
3. The rule condition evaluates to a value whose type is not boolean.

For example, if we want to run a rule when the microservice "msi" succeeds, we can write the rule as:

```
testrule {
    on (msi >= 0) { ... }
}
```

Conversely, if we want to run a rule when the microservice fails, we need to write the rule as:

```
testrule {
    on (errorcode(msi) < 0) { ... }
}
```

The following rule condition always fails by failure condition 3 listed above because msi returns an integer value, not a boolean value:

    on(msi) { ... }

2.7 Types

2.7.1 Introduction

Types are useful for capturing errors before rules are executed, but a restrictive type system may also rule out meaningful expressions. As the rule language is a highly dynamic language, the main goals of introducing a type system are twofold:

1) To enable the discovery of some errors statically without ruling out most valid rules written for the old rule engine, and
2) To help remove some repetitive type checking and conversion code in microservices by viewing types as contracts of what kinds of values are passed between the rule engine and microservices.

The type system is designed so that the rule language is dynamically typed when no type information is given, while providing certain static guarantees when some type information is given. The key is combining static typing with dynamic typing, so that we only need to check the statically typed part of a program statically and leave the rest of the program to dynamic typing.

The rule engine distinguishes between two groups of microservices. System-provided microservices such as string operators are called internal microservices. The rest are called external microservices. Most internal microservices are statically typed. They come with type information which the type checker can make use of to check for errors statically. By default, external microservices are dynamically typed, but they can be assigned a static type by a programmer using type declaration.

A type declaration specifies types for parameters of microservices and rules and their return values. The primitive types include: boolean, integer, double, time, string, and iRODS types. From the primitive types, complex types such as list types, tuple types, and algebraic data types can be built. A type called dynamic is included for dynamically typed values.

Typing constraints are used in the rule engine to encode typing requirements that need to be checked at compile time or at runtime. The type constraints are solved against a type coercion relation, a model of whether one type can be coerced to another type and how their values should be converted. For example, in the rule engine integers can be implicitly coerced to doubles, but not the other way around.

2.7.2 Variable Typing

As in C, all variables in the rule language have a fixed type that can not be updated through an assignment. For example, the following does not work:

```
testTyping1 {
    *A = 1;
    *A = "str";
}
```

Once a variable *A is assigned a value X the type of the variable is given by a typing constraint:

    type of X can be coerced to type of *A

For example:

```
testTyping2 {
    *A = 1;   # integer can be coerced to type of *A
    *A = 2.0; # double can be coerced to type of *A
}
```

Solving the typing constraints, we have:

    type of *A must be double

For another example, the following generates a type error:

```
testTyping3 {
    *A = 1; # integer can be coerced to type of *A
    if(*A == "str") { # type error occurs here
    }
}
```

2.7.3   Types by Examples

In this subsection, we look at a few simple examples of how the rule engine works with types. In the rule engine, binary arithmetic operators such as addition and subtraction are given the type:

forall X in {integer double}, f X * f X -> X

This type indicates that the operator takes in two parameters of the same type and returns a value of the same type as its parameters. The parameter type is bound by {integer double}, which means that the operator applies to only integers or doubles. The "f" indicates that if any type can be coerced to these types, it can also be accepted with a runtime coercion inserted.

Examples:

(a) When both parameter types are double, the return type is also double:

1.0 + 1.0 # returns double

(b) When one of the parameter types is integer and the other is double, the return type is double, because integer can be coerced to double, but not conversely:

1 + 1.0   # returns double

(c) When both parameter types are integer, the return type is integer, which can also be coerced to double:

1 + 1   # returns integer

(d) If one of the parameter types is dynamic, and the other is double, the return type is double, with a runtime constraint:

*A + 1.0 # returns double

The type checker generates a constraint that the type of *A can be coerced to double.

(e) If both parameter types are dynamic, the return type can be either integer or double:

*A + *B # unclear return type without more context

The type checker generates a constraint that both type of *A and type of *B can be coerced to either integer or double.

Some typing constraints can be solved within a certain context. For example, we put (e) into the following context:

```
*B = 1.0;
*B = *A + *B;   # returns double
```

We can eliminate the possibility that *B is an integer, thereby narrowing the type of the return value to double.

Some typing constraints can be proved unsolvable:

```
*B = *A + *B;
*B == "";
```

By the second action we know that *B has to have type string. In this case the rule engine reports a type error.

If some typing constraints can not be solved statically, they are left to be solved at runtime.

2.7.4   Type Declaration

In the rule engine, you can declare the type of a rule or a microservice. The syntax for type declaration is:

```
<name> : <type>
```

A typical <type> looks like:

$$P_1 * P_2 * ... * P_n -> R$$

P_1, P_2, ..., and P_n are the parameter types and R is the return type.

If the type of an action is declared, then the rule engine will do more static type checking. For example, although this does not generate a static type error:

```
concat(*a, *b) = *a ++ *b
add(*a, *b) = concat(*a, *b)
```

"add(0, 1)" would generate a dynamic type error. This can be solved (generate static type errors instead of dynamic type errors) by declaring the types of the functions:

```
concat : string * string -> string
concat(*a, *b) = *a ++ *b
add : integer * integer -> integer
add(*a, *b) = concat(*a, *b)
```

2.8   Microservices

2.8.1   Automatic Evaluation of Arguments

The rule engine automatically evaluates expressions within arguments of actions, which is useful when a program needs to pass in the result of an expression as an argument to an action. For example, in the old rule engine, if we want to pass the result of an expression "1+2" as an argument to microservice "msi", then we need to either write something like this:

```
*A=1+2;
msi(*A);
```

Or, we have to pass "1+2" in as a string to "msi" and write code in the microservice which parses and evaluates the expression. With the rule engine, the programmer can write:

```
msi(1+2);
```

and the rule engine will evaluate the expression "1+2" and pass the result of 3 into the microservice.

2.8.2   The Return Value of User Defined Microservices

Both the old rule engine and the rule engine view the return value of user defined microservices as an integer "errorcode". If the return value of a microservice is less than zero, both rule engines interpret it as a failure, rather than as an integer value; and if the return value is greater than zero, both rule engines interpret it as an integer. Therefore, the following expression:

```
msi >= 0
```

either evaluates to true or fails (and never evaluates to false), because when "msi" returns a negative integer, the rule engine interprets the value as a failure and the comparison is never evaluated. In some applications, there is a need for capturing all possible return values as regular integers. The "errorcode" microservice provided by the rule engine can be used to achieve this. In the previous example, we can modify the code as follows:

```
errorcode(msi) >= 0
```

This expression does not fail on negative return values from msi and then allows the greater than or equal to comparison to be evaluated as expected.

2.9   Rule Indexing

To improve the performance of rule execution, the rule engine provides a two level indexing scheme on applicable rules. The first level of indexing is based on the rule names. The second level of indexing is based on the rule conditions. The rule condition indexing can be demonstrated by the following example:

```
testRule(*A) {
      on (*A == "a") { ... }
      on (*A == "b") { ... }
}
```

In this example, we have two rules with the same rule name, but different rule conditions. The first level of indexing does not improve the performance in rule applications like:

```
testRule("a")
```

However, the second level indexing does improve performance. The second level indexing works on rules with similar rule conditions. In particular, the rule conditions have to be of the form:

<expr> == <string>

The syntactical requirement for the rule indexing to work are: all rules have to have the same number of parameters, but they may have different parameter names; the expression has to be the same for all rules modulo variable renaming; and the strings have to be different for different rules. The rule engine indexes the rules by the string. When the rule is called, the rule engine evaluates the expression once and looks up the rule using the second level indexing.

Rule indexing also works on subsets of rules that satisfy the syntactical requirement:

```
testRule(*A) {
     on (msi(*A)) { ... }
     on (*A == "a") { ... }
     on (*A == "b") { ... }
}
```

Rule indexing works on the second and third rule, but not the first. When the rule is called, the rule engine tries the first rule first, if the first rule fails, it tries to look up an applicable rule using the second level indexing.

PART III iRODS MICROSERVICE CATEGORIES AND CONVENTIONS

In this chapter:
Microservices Overview
Microservices Categories
Microservices Input/Output Arguments
Microservices Naming Conventions
Examples of Writing Advanced Microservices
Summary

3.1   Microservices Overview

Microservices are small, well-defined C procedures (functions) developed by systems programmers and applications programmers to perform a certain task. This task may be very complicated or quite small. If a task is large, it may be best to be divided into smaller tasks as multiple microservices. However, if two sub-tasks are usually used together, they may be best combined into a single microservice. There is tension between making a large task into a single microservice that does not allow an end user or administrator to choose which part of a task to run, and creating microservices that are so fine-grained that the implementation of the task becomes cumbersome. As with all programming, use of normal coding practices and good design principles in deciding the granularity of a microservice is recommended. The microservices are compiled into the iRODS server code for installation at each storage location. The data grid administrator has control over the operations that will be performed within the data grid.

3.2   Microservices Categories

Microservices are divided into the following three categories:

1. **Core Microservices** - These microservices are functions for Rule Engine control, workflow creation, and low-level and higher-level data object manipulation. Low-level data operations include opening a file, closing a file, reading data, and writing data. High-level data operations include replication, checksumming, registration, and the staging of files.

2. **Framework Services** - These are functions for rule-oriented remote database access, message passing with the high-performance Xmessaging system, sending e-mail, manipulating Keyword–Value attribute pairs, and supporting user-defined services.

3. **iCAT Services** - These are functions for manipulating system metadata, and for interacting with the iCAT catalog.

If more sophisticated macro functionality is required, then end users and administrators may chain together a series of microservices. This macro-level functionality provides full control over any actions performed. An end user or administrator may also chain together different microservices to provide different ways to perform the same or similar action. The system itself "chooses" the best microservice chain to be executed using priorities and validation conditions at run-time.

Some examples of microservices are: **msiCreateUser**, **msiDeleteUser**, **msiTarFileExtract**, **msiTarFileCreate**, **msiCollCreate**, and **msiRenameCollection**. A complete list of microservices available at publication time is provided in the index of microservices. The most recent list of microservices may be found online at https://wiki.irods.org/doxygen/. The list of microservices enabled on your data grid can be generated by running the rule:

irule –F iRODS/clients/icommands/test/rules4.0/rulemsiListEnabledMS.r

3.3 The Microservice Interface and *msParam_t*

Any normal C procedure can be a microservice, provided it is embedded in a standard interfacing template. The C procedure you want to use as a microservice can have any number of arguments, type or structure. The iRODS Rule Engine interacts with a microservice through the *msParam_t* structure. This is a published parametric structure that is standardized within iRODS. A microservice interface (msi) is used to convert from *msParam_t* to the argument types required by the underlying C code within the microservice. The msi routine maps *msParam_t* to the call arguments and converts back any output parameters to the *msParam_t* structure; it is glue code. Thus, a C procedure called "createUser" will have an interface routine called **msicreateUser**; the Rule Engine invokes **msicreateUser**, and this invokes the "createUser" function. Microservices that are statically compiled with the core are listed in the header file /var/lib/irods/iRODS/server/re/include/reAction.hpp. Others that have been added via plug-ins will be contained in the dynamic libraries in /var/lib/irods/plugins/microservices.

msParam_t provides the following uniform type definitions for use by the Rule Engine to handle the distributed operation of microservices:

```
typedef struct MsParam {
        char *label;
        char *type;        /* This is the name of the packing instruction in rodsPackTable.hpp */
        void *inOutStruct;
        bytesBuf_t *inpOutBuf;
} msParam_t;
```

In the example above, "label" is the name of the argument in the call; "type" is the C structure type supported by iRODS; "inOutStruct" is a pointer to the value of the input structure being passed (it can be "NULL"); and "inpOutBuf" is used to specify any binary buffers that need to be passed as part of the argument. Each type has a packing instruction that defines how the structure can be serialized for transmission over the network.

3.4 Microservice Input/Output Parameters

For input/output parameters, a user or administrator may pass a variable to a microservice through explicit arguments, exactly as in the case of C function or procedure calls. The input parameters may take two forms:

- **Literal**: If an argument does not begin with a special character (#, $ or *), it is treated as a character string input if it is quoted. For example, in the microservice

  msiSortDataObj("random");

  the character string "random" will be passed in as input. Literals can only be used as input parameters and not as output parameters. Literals can be of type string, integer, and double.

- **Variable**: If an argument begins with the * character, it is treated as a variable argument. Variable arguments can be used both as input and output parameters. The output parameter from one microservice can be explicitly specified as the input parameter of another microservice. This powerful capability allows very complex workflow-like rules to be constructed.

For example, in the following workflow chain:

```
myStagingRule {
# Periodic execution of the staging of files
 delay("<PLUSET>1m</PLUSET><EF>1d</EF>") {
# Loop over files in a staging area, /$rodsZoneClient/home/$userNameClient/*stage
```

```
# Put all files with .r into collection /$rodsZoneClient/home/$userNameClient/*Coll
  *Src = "/$rodsZoneClient/home/$userNameClient/" ++ *Stage;
  *Dest= "/$rodsZoneClient/home/$userNameClient/" ++ *Coll;

#============get current time, Timestamp is YYY-MM-DD.hh:mm:ss ==========
  msiGetSystemTime(*TimeH,"human");

#============ create a collection for log files if it does not exist ================
  *LPath = "*Dest/log";
  msiIsColl(*LPath,*Result, *Status);
  if(*Result == 0 || *Status < 0) {
    msiCollCreate(*LPath, "0", *Status);
    if(*Status < 0) {
      writeLine("serverlog","Could not create log collection");
      fail;
    } # end of check on status
  } # end of log collection creation

#============ create file into which results will be written ====================
  *Lfile = "*LPath/Check-*TimeH";
  *Dfile = "destRescName=*Res++++forceFlag=";
  msiDataObjCreate(*Lfile, *Dfile, *L_FD);

#============ find files to stage
  *Query = select DATA_NAME where COLL_NAME = '*Src' and DATA_NAME like '%.r';
  foreach(*Row in *Query) {
    *File = *Row.DATA_NAME;
    *Src1 = *Src ++ "/" ++ *File;
    *Dest1 = *Dest ++ "/" ++ *File;
#Check whether file already exists
    msiIsData(*Dest1,*DataID,*Status);
# Move file and set access permission
    if(*DataID == "0") {
      msiDataObjAutoMove(*Src1,*Src,*Dest, $userNameClient, "true");
      msiSetACL("default","own",$userNameClient, *Dest1);
      writeLine("*Lfile", "Moved file *Src1 to *Dest1");
    }
  }
 }
}
INPUT *Stage =$"stage", *Coll=$"Rules", *Res=$"lifelibResc1"
OUTPUT ruleExecOut
```

(Please note in the example above, the line beginning with "INPUT" and ending with "lifelibResc1" should be a single line when executed. In examples it may be displayed as multiple lines due to limitations of the printed page.)

msiCollCreate uses as an input variable the path name constructed for the log collection. Files in a staging area are identified through a query on the metadata catalog. The files are moved to a destination directory if they are not present in the destination directory. Each operation is recorded in the log file which is also stored in the data grid.

For information on how to pass arguments to a rule or action, please see Section 6.1 "Microservice Input/Output Arguments" in the iRODS Primer.

3.5 How to Create a New Microservice

Microservices can be added dynamically to the system through creation of microservice plugins. Once a microservice is written, a plugin factory function can also be written that provides the information needed by iRODS to support execution of the new microservice. The steps are outlined below as a generic template for writing iRODS microservice plugins.

To run this tutorial:

- Download iRODS binary package and Development Tools from http://www.irods.org/download
- Install iRODS
- Install the iRODS Development Tools

1. Create the microservice function as needed.

```
int myPetProc(char *in1, int in2, char *out1, int *out2)
{
  ... my favorite code ...
}
```

2. Create the microservice interface (msi) glue procedure.

```
int my_microservice(msParam_t *mPin1, msParam_t *mPin2,
        msParam_t *mPout1, msParam_t *mPout2,
        RuleExecInfo_t *rei)
{
  char *in1,  out1;
  int i, in2, out2;

  RE_TEST_MACRO ("    Calling myPetProc")
  /* the above line is needed for loopback testing using the irule -i option */

  in1  = (char *) mPin1->inOutStruct;
  in2  = (int)    mPin2->inOutStruct;
  out1 = (char *) mPout1->inOutStruct;
  out2 = (int)    mPout2->inOutStruct;

  i = myPetProc(in1, in2, out1, &out2);
  mPout2->inOutStruct = (int) out2;

  return(i);
}
```

3. Create a package with the microservice and a plugin factory function

```
// =_=_=_=_=_=_=_=_
// iRODS Includes
#include "msParam.hpp"
#include "reGlobalsExtern.hpp"
#include "irods_ms_plugin.hpp"

// =_=_=_=_=_=_=_=_
// STL Includes
#include <iostream>

extern "C" {
```

```
// =-=-=-=-=-=-=-
// 1. Write a standard issue microservice
int my_microservice(msParam_t *mPin1, msParam_t *mPin2,
        msParam_t *mPout1, msParam_t *mPout2,
        RuleExecInfo_t *rei)
}
```

4. Add the plugin factory function

```
// =-=-=-=-=-=-=-
// 2. Create the plugin factory function which will
//    return a microservice table entry
irods::ms_table_entry* plugin_factory() {

    // =-=-=-=-=-=-=-
    // 3. Allocate a microservice plugin which takes the number of function
    //    params as a parameter to the constructor, not including _rei. With
    //    N as the total number of arguments of my_microservice() we would have:
    irods::ms_table_entry* msvc = new irods::ms_table_entry( N-1 );

    // =-=-=-=-=-=-=-
    // 4. Add the microservice function as an operation to the plugin
    //    the first param is the name / key of the operation, the second
    //    is the name of the function which will be the microservice
    msvc->add_operation( "my_microservice", "my_microservice" );

    // =-=-=-=-=-=-=-
    // 5. Return the newly created microservice plugin
    return msvc;
    }
}; // extern "C"
```

3.6   How to Load a Microservice

To run this example from your test directory type:

    $ make my_microservice

This should create a shared object: libirods_my_microservice.so

Copy libirods_my_microservice.so to the microservices plugin directory (as irods):

    $ sudo -u irods cp -f libirods_my_microservice.so /var/lib/irods/plugins/microservices/

Now that you have "loaded" your new microservice plugin you can test it with its corresponding rule:

    $ irule –F irods_my_microservice.r

3.7   Microservice Naming Conventions

When users or system administrators add files and functions, we recommend using standard naming conventions for ease of maintenance. Following a standard naming convention is useful for maintaining the programs and functions our users create. While we do not force these conventions on volunteer developers, we recommend their usage for maintaining good programming practice.

3.8 Microservice Variable Naming Conventions

We recommend that variable names use multiple descriptive words.

> Example: myRodsArgs

Variable names use camel-case to distinguish words, with the first letter of each word component capitalized.

> Example: genQueryInp

3.9 Microservice Constant Naming Conventions

We recommend using one of the two following conventions:

1. Constant string names use multiple descriptive words and start with an uppercase letter.

    > Example: Msg_Header_PI

2. Constant string names use uppercase letters separated with an underscore.

    > Example: NAME_LEN

3.10 Microservice Function Naming Conventions

All C functions in iRODS occupy the same namespace. To avoid function name collisions, we recommend that:

- Function names use multiple descriptive words.

  Example: getMsParamByLabel

- Function names use camel-case to distinguish words.

  Example: printMsParam

- Microservice function names start with "msi".

  Example: msiDataObjGet

- Microservice helper function names start with "mh".

  Example: mht

- Server function names start with "rs".

  Example: rsCollCreate

- Client function names start with "rc".

  Example: rcCollCreate

3.11   Microservice File Naming Conventions

The purpose of a file may be inferred by the location of the file in the iRODS directory tree. For instance, those in the "server/re/src" directory are part of the Rule Engine, whereas those in the "clients/icommands/src" directory are command-line tools. Beyond this, we recommend that:

- File names use multiple descriptive words.

  Example: rodsServer.cpp contains the iRODS Server main program.

- File names reflect the names of functions in the file.

  Example: msParam.cpp contains utility functions that work with the msParam structure.

- File names use camel-case to distinguish words.

  Example: irodsReServer.cpp

- *No two files in the same directory may have names that differ only by case.* Case-insensitive names cause problems with Windows and legacy Mac (OS 9 and earlier) file systems.

3.12   Delaying the Execution of a Microservice

We can delay the execution of any microservice either in the irule execution or in a rule at the server side.

For example, the microservice **msiSysReplDataObj(*R,*Flag)** replicates an existing iRODS file. In order to delay the replication by two minutes we can use:

```
delay("<PLUSET>2m</PLUSET>") {
   msiSysReplDataObj("tgrReplResc");
}
```

In a "core.re" file this might be used as follows:
```
acPostProcForPut{
   on($objPath like "/tempZone/home/tgr/*") {
      delay("<PLUSET>2m</PLUSET>") {
         msiSysReplDataObj("tgrReplResc");
      }
   }
}

acPostProcForPut {
   on($objPath like "/tempZone/home/nvo/*") {
      msiSysReplDataObj("nvoReplResc", "null" );
   }
}

acPostProcForPut {
}
```

Three versions of the acPostProcForPut action are listed above. The order is important, as the rule engine will execute the first policy that is satisfied. Thus the last policy should be a generic policy that handles all otherwise non-exceptional cases (it has no condition that must be matched, so it matches everything).

3.13 Summary

We designed and wrote microservices to extract and ingest template-identified metadata. We coded each module to be microservice compliant. We tested the microservices from the command line, and we used the microservices as a workflow.

PART IV iRODS MICROSERVICES

In this chapter:
Introduction
Doxygen Output
Core Microservices Descriptions
Module Microservices Descriptions
Rule Microservices Descriptions
What about Framework and iCAT microservices?

The iRODS data grid composes procedures by chaining together microservices. Information can be passed between microservices through an in-memory structure called "rei" or the Rule Execution Information. Each input and output parameter has a well-defined data structure, which is stored in the "rei" structure. Thus, the development of a procedure requires knowledge of the expected data types used by each microservice.

For each of the microservices provided in the iRODS release version 4.0, a description of the input and output parameters is provided, along with an example of how the microservice might be used within a rule. The examples are written using the iRODS 3.0 rule language, a later variant of the "rulegen" language referenced in the iRODS Primer and used up to iRODS 2.5. The text in the examples can be copied into a ".r" file, and then executed using an "irule" command. Further examples can also be found in the code under "/iRODS/clients/icommands/test/rules4.0/". There are several caveats that must be observed:

- Microservice invocations may be broken across multiple lines in the example because of formatting limitations. These should be combined into a single line that is terminated with the ";" symbol.
- All of the parameters specified in an INPUT line should be combined into a single line. The parameters are separated by commas. Spaces are ignored.
- All of the parameters specified in an OUTPUT line should be combined into a single line.
- All double quotes should be straight quotes, not curly or "smart" ("") quotes. A valid quote example is:
  "Select DATA_ID where DATA_NAME = '*File' "
- All single quotes should be straight quotes.

The "rule.r" file can be executed directly by the irule command:

irule –F rule.r

Rule files (ending in ".r") that are loaded into the iRODS data grid can also be executed using the iDrop-Web web browser interface.

The data grid test environment in which the examples execute is assumed to have the following attributes:
irodsHost=localhost
irodsPort=1247
irodsDefResource=demoResc
irodsHome=/$rodsZoneClient/home/rods
irodsCwd=/$rodsZoneClient/home/rods
irodsUserName=rods
irodsZone=tempZone

These attributes can be changed by modifying the INPUT parameters for the rule. In addition, the following directories and resources need to be set up to use the rules as listed. Note that session variables are used to pick up the name of the data grid, $rodsZoneClient, and the name of the user account, $userNameClient. See Appendix C for other session variables.

Test user account with name	testuser
Test directory at location	/$rodsZoneClient/home/$userNameClient/ruletest
Test sub-directory at location	/$rodsZoneClient/home/$userNameClient/ruletest/sub
Test sub-directory at location	/$rodsZoneClient/home/$userNameClient/test
Test storage resource	testResc
Test storage group	testgroup (consisting of testResc and demoResc)
E-mail address	test@irods.org

A shortened version of the microservice documentation is provided below. To view the full documentation of the latest release, please go online to https://wiki.irods.org/doxygen/.

Rules that can be used to try each microservice are listed in the directory "clients/icommands/test/rules4.0/". The example rule name for a given microservice can be formed by prepending the microservice name with "rule" and then appending ".r". Thus the rule that can be used to try the **msiGetSystemTime** microservice is "rulemsiGetSystemTime.r".

Some rules are illustrated using policies within the core.re file, and the name of the file will start with "ac". For example "acmsiAclPolicy" is implemented as a policy that cannot be executed by the irule command. Instead, this policy is inserted into the core.re file for automated enforcement. In many cases, these rules rely upon session variables that are only set when an appropriate policy enforcement point is invoked.

    acAclPolicy { msiAclPolicy("STRICT"); }

Rules are also provided for the workflow functions used by the rule language. They are named "ruleworkflow*function*.r" where *function* is replaced by the workflow operator. Thus the rule for illustrating the "if" operator is "ruleworkflowif.r".

Rules are provided for the arithmetic and string manipulation operations. They are named ruleoper*function*.r where *function* is replaced by the name of the operation. Thus the rule for illustrating the "minus" operation is "ruleoperMinus.r".

Rules are also provided that illustrate additional use cases. They are named:

rulegenerateBagIt.r	Generate a BagIt file
ruleintegrityACL.r	Verify ACLs
ruleintegrityAVU.r,	Verify required AVUs
ruleintegrityAVUvalue.r	Verify value of an AVU
ruleintegrityExpiry.r	Check retention period
ruleintegrityFileSize.r	Check file sizes
ruleintegrityFileOwner.r	Verify file owners
ruleshowCore.r	List rules invoked at policy enforcement points

In the following sections, please note that all input parameters for a rule are assumed to be entered on a single line. The code examples may have wrapped due to limitations of the printed text.

4.1   Core :: Operations :: abs

Absolute value operation

Description:
Absolute value operation for integers and floating point numbers. The rule example is in iRODS/clients/icommands/test/rules4.0/absval.r

Example Usage:

```
mytestrule{
#rule to test the absolute value operation
 *out=abs(*int1);
 writeLine("stdout", "absolute value of *int1 is *out");
}
INPUT *int1=$-1
OUTPUT ruleExecOut
```

4.2   Core :: Operations :: and

Boolean and operation

Description:
AND operation between two boolean variables, expressed using the symbol "&&".
The rule example is in iRODS/clients/icommands/test/rules4.0/booleanAnd.r.

Example Usage:

```
mytestrule{
#rule to test the boolean and operation, &&
 *A = false;
 *B = true;
 if(!*A && *B) {
   writeLine("stdout", "Verified AND (&&) operation");
 }
}
INPUT null
OUTPUT ruleExecOut
```

4.3   Core :: Operations :: average

Averaging operation

Description:
Average two integers or two floating point numbers. The rule example is in
iRODS/clients/icommands/test/rules4.0/average.r.

Example Usage:

```
mytestrule{
#rule to test averaging operation, average
 *out=average(*int1,*int2);
 writeLine("stdout", "average of *int1 and *int2 is *out");
 *A = 2.2;
 *B = 5.2;
 *out2 = average(*A, *B);
```

```
  writeLine("stdout", "average of *A and *B is *out2");
}
INPUT *int1=$1,*int2=$2
OUTPUT ruleExecOut
```

4.4   Core :: Operations :: bool

Boolean value conversion routine

Description:
Convert a string to a boolean value, or convert an integer to a boolean value. The rule example is in
iRODS/clients/icommands/test/rules4.0/convert-to-boolean.r.

Example Usage:

```
mytestrule{
#rule to test conversion of string to boolean value
  *out=bool(*input);
  writeLine("stdout", "boolean of string *input is *out");
  *A = 1;
  *out2 = bool(*A);
  writeLine("stdout", "boolean of integer *A is *out2");
  *B = 0;
  *out3 = bool(*B);
  writeLine("stdout", "boolean of integer *B is *out3");
}
INPUT *input=$"true"
OUTPUT ruleExecOut
```

4.5   Core :: Operations :: ceiling

Ceiling arithmetic operation

Description:
Convert a floating point number to an integer by rounding up to the closest integer. The rule example is in
iRODS/clients/icommands/test/rules4.0/ceiling.r.

Example Usage:

```
mytestrule{
#rule to test ceiling operation
  *out=ceiling(*val1);
  writeLine("stdout", "ceiling of *val1 is *out");
}
INPUT *val1=$1.1
OUTPUT ruleExecOut
```

4.6   Core :: Operations :: concatenate

String concatenation operation

Description:
Concatenate two strings using the string operator ++. The rule example is in
iRODS/clients/icommands/test/rules4.0/strConcatenate..r.

Example Usage:

```
mytestrule{
#rule to concatenate two strings using ++
  *out= *string1 ++ *string2;
  writeLine("stdout", "\"*string1\" concatenated to \"*string2\" is \"*out\"");
}
INPUT *string1=$"concatenate", *string2=$" strings"
OUTPUT ruleExecOut
```

4.7   Core :: Operations :: cons

Cons list addition function

Description:
Add a string to the start of a list using the cons (construct) operation. The rule example is in
iRODS/clients/icommands/test/rules4.0/prependToList.r.

Example Usage:

```
mytestrule{
#rule to test operation to add an item to a list, cons
  *A = list("is", "a", "list");
  *1 = cons("This",*A);
  writeLine("stdout", "Original list is *A");
  writeLine("stdout", "cons output is *1");
}
INPUT null
OUTPUT ruleExecOut
```

4.8   Core :: Operations :: datetime

Datetime time conversion function

Description:
Create a datetime variable from a string, integer, or double. The datetime variable will be correctly interpreted by the writeLine output command and changed into a human readable form. The rule example is in iRODS/clients/icommands/test/rules4.0/datetime.r.

Example Usage:

```
myTestRule {
# Use the datetime function to list the date a user account was created.
  *Query = select USER_ID, USER_CREATE_TIME where USER_NAME = '$userNameClient';
  foreach (*Row in *Query) {
   *userid = *Row.USER_ID;
   *usercreate = *Row.USER_CREATE_TIME;
   *usercreatetime = datetime(double(*usercreate));
   writeLine("stdout", "User: $userNameClient  UserID: *userid  CreateTime: *usercreatetime");
  }
}
INPUT null
OUTPUT ruleExecOut
```

4.9   Core :: Operations :: datetimef

Datetime formatted time conversion function

Description:
Convert a string, integer or double variable to a datetime varible, using a specified format. Note that %y %m %d %H:%M:%S corresponds to Year Month Day Hour:Minute:Second. The rule example is in iRODS/clients/icommands/test/rules4.0/datetimeF.r.

Example Usage:

```
mytestrule{
# rule to test datetimef function to convert a string/integer/double
# to a variable of type dateime.
  msiGetSystemTime(*Time,"unix");
  *out = timestrf(datetime(double(*Time)), "%y %m %d");
  writeLine("stdout", "datetime of *Time is *out");
}
INPUT null
OUTPUT ruleExecOut
```

4.10   Core :: Operations :: division

Division operation

Description:
Perform the arithmetic operation of dividing two numbers. The rule example is in iRODS/clients/icommands/test/rules4.0/division.r.

Example Usage:

```
mytestrule{
#rule to test division operation
  *out= *int1/*int2;
  writeLine("stdout", "output of *int1 / *int2 is *out");
}
INPUT *int1=$1,*int2=$2
OUTPUT ruleExecOut
```

4.11   Core :: Operations :: dot – included in version 4.0.1+

Dot structure operation

Description:
Extract or set information within a structure. This is used to simplify extraction of values from key-value pairs. The rule example is in iRODS/clients/icommands/test/rules4.0/ruleDot.r.

Example Usage:

```
mytestRule {
# demonstrate use of the dot operator
# generate summaries of the extensions used in a collection
  *c = "/$rodsZoneClient/home/$userNameClient"
  *rs = select DATA_NAME, DATA_SIZE where COLL_NAME = *c;
  *res.total = str(0);
  *total.total = str(0);
  foreach(*r in *rs) {
   *fn = *r.DATA_NAME;
   *ds = *r.DATA_SIZE;
   *ext = ext(*fn);
   *res.total = str(int(*res.total) + 1);
   *total.total = str(double(*total.total) + double(*ds));
   if (contains(*res, *ext)) {
     *res.*ext = str(int(*res.*ext) + 1)
     *total.*ext = str(double(*res.*ext) + double(*ds))
   } else {
     *res.*ext = str(1);
     *total.*ext = *ds;
   }
  }
  writeLine("stdout", "ext\tcount\tavg\ttotal");
  foreach(*ext in *res) {
   if(*ext != "total") {
     writeLine("stdout",
"*ext\t"++*res.*ext++"\t"++str(double(*total.*ext)/int(*res.*ext))++"\t"++*total.*ext);
   }
  }
  writeLine("stdout",
"total\t"++*res.total++"\t"++str(double(*total.total)/int(*res.total))++"\t"++*total.total);
```

```
}
ext(*p) {
 *b = trimr(*p, ".");
 *ext = if *b == *p then "no ext" else substr(*p, strlen(*b)+1, strlen(*p));
 *ext;
}
contains(*kvp, *k) {
 *c = false;
 foreach(*k1 in *kvp) {
  if (*k1 == *k) {
   *c = true;
   break;
  }
 }
 *c;
}
input null
output ruleExecOut
```

4.12   Core :: Operations :: double

Double type conversion operation

Description:
Convert a string or integer to a double type. The rule example is in
iRODS/clients/icommands/test/rules4.0/convert-to-double.r.

Example Usage:

```
mytestrule{
#rule to test conversion of string to double
 *out=double(*int1);
 writeLine("stdout", "double conversion of *int1 is *out");
}
INPUT *int1=$"1.1"
OUTPUT ruleExecOut
```

4.13   Core :: Operations :: elem

List element extraction operation

Description:
Extract an element from a list. The second parameter contains the element number to extract, starting at
element number "0". The rule example is in iRODS/clients/icommands/test/rules4.0/ruleElem.r.

Example Usage:

```
mytestrule{
#rule to extract element from a list using  elem
  *A = list("This", "is", "a", "list");
  writeLine("stdout",*A);
  *out=elem(*A, *elno)
  writeLine("stdout", "*elno th element of list is *out");
}
INPUT *elno=$0
OUTPUT ruleExecOut
```

4.14   Core :: Operations :: equal

Conditional equal operation

Description:
Test the equivalence of two numbers within an IF statement using the operation "==". The rule example is in iRODS/clients/icommands/test/rules4.0/booleanEqual.r.

Example Usage:

```
mytestrule{
#rule to test conditional equal operation, ==
  if(*int1==*int2) {
  writeLine("stdout", "Value of \*int1 equals value of \*int2, *int1 == *int2");
  } else {
  writeLine("stdout", "Value of \*int1 does not equal value of \*int2, *int1 != *int2");
  }
}
INPUT *int1=$2,*int2=$2
OUTPUT ruleExecOut
```

4.15   Core :: Operations :: eval

String evaluation operator

Description:
Convert the operation specified between two arguments within a string to a floating point or integer, using the eval function. The rule example is in iRODS/clients/icommands/test/rules4.0/strEval.r.

Example Usage:

```
mytestrule{
# rule to test conversion of an arithmetic operation specified in a string
# to a number, using eval
  *out=eval("*int1+*int2");
  writeLine("stdout", "eval of *int1+*int2 is *out");
```

```
}
INPUT *int1=$1,*int2=$2
OUTPUT ruleExecOut
```

4.16   Core :: Operations :: exp

Exponentiation operation

Description:
Apply the arithmetic exponential operator to a number. The rule example is in
iRODS/clients/icommands/test/rules4.0/exponentiate.r.

Example Usage:

```
mytestrule{
# rule to test evaluation of an exponential using exp
# raises e to input value
  *out=exp(*A);
  writeLine("stdout", "output is *out");
}
INPUT *A=$2
OUTPUT ruleExecOut
```

4.17   Core :: Operations :: floor

Floor arithmetic operation

Description:
Convert a floating point number to an integer by rounding down to the closest integer. The rule example is
in iRODS/clients/icommands/test/rules4.0/floor.r.

Example Usage:

```
mytestrule{
#rule to test arithmetic operation operation to find nearest lower integer, floor
  *out=floor(*val1);
  writeLine("stdout", "floor of *val1 is *out");
}
INPUT *val1=$1.1
OUTPUT ruleExecOut
```

4.18   Core :: Operations :: greater

Conditional greater than operation

Description:
Compare the size of two numbers within an IF statement using the greater than operation ">". The rule example is in iRODS/clients/icommands/test/rules4.0/greaterThan.r.

Example Usage:

```
mytestrule{
# rule to apply condition test greater than, >
  if(*int1>*int2) {
    writeLine("stdout", "Value of \*int1 is greater than value of \*int2, *int1 > *int2");
  }
}
INPUT *int1=$2,*int2=$1
OUTPUT ruleExecOut
```

4.19 Core :: Operations :: greater than or equal

Conditional greater than or equal operation

Description:
Compare the size of two numbers within an IF statement using the greater than or equal operation ">=".
The rule example is in iRODS/clients/icommands/test/rules4.0/greaterThanOrEqual.r.

Example Usage:

```
mytestrule{
# rule to apply condition test greater than or equal, >=
  if(*int1>=*int2) {
    writeLine("stdout", "Value of \*int1 is greater than or equal to value of \*int2, *int1 >= *int2");
  }
}
INPUT *int1=$2,*int2=$1
OUTPUT ruleExecOut
```

4.20 Core :: Operations :: hd

Extract head of a list

Description:
Extract the head of a list. The rule example is in iRODS/clients/icommands/test/rules4.0/listHead.r.

Example Usage:

```
mytestRule {
# Extract the head of a list
  *L = list("This", "is", "a", "list");
  *A = hd(*L);
```

```
  writeLine("stdout", "For list *L");
  writeLine("stdout", "Head of the list is \"*A\"");
}
INPUT null
OUTPUT ruleExecOut
```

4.21   Core :: Operations :: int

String conversion to integer

Description:
Convert a string to an integer. The rule example is in iRODS/clients/icommands/test/rules4.0/string-to-int.r.

Example Usage:

```
mytestrule{
#rule to apply conversion of string to integer using int
  *Int = int (*A);
  writeLine("stdout", "String *A is integer *Int");
}
INPUT *A=$"1"
OUTPUT ruleExecOut
```

4.22   Core :: Operations :: less

Conditional less than operation

Description:
Compare the size of two numbers within an IF statement using the less than operation "<". The rule example is in iRODS/clients/icommands/test/rules4.0/lessThan.r.

Example Usage:

```
mytestrule{
#rule to apply condition less than test,  <
  if(*int1<*int2) {
    writeLine("stdout", "Value of \*int1 is less than value of \*int2, *int1 < *int2");
  }
}
INPUT *int1=$1, *int2=$2
OUTPUT ruleExecOut
```

4.23   Core :: Operations :: less than or equal

Conditional less than or equal operation

Description:
Compare the size of two numbers within an IF statement using the less than or equal operation "<=". The rule example is in iRODS/clients/icommands/test/rules4.0/lessThanOrEqual.r.

Example Usage:

```
mytestrule{
#rule to apply the conditional test less than or equal,  <=
  if(*int1 <= *int2) {
    writeLine("stdout", "Value of \*int1 is <= value of \*int2, *int1 <= *int2");
  }
}
INPUT *int1=$1, *int2=$2
OUTPUT ruleExecOut
```

4.24   Core :: Operations :: let

Functional equivalence operator

Description:
Define a functional dependence. An example is
          quad(*n) = let *t = *n * *n in *t * *t
This replaces the values of *t with *n * *n in the expression. Rule examples in iRODS/clients/icommands/test/rules4.0/ruleLet1.r, ruleLet2.r, and ruleLet3.r.

Example Usage:

```
mytestrule{
#rule to assign functional dependence using let
# define quartic operation from square
  *C = quad(*A);
  writeLine("stdout", "*A\*\*4 = *C");
}
quad(*n)=let *t = *n * *n in *t * *t
INPUT *A=3
OUTPUT ruleExecOut
```

4.25   Core :: Operations :: like

String comparison operator like

Description:
Compare two strings using a wild card operator and the "like" operator. An example is "abcd" like "a*d". Note that the wild card character is escaped. The rule example is in iRODS/clients/icommands/test/rules4.0/strLike.r.

Example Usage:

```
mytestrule{
# rule to test whether two strings have similar text using like
# and the wild card symbol *
 *C = *B ++ "\*";
 if(eval(" '*A' like '*C' ")) {
  writeLine("stdout","\"*A\" is like \"*C\"");
 }
 else {
  writeLine("stdout","\"*A\" is not like \"*C\"");
 }
}
INPUT *A=$"this try", *B=$"this"
OUTPUT ruleExecOut
```

4.26   Core :: Operations :: like regex

String comparison operator like regex

Description:
Compare two strings using a regular expression and the "like regex" operator. An example is "abcd" like regex "a.*". The rule example is in iRODS/clients/icommands/test/rules4.0/regexLike.r.

Example Usage:

```
mytestrule{
# rule to compare strings using a regular expression with like regex
 if(eval(" '*A' like regex '*B' ")) {
  writeLine("stdout","\"*A\" is like regex \"*B\"");
 }
 else {
  writeLine("stdout","\"*A\" is not like regex \"*B\"");
 }
}
INPUT *A=$"this",*B=$"t.*"
OUTPUT ruleExecOut
```

4.27   Core :: Operations :: list

List creation operator

Description:
Create a list by specifying the elements. The rule example is in iRODS/clients/icommands/test/rules4.0/list.r.

Example Usage:

```
mytestrule{
#rule to generate a list
  *l=list("this", "is", "a", "list");
  writeLine("stdout","Created demo list *l");
}
INPUT null
OUTPUT ruleExecOut
```

4.28　Core :: Operations :: log

Natural logarithm arithmetic operation

Description:
Generate the natural logarithm of a number using the natural logarithm operator, log. The rule example is
in iRODS/clients/icommands/test/rules4.0/naturalLog.r.

Example Usage:

```
mytestrule{
#rule to apply logarithm, log
  *B=log(*A);
  writeLine("stdout", "Log of *A is *B");
}
INPUT *A=$2.718281
OUTPUT ruleExecOut
```

4.29　Core :: Operations :: match

Match operation for constants

Description:
Determine whether a constant or variable is being used.. The rule example is in
iRODS/clients/icommands/test/rules4.0/ruleMatch.r.

Example Usage:

```
mytestRule {
# Define the natural number that represents "1"
  *one = succ(zero);
# Convert the natural number to an integer and print
  writeLine("stdout", natToInt(*one));
# define the next natural number
  *two = succ(*one);
  writeLine("stdout", natToInt(*two));
}
# Definition of a data type for natural numbers
data nat =
```

```
| zero : nat
| succ : nat -> nat
# Type the function that converts natural numbers to integers
natToInt : nat -> int
# This is a function for manipulating the natural numbers.
# It converts the natural number data type to integer
# Demonstrate matching the natural number data type and convert to an integer
natToInt(*x) =
  match *x with
   | zero => 0
   | succ(*z) => natToInt(*z) + 1
INPUT null
OUTPUT ruleExecOut
```

4.30   Core :: Operations :: max

Maximum arithmetic operation

Description:
Find the maximum of two numbers. The rule example is in iRODS/clients/icommands/test/rules4.0/max.r.

Example Usage:

```
mytestrule{
#rule to test arithmetic maximum operation
  *out=max(*A, *B);
  writeLine("stdout", "Maximum of *A and *B is *out");
}
INPUT *A=$1, *B=$2
OUTPUT ruleExecOut
```

4.31   Core :: Operations :: min

Minimum arithmetic operation

Description:
Find the minimum of two numbers. The rule example is in iRODS/clients/icommands/test/rules4.0/min.r.

Example Usage:

```
mytestrule{
#rule to test the arithmetic  minimum operation
  *out=min(*A, *B);
  writeLine("stdout", "Minimum between *A and *B is *out");
}
INPUT *A=$1, *B=$2
OUTPUT ruleExecOut
```

4.32 Core :: Operations :: minus

Minus aritmetic operation

Description:
Subtraction operation for integers and floating point numbers. The rule example is in iRODS/clients/icommands/test/rules4.0/minus.r.

Example Usage:

```
mytestrule{
#rule to test the arithmetic operation, minus
 *out=(*int1-*int2);
 writeLine("stdout", "output of *int1 - *int2 is *out");
}
INPUT *int1=$1,*int2=$2
OUTPUT ruleExecOut
```

4.33 Core :: Operations :: modulus

Modulus arithmetic operation

Description:
Find the modulus of two numbers using the "%" operator. The rule example is in iRODS/clients/icommands/test/rules4.0/modulo.r.

Example Usage:

```
mytestrule{
#rule to test modulo operation (%)
 *out=(*A % *B);
 writeLine("stdout", "modulo of *A and *B is *out");
}
INPUT *A=$4, *B=$3
OUTPUT ruleExecOut
```

4.34 Core :: Operations :: multiply

Multiplication arithmetic operation

Description:
Find the product of two numbers using the multiplication "*" operator. The rule example is in iRODS/clients/icommands/test/rules4.0/multiply.r.

Example Usage:

```
mytestrule{
#rule to test multiplication operation, *
  *out=*int1 * *int2;
  writeLine("stdout", "output of *int1 * *int2 is *out");
}
INPUT *int1=$1, *int2=$2
OUTPUT ruleExecOut
```

4.35   Core :: Operations :: negation

Conditional negation operation

Description:
Apply the conditional negation operation, !. The rule example is in
iRODS/clients/icommands/test/rules4.0/booleanNot.r.

Example Usage:

```
mytestrule{
#rule to test logical negation operation, !
#! operator works on boolean values, evaluating as opposite of input
  if(!false){
    writeLine("stdout", "negation ! worked")
  }
}
INPUT null
OUTPUT ruleExecOut
```

4.36   Core :: Operations :: not equal

Conditional not equal operation

Description:
Apply the conditional not equal operation, !=. The rule example is in
iRODS/clients/icommands/test/rules4.0/notEqual.r.

Example Usage:

```
mytestrule{
#rule to apply conditional not equal test, !=
  if(*int1 != *int2) {
    writeLine("stdout","Value of \*int1 is != to value of \*int2, *int1 != *int2");
  }
}
INPUT *int1=$1, *int2=$2
```

4.37 Core :: Operations :: not like

String comparison operator not like

Description:
Compare two strings and determine whether they are not similar, using the not like operator. The rule example is in iRODS/clients/icommands/test/rules4.0/notLike.r.

Example Usage:

```
mytestrule{
#rule to test string comparison not like
  if(eval(" '*A' not like '*B' ")) {
    writeLine("stdout", "\"*A\" is not like \"*B\"");
  }
  else {
    writeLine("stdout","\"*A\" is like \"*B\"");
  }
}
INPUT *A=$"this", *B=$"these"
OUTPUT ruleExecOut
```

4.38 Core :: Operations :: or

Conditional or operation

Description:
Apply the conditional or operation, ||. An alternate form is %%. The rule example is in iRODS/clients/icommands/test/rules4.0/booleanOr.r.

Example Usage:

```
mytestrule{
#rule to test conditional OR || %%
  if(!false || 1>2){
    writeLine("stdout", "output is true for ||");
  }
  if(!false %% 1>2){
    writeLine("stdout", "output is true for %%");
  }
}
INPUT null
OUTPUT ruleExecOut
```

4.39   Core :: Operations :: plus

Addition arithmetic operation

Description:
Add two numbers using the addition operator, +|. The rule example is in
iRODS/clients/icommands/test/rules4.0/plus.r.

Example Usage:

```
mytestrule{
#rule to test arithmetic addition operation, +
  *out=*int1 + *int2;
  writeLine("stdout", "output of *int1 + *int2 is *out");
}
INPUT *int1=$1, *int2=$2
OUTPUT ruleExecOut
```

4.40   Core :: Operations :: power

Power arithmetic operation

Description:
Raise a number to an integer power. Example in iRODS/clients/icommands/test/rules4.0/powerRule.r.

Example Usage:

```
mytestRule {
# Demonstrate use of arithmetic power operator, ^
  *A = 2;
  *B = *A ^ 3;
  writeLine("stdout", "A = *A, B = A ^ 3 = *B");
}
INPUT null
OUTPUT ruleExecOut
```

4.41   Core :: Operations :: root

Root arithmetic operation

Description:
Take a root of a number. Example in iRODS/clients/icommands/test/rules4.0/rootRule.r.

Example Usage:

```
mytestRule {
# Take the root of a number.
 *B = *A ^^ *C;
 writeLine("stdout", "A = *A, B = A ^^ *C = *B");
 *D = *B ^ *C;
 writeLine("stdout", "B = *B, D = B ^ *C = *D");
}
INPUT *A = 2., *C = 3.
OUTPUT ruleExecOut
```

4.42   Core :: Operations :: setelem

List update operator

Description:
The "setelem" microservice takes three parameters, a list, an index, and a value, and returns a new list that is identical to the list given by the first parameter except that the element at the index given by the second parameter is replaced by the value given by the third parameter:

setelem(list("This", "is", "a", "list"),1,"isn't") # evaluates to list("This", "isn't", "a", "list")

The rule example is in iRODS/clients/icommands/test/rules4.0/setelemRule.r..

Example Usage:

```
mytestrule {
# Change an element in a list
 *l = list("1", "2", "3", "4");
 writeLine("stdout", "Initial list is *l");
 *B = setelem (*l, 0, "5");
 writeLine("stdout", "Revised list is *B");
}
INPUT null
OUTPUT ruleExecOut
```

4.43   Core :: Operations :: size

List length operator

Description:
Determine the number of items in a list, using the list operator size. The rule example is in iRODS/clients/icommands/test/rules4.0/size.r.

Example Usage:

```
mytestrule{
#rule to find the number of elements in a list using size
 *A=split(" true, false ", ", ");
```

```
*size=size(*A);
  writeLine("stdout", "size of *A = *size");
}
INPUT null
OUTPUT ruleExecOut
```

4.44   Core :: Operations :: str

String conversion operator

Description:
Convert an integer into a string. The rule example is in iRODS/clients/icommands/test/rules4.0/integer-to-string.r.

Example Usage:

```
mytestrule{
#rule to convert an integer into a string
  *str=str(*A);
  writeLine("stdout","*A in string format is *str");
}
INPUT *A=$919
OUTPUT ruleExecOut
```

4.45   Core :: Operations :: time

Retrieve the current time

Description:
Get the time in the format Month Day Year Hour:Minute:Second. The rule example is in iRODS/clients/icommands/test/rules4.0/time.r.

Example Usage:

```
mytestrule{
#rule to get the current time
  *time=time();
  writeLine("stdout","Time is currently *time");
}
INPUT null
OUTPUT ruleExecOut
```

4.46   Core :: Operations :: timestr

Datetime variable conversion

Description:
Convert from a datetime variable to a string. The rule example is in iRODS/clients/icommands/test/rules4.0/timeStr.r.

Example Usage:

```
mytestrule{
#rule to convert a datetime variable to a string using timestr
 *time=time();
 *timestr=timestr(*time);
 writeLine("stdout","Time in string output is currently *timestr");
}
INPUT null
OUTPUT ruleExecOut
```

4.47   Core :: Operations :: timestrf

Datetime variable conversion using a format

Description:
Convert from a datetime variable to a string by specifying the desired formt. Any variation on %y %m %d %H:%M:%S is valid. The rule example is in iRODS/clients/icommands/test/rules4.0/timeStrF.r.

Example Usage:

```
mytestrule{
#rule to convert a datetime variable to a string using a format
 msiGetSystemTime(*Time, "unix");
 *out = timestrf(datetime(double(*Time)), "%y %m %d");
 writeLine("stdout", "Convert *Time to a string *out");
}
INPUT null
OUTPUT ruleExecOut
```

4.48   Core :: Operations :: tl

Extract the tail of a list

Description:
Extract the tail of a list. The rule example is in iRODS/clients/icommands/test/rules4.0/listTail.r.

Example Usage:

```
mytestRule {
# Extract the tail of a list
  *L = list("This", "is", "a", "list");
  *A = tl(*L);
  writeLine("stdout", "The tail of the list \"*L\" is \"*A\"");
}
INPUT null
OUTPUT ruleExecOut
```

4.49   Core :: Operations :: triml

Trim prefix of a string

Description:
Trim the prefix of a string from the left.
Input   String
          Characters that end the prefix
The rule example is in iRODS/clients/icommands/test/rules4.0/trimleft.r.

Example Usage:

```
mytestrule{
#rule to trim string from the left.
#Input   String
#       Characters that end the prefix
  *str = "abcdxyz"
  *out1 = triml(*str,"b");
  writeLine("stdout","Trim string \"*str\" after character \"b\" to get \"*out1\"");
}
INPUT null
OUTPUT ruleExecOut
```

4.50   Core :: Operations :: trimr

Trim suffix of a string

Description:
Trim the suffix of a string from the right.
Input   String
          Characters that begin the prefix
The rule example is in iRODS/clients/icommands/test/rules4.0/trimright.r.

Example Usage:

```
mytestrule{
#rule to trim the suffix of a string from the right using trimr
# Input String
```

```
#        Leading character of the suffix
 *str = "abcdxyz";
 *out = trimr(*str, "x");
 writeLine("stdout","String \"*str\" is trimmed at character \"x\" to give \"*out\"");
}
INPUT null
OUTPUT ruleExecOut
```

4.51   Core :: Collection :: msiCollCreate

Example rule contained in iRODS/clients/icommands/test/rules4.0/rulemsiCollCreate.r

msiCollCreate (	msParam_t *	inpParam1,
	msParam_t *	inpParam2,
	msParam_t *	outParam)

Parameters:
[in]   inpParam1   - a CollInp_MS_T or a STR_MS_T which would be taken as
                dataObj path.
[in]   inpParam2   - a STR_MS_T which specifies the flags integer. A flags value of 1
                means the parent collections will be created too.
[out]   outParam   - a INT_MS_T containing the status.

Description:
This microservice creates a new collection by calling rsCollCreate.

Example Usage:

```
myTestRule
{
        # Input parameters are:
        #  Collection that will be created
        #  Flag specifying whether to create parent collection
        #   Value of 1 means create parent collection
        # Output parameter:
        #  Result status for the operation
        # Output from running the example
        #  Create collection /$rodsZoneClient/home/$userNameClient/ruletest/sub1
        #  Collection created was
        #  COLL_NAME = /$rodsZoneClient/home/$userNameClient/ruletest/sub1

         msiCollCreate(*Path,"0", *Status);

         #  Verify collection was created
         writeLine("stdout", "Create collection *Path");
         writeLine("stdout", "Collection created was");
         *Query = select COLL_NAME where COLL_NAME = '*Path';
         foreach(*Row in *Query) { msiPrintKeyValPair("stdout", *Row); }
}
INPUT *Path="/$rodsZoneClient/home/$userNameClient/ruletest/sub1"
OUTPUT ruleExecOut
```

4.52   Core :: Collection ::   msiCollRepl

Example rule contained in iRODS/clients/icommands/test/rules4.0/rulemsiCollRepl.r

msiCollRepl   (msParam_t *   collection,
                       msParam_t *   msKeyValStr,
                       msParam_t *   status   )

Parameters:

[in]   collection   - A CollInp_MS_T or a STR_MS_T with the iRODS path of the collection to replicate.

[in]   msKeyValStr   - Optional - a STR_MS_T. This is the special msKeyValStr format of keyWd1=value1++++keyWd2=value2++++keyWd3=value3... If the keyWd is not specified (without the '=' char), the value is assumed to be the target resource ("destRescName") for backward compatibility. Valid keywords are:

"destRescName"   - the target resource to replicate to.

"backupRescName"   - the target resource to backup the data. If this keyWd is used, the backup mode will be switched on.

"rescName"   - the resource of the source copy.

"updateRepl"   - update other replicas with the latest copy. This keyWd has no value. But the '=' character is still needed.

"replNum"   - the replica number to use as source.

"numThreads"   - the number of threads to use.

"all"   - replicate to all resources in the resource group. This keyWd has no value.

"irodsAdmin"   - admin user replicate other users' files. This keyWd has no value.

"verifyChksum"   - verify the transfer using checksum. This keyWd has no value.

[out]   status   - a CollOprStat_t for detailed operation status.

Description:

This microservice wraps the rsCollRepl() routine to replicate a collection.

Note:

This call does not require client interaction, which means it can be used through rcExecMyRule (irule) or internally by the server.

Example Usage:

```
myTestRule
{
      #
      # Input parameters are:
      #  Collection that will be replicated, it must contain at least one file
      #  Target resource in keyword-value form
      # Output parameter is:
      #  Status of operation
      # Output from running the example is:
      #  Replicate collection /$rodsZoneClient/home/$userNameClient/sub1 to location
      destRescName=testResc
```

```
        # Put a file in the collection
        msiDataObjPut(*Path,*Resource, "localPath=*LocalFile++++forceFlag=", *Status);
        msiSplitPath(*Path, *Coll, *File);
        msiCollRepl(*Coll, *RepResource, *status);
        writeLine("stdout","Replicate collection *Coll to location *RepResource");
}
INPUT *RepResource="destRescName=testResc",
*Path="/$rodsZoneClient/home/$userNameClient/sub1/foo1", *Resource="demoResc", *LocalFile="foo1"
OUTPUT ruleExecOut
```

4.53   Core :: Collection :: msiPhyBundleColl

msiPhyBundleColl   (msParam_t *   inpParam1,
                                      msParam_t *   inpParam2,
                                      msParam_t *   outParam   )

Parameters:
[in]   inpParam1   - A StructFileExtAndRegInp_MS_T or a STR_MS_T which would
                            be taken as the collection for the physical bundle.
[in]   inpParam2   - optional - a STR_MS_T which specifies the target resource.
[out]   outParam   - An INT_MS_T containing the status.

Description:
This microservice bundles a collection into a number of tar files, similar to the iphybun command

Note:
The tar file is written to the /<zone_name>/bundle/home/<user_name> directory. If user running the rule is
an admin user, the directory will be created and the tar bundle written into it. For a rodsuser, the admin
must create the /<zone_name>/bundle/home/<user_name> directory and give the rodsuser ownership of it
so that the tar bundle can be written there by the user running the rule.

Example Usage:

myTestRule
{
        # Input parameters are:
        #   Collection that will be bundled into a tar file
        #   Resource where the tar file will be stored
        # Output parameter is:
        #   Status flag for the operation
        #   The file is stored under the /$rodsZoneClient/bundle/home/$userNameClient directory in iRODS
        # Output from running the example is
        #   Create tar file of collection /$rodsZoneClient/home/$userNameClient/test on resource testResc
        msiPhyBundleColl(*Coll, *Resc, *status);
        writeLine("stdout","Create tar file of collection *Coll on resource *Resc");
}
INPUT *Coll="/$rodsZoneClient/home/$userNameClient/test", *Resc="testResc"
OUTPUT ruleExecOut

4.54   Core :: Collection :: msiRmColl

Example rule contained in iRODS/clients/icommands/test/rules4.0/rulemsiRmColl.r

msiRmColl   (msParam_t *   inpParam1,
                          msParam_t *   msKeyValStr,
                          msParam_t *   outParam   )

Parameters:
[in]   inpParam1   - a CollInp_MS_T or a STR_MS_T which would be taken as
                         dataObj path.
[in]   msKeyValStr   - This is the special msKeyValStr format of
                         keyWd1=value1++++keyWd2=value2++++keyWd3=value3...
                         If the keyWd is not specified (without the '=' char), the value is
                         assumed to be one of the keywords listed below for backwards
                         compatibility. Valid keyWds are :
                         "forceFlag"   - Remove the data object instead of putting it
                                                        in the trash. This keyWd has no value. But
                                                        the '=' character is still needed.
                         "irodsAdminRmTrash"   - Admin remove trash. This keyWd has no value.
                         "irodsRmTrash"   - Remove trash. This keyWd has no value.
[out]   outParam   - an INT_MS_T containing the status.

Description:
Microservice msiRmColl calls rsRmColl to recursively remove a collection.

Example Usage:

```
myTestRule
{
        # Input parameters are:
        #   Collection that will be removed
        #   Flag controlling options in the form keyword=value
        # Output parameter is:
        #   Status flag for the operation
        # Output from running the example is:
        # Removed collection /$rodsZoneClient/home/$userNameClient/ruletest/sub
        msiRmColl(*Coll,*Flag,*Status);
        writeLine("stdout","Removed collection *Coll");
}
INPUT *Coll="/$rodsZoneClient/home/$userNameClient/ruletest/sub", *Flag="forceFlag="
OUTPUT ruleExecOut
```

4.55   Core :: Collection :: msiTarFileCreate

Example rule: iRODS/clients/icommands/test/rules4.0/rulemsiTarFileCreate.r

msiTarFileCreate (msParam_t * inpParam1,
            msParam_t * inpParam2,
            msParam_t * inpParam3,
            msParam_t * inpParam4   )

Parameters:
[in] inpParam1   - A StructFileExtAndRegInp_MS_T or a STR_MS_T which would
          be taken as dataObj path.
[in] inpParam2   - A STR_MS_T which specifies the target collection.
[in] inpParam3   - optional - A STR_MS_T which specifies the target resource.
[in] inpParam4   - optional - A STR_MS_T which specifies if the force flag is set.
          Set it to "force" if the force option is needed, otherwise no force
          option will be used.

Description:
Creates a tar object file from a target collection

Note:
This microservice calls rsStructFileBundle to create a tar file (inpParam1) from a target collection
(inpParam2). The content of the target collection is stored on the physical resource (inpParam3).

Example Usage:

```
myTestRule
{
        # Input parameters are:
        #   Tar file path name that will be created
        #   Collection that will be turned into a tar file
        #   Resource where the tar file will be stored
        #   Flag controlling options in form keyword=value
        # Output from running the example is:
        #   Created tar file /$rodsZoneClient/home/$userNameClient/test/testcoll.tar for collection
        /$rodsZoneClient/home/$userNameClient/ruletest/sub on resource demoResc
        msiTarFileCreate(*File,*Coll,*Resc,*Flag);
        writeLine("stdout","Created tar file *File for collection *Coll on resource *Resc");
}
INPUT *File="/$rodsZoneClient/home/$userNameClient/test/testcoll.tar",
*Coll="/$rodsZoneClient/home/$userNameClient/ruletest/sub", *Resc="demoResc", *Flag=""
OUTPUT ruleExecOut
```

4.56   Core :: Collection :: msiTarFileExtract

Example rule: iRODS/clients/icommands/test/rules4.0/rulemsiTarFileExtract.r

msiTarFileExtract (msParam_t * inpParam1,
            msParam_t * inpParam2,
            msParam_t * inpParam3,
            msParam_t * outParam   )

Parameters:

[in]	inpParam1	- A StructFileExtAndRegInp_MS_T or a STR_MS_T which would be taken as dataObj path.
[in]	inpParam2	- A STR_MS_T which specifies the target collection.
[in]	inpParam3	- optional - A STR_MS_T which specifies the target resource.
[out]	outParam	- An INT_MS_T containing the status.

Description:
Extracts a tar object file into a target collection.

Note:
This microservice calls rsStructFileExtAndReg to extract a tar file (inpParam1) into a target collection (inpParam2). The content of the target collection is stored on the physical resource (inpParam3).

Example Usage:

```
myTestRule
{
        # Input parameters are:
        #   Tar file within iRODS that will have its files extracted
        #   Collection where the extracted files will be placed
        #   Resource where the extracted files will be written
        # Output parameter:
        #   Status flag for the operation
        # Output from running the example is:
        #   Extract files from a tar file into collection /$rodsZoneClient/home/$userNameClient/ruletest/sub
        on resource demoResc
        msiTarFileExtract(*File,*Coll,*Resc,*Status);
        writeLine("stdout","Extract files from a tar file *File into collection *Coll on resource *Resc");
}
INPUT *File="/$rodsZoneClient/home/$userNameClient/test/testcoll.tar",
*Coll="/$rodsZoneClient/home/$userNameClient/ruletest/sub", *Resc="demoResc"
OUTPUT ruleExecOut
```

4.57   Core :: Data Object Low-level :: msiDataObjClose

Example rule: iRODS/clients/icommands/test/rules4.0/rulemsiDataObjClose.r

msiDataObjClose	(	msParam_t *	inpParam,	
		msParam_t *	outParam	)

Parameters:
[in]	inpParam	- inpParam is a msParam of type INT_MS_T or STR_MS_T for the file descriptor.
[out]	outParam	- outParam is a msParam of type INT_MS_T for a status flag.

Description:
This microservice performs a low-level close for an opened/created data object.

Note:

Can be called by client through irule.

Example Usage:

```
myTestRule
{
        # Input parameters are:
        #   Path
        #   Flags specifying resource, and force option in format keyword=value
        # Output parameter is:
        #   File descriptor for the file
        # Output from running the example is
        #   Created and closed file /$rodsZoneClient/home/$userNameClient/test/foo4
        msiDataObjCreate(*ObjB,*OFlagsB,*D_FD);
        writeLine("stdout","Created and closed file *ObjB");
        msiDataObjClose(*D_FD,*Status2);
}
INPUT *Resc="demoResc", *ObjB="/$rodsZoneClient/home/$userNameClient/test/foo4",
*OFlagsB="destRescName=demoResc++++forceFlag="
OUTPUT ruleExecOut
```

4.58   Core :: Data Object Low-level :: msiDataObjCreate

Example rule: iRODS/clients/icommands/test/rules4.0/rulemsiDataObjCreate.r

msiDataObjCreate	(	msParam_t *	inpParam1,	
		msParam_t *	msKeyValStr,	
		msParam_t *	outParam	)

Parameters:

[in]   inpParam1   - A DataObjInp_MS_T or STR_MS_T which would be taken as
                                        dataObj path.

[in]   msKeyValStr   - Optional - a STR_MS_T. This is the special msKeyValStr format
                                        of keyWd1=value1++++keyWd2=value2++++keyWd3=value3...
                                        If the keyWd is not specified (without the '=' char), the value is
                                        assumed to be the target resource ("destRescName") for
                                        backward compatibility. Valid keyWds are:
                                        "destRescName"   - the target resource.
                                        "forceFlag"   - overwrite existing copy. This keyWd has
                                                                        no value. But the '=' character is needed.
                                        "createMode"   - the file mode of the data object.
                                        "dataType"   - the data type of the data object.
                                        "dataSize"   - the size of the data object. This input is optional.

[out]   outParam   - a INT_MS_T containing the file
            descriptor of the create.

Description:
Creates a file descriptor for a data object, for subsequent reading or writing.

Note:

Example Usage:

myTestRule
{
       # Input parameters are:
      # Path
      # Flags specifying resource, and force option in format keyword=value
      # Output parameter is:
      # File descriptor for the file
      # Output from running the example is
      # Created and closed file /$rodsZoneClient/home/$userNameClient/test/foo4
      msiDataObjCreate(*ObjB,*OFlagsB,*D_FD);
      msiDataObjClose(*D_FD,*Status2);
      writeLine("stdout","Created and closed file *ObjB");
}
INPUT *Resc="demoResc", *ObjB="/$rodsZoneClient/home/$userNameClient/test/foo4",
*OFlagsB="destRescName=demoResc++++forceFlag="
OUTPUT ruleExecOut

4.59   Core :: Data Object Low-level :: msiDataObjLseek

Example rule: iRODS/clients/icommands/test/rules4.0/rulemsiDataObjLseek.r

msiDataObjLseek	(	msParam_t *	inpParam1,	
		msParam_t *	inpParam2,	
		msParam_t *	inpParam3,	
		msParam_t *	outParam	)

Parameters:

[in]	inpParam1	- a msParam of type DataObjLseekInp_MS_T or INT_MS_T or a STR_MS_T which would be the file descriptor.
[in]	inpParam2	- Optional - a msParam of type DOUBLE_MS_T or a STR_MS_T which would be the offset.
[in]	inpParam3	- Optional - a msParam of type INT_MS_T or a STR_MS_T which would be location for offset. Can be SEEK_SET, SEEK_CUR, and SEEK_END.
[out]	outParam	- a msParam of type Double_MS_T or DataObjLseekOut_MS_T which is the return status.

Description:
This is a microservice that performs a low-level (file) seek of an opened data object.

Note:
Can be called by client through irule

Example Usage:

myTestRule
{
      # Input parameters are:

```
    # File descriptor
    # Optional Offset from specified location
    # Optional location for offset: SEEK_SET, SEEK_CUR, and SEEK_END
    # Output Parameter is:
    #   Status of operation
    # Output from running the example is:
    # Open file /$rodsZoneClient/home/$userNameClient/test/foo1, create file
    /$rodsZoneClient/home/$userNameClient/test/foo4, copy 100 bytes starting at location 10
    msiDataObjOpen(*OFlags,*S_FD);
    msiDataObjCreate(*ObjB,*OFlagsB,*D_FD);
    msiDataObjLseek(*S_FD,*Offset,*Loc,*Status1);
    msiDataObjRead(*S_FD,*Len,*R_BUF);
    msiDataObjWrite(*D_FD,*R_BUF,*W_LEN);
    msiDataObjClose(*S_FD,*Status2);
    msiDataObjClose(*D_FD,*Status3);
    writeLine("stdout","Open file *Obj, create file *ObjB, copy *Len bytes starting at location
    *Offset");
}
INPUT *Obj="/$rodsZoneClient/home/$userNameClient/test/foo1",
*OFlags="objPath=/$rodsZoneClient/home/$userNameClient/test/foo1++++rescName=demoResc++++rep
lNum=0++++openFlags=O_RDONLY", *ObjB="/$rodsZoneClient/home/$userNameClient/test/foo4",
*OFlagsB="destRescName=demoResc++++forceFlag=", *Offset="10", *Loc="SEEK_SET", *Len="100"
OUTPUT ruleExecOut
```

4.60   Core :: Data Object Low-level :: msiDataObjOpen

Example rule: iRODS/clients/icommands/test/rules4.0/rulemsiDataObjOpen.r

msiDataObjOpen   (msParam_t *   inpParam,
                                       msParam_t *   outParam   )

Parameters:

[in]   inpParam   - a msParam of type DataObjInp_MS_T or a STR_MS_T which
                       would be taken as msKeyValStr. msKeyValStr - This is the
                       special msKeyValStr format of
                       keyWd1=value1++++keyWd2=value2++++keyWd3=value3...
                       If the keyWd is not specified (without the '=' char), the value is
                       assumed to be the path of the data object("objPath") for backward
                       compatibility. Valid keyWds are:
                       "objPath"   - the path of the data object to open.
                       "rescName"   - the resource of the data object to open.
                       "replNum"   - the replica number of the copy to open.
                       "openFlags"   - the open flags. Valid open flags are: O_RDONLY,
                                        O_WRONLY, O_RDWR and O_TRUNC. These
                                        can be combined by concatenation, e.g.
                                        O_WRONLYO_TRUNC (without the '|'
                                        character). The default open flag is O_RDONLY.
[out]   outParam   - a msParam of type INT_MS_T containing the descriptor of the
                       opened file.

Description:
This microservice performs a low-level open for an existing data object

Note:
Can be called by client through irule

Example Usage:

myTestRule
{
        # Input parameters are:
        #   File descriptor
        #   Optional length to read
        # Output parameter is:
        #   Buffer holding the data read
        # Output from running the example is:
        #   Open file /$rodsZoneClient/home/$userNameClient/test/foo1, create file
        /$rodsZoneClient/home/$userNameClient/test/foo4, copy 100 bytes starting at location 10
        msiDataObjOpen(*OFlags,*S_FD);
        msiDataObjCreate(*ObjB,*OFlagsB,*D_FD);
        msiDataObjLseek(*S_FD,*Offset,*Loc,*Status1);
        msiDataObjRead(*S_FD,*Len,*R_BUF);
        msiDataObjWrite(*D_FD,*R_BUF,*W_LEN);
        msiDataObjClose(*S_FD,*Status2);
        msiDataObjClose(*D_FD,*Status3);
        writeLine("stdout","Open file *Obj, create file *ObjB, copy *Len bytes starting at location
        *Offset");
}
INPUT *Obj="/$rodsZoneClient/home/$userNameClient/test/foo1",
*OFlags="objPath=/$rodsZoneClient/home/$userNameClient/test/foo1++++rescName=demoResc++++rep
lNum=0++++openFlags=O_RDONLY", *ObjB="/$rodsZoneClient/home/$userNameClient/test/foo4",
*OFlagsB="destRescName=demoResc++++forceFlag=", *Offset="10", *Loc="SEEK_SET", *Len="100"
OUTPUT ruleExecOut

4.61   Core :: Data Object Low-level :: msiDataObjRead

Example rule: iRODS/clients/icommands/test/rules4.0/rulemsiDataObjRead.r

msiDataObjRead	(	msParam_t *	inpParam1,	
		msParam_t *	inpParam2,	
		msParam_t *	outParam	)

Parameters:
[in]	inpParam1	- a msParam of type DataObjReadInp_MS_T or INT_MS_T or STR_MS_T which would be the file descriptor.
[in]	inpParam2	- a msParam of type INT_MS_T or STR_MS_T which would be the length.
[out]	outParam	- a msParam of type BUF_LEN_MS_T.

Description:
This microservice performs a low-level read of an opened data object.

Note:
Can be called by client through irule.

Example Usage:

myTestRule
{
        # Input parameters are:
        # File descriptor
        # Optional length to read
        # Output Parameter is:
        # Buffer holding the data read
        # Output from running the example is:
        # Open file /$rodsZoneClient/home/$userNameClient/test/foo1, create file
        /$rodsZoneClient/home/$userNameClient/test/foo4, copy 100 bytes starting at location 10
        msiDataObjOpen(*OFlags,*S_FD);
        msiDataObjCreate(*ObjB,*OFlagsB,*D_FD);
        msiDataObjLseek(*S_FD,*Offset,*Loc,*Status1);
        msiDataObjRead(*S_FD,*Len,*R_BUF);
        msiDataObjWrite(*D_FD,*R_BUF,*W_LEN);
        msiDataObjClose(*S_FD,*Status2);
        msiDataObjClose(*D_FD,*Status3);
        writeLine("stdout","Open file *Obj, create file *ObjB, copy *Len bytes starting at location *Offset
        to *ObjB");
}
INPUT *Nu="", *Obj="/$rodsZoneClient/home/$userNameClient/test/foo1", *Resc="demoResc",
*Repl="0", *Flag="O_RDONLY",
*OFlags="objPath=*Obj++++rescName=*Resc++++replNum=*Repl++++openFlags=*Flag",
*ObjB="/$rodsZoneClient/home/$userNameClient/test/foo4",
*OFlagsB="destRescName=*Resc++++forceFlag=*Nu", *Offset=10, *Loc="SEEK_SET", *Len=100
OUTPUT ruleExecOut

4.62   Core :: Data Object Low-level :: msiDataObjWrite

Example rule: iRODS/clients/icommands/test/rules4.0/rulemsiDataObjWrite.r

msiDataObjWrite   (msParam_t *   inpParam1,
                         msParam_t *   inpParam2,
                         msParam_t *   outParam   )

Parameters:

[in]	inpParam1	- a msParam of type DataObjWriteInp_MS_T or INT_MS_T or a STR_MS_T which would be the file descriptor.
[in]	inpParam2	- Optional - a msParam of type BUF_LEN_MS_T or a STR_MS_T, the input can be an inpOutBuf from a previous read. "stderr", "stdout" can be passed as well.
[out]	outParam	- a msParam of type INT_MS_T for the length written.

Description:
This microservice performs a low-level write to an opened data object.

Note:
Can be called by client through irule.

Example Usage:

myTestRule
{
        # Input parameters are:
        # File descriptor
        # Buffer that is being written
        # Output parameter is:
        # Length that is written
        # Output from running the example is:
        # Open file /$rodsZoneClient/home/$userNameClient/test/foo1, create file
        /$rodsZoneClient/home/$userNameClient/test/foo4, copy 100 bytes starting at location 10
        msiDataObjOpen(*OFlags,*S_FD);
        msiDataObjCreate(*ObjB,*OFlagsB,*D_FD);
        msiDataObjLseek(*S_FD,*Offset,*Loc,*Status1);
        msiDataObjRead(*S_FD,*Len,*R_BUF);
        msiDataObjWrite(*D_FD,*R_BUF,*W_LEN);
        msiDataObjClose(*S_FD,*Status2);
        msiDataObjClose(*D_FD,*Status3);
        writeLine("stdout","Open file *Obj, create file *ObjB, copy *Len bytes starting at location
        *Offset");
}
INPUT *Obj="/$rodsZoneClient/home/$userNameClient/test/foo1",
*OFlags="objPath=/$rodsZoneClient/home/$userNameClient/test/foo1++++rescName=demoResc++++rep
lNum=0++++openFlags=O_RDONLY", *ObjB="/$rodsZoneClient/home/$userNameClient/test/foo4",
*OFlagsB="destRescName=demoResc++++forceFlag=", *Offset="10", *Loc="SEEK_SET", *Len="100"
OUTPUT ruleExecOut

4.63   Core :: Data Object :: msiCheckAccess

Example rule: iRODS/clients/icommands/test/rules4.0/rulemsiCheckAccess.r

msiCheckAccess (	msParam_t *inObjName,
	msParam_t *inOperation,
	msParam_t *outResult)

Parameters:
[in]	inObjName	- a msParam of type STR_MS_T with the object name
[in]	inOperation	- a msParam of type STR_MS_T with the type of desired access
[out]	outResult	- a msParam of type STR_MS_T for the result of the check, with 0 for failure and 1 for success

Description:
This microservice checks whether the desired access is permitted.

Note:
The microservice relies upon session variables defined for user access to define whose permissions are being checked. Only the access permissions of the person executing the microservice can be checked. See ruleintegrityFileOwner.r for how to check access permission for any person. The following types of

hierarchical access can be checked. The list is ordered from lowest to highest access permission. A higher access permission grants all lower access permissions.

     null
     execute
     read annotation
     read system metadata
     read object
     write annotation
     create metadata
     modify metadata
     administer object
     create object
     modify object
     delete object
     create token
     delete token
     curate
     own

Example Usage:

```
myTestRule
{
     #Input parameters are:
     # Name of object
     # Access permission that will be checked
     #Output parameter is:
     # Result, 0 for failure and 1 for success
     msiCheckAccess(*Path,*Acl,*Result);
     if(*Result == 0) {
        writeLine("stdout","File *Path does not have access *Acl"); }
     else {writeLine("stdout","File *Path has access *Acl"); }
}
INPUT *Path = "/$rodsZoneClient/home/$userNameClient/sub1/foo1", *Acl = "own"
OUTPUT ruleExecOut
```

4.64   Core :: Data Object :: msiCheckOwner

Example rule: iRODS/clients/icommands/test/rules4.0/acmsiCheckOwner.r

msiCheckOwner(   )

Parameters:
None.

Description:
This microservice checks whether the user is the owner for a file operation.

Note:

This microservice can only be used within the "core.re" file for policies that have the S3 session variable $userNameClient set as defined in the iRODS Primer. The rule example is in iRODS/clients/icommands/test/rules4.0/acmsiCheckOwner.r.

Example Usage:

```
acPostProcForPut
{
        # The msiCheckOwner microservice reads the data object rei structure
        # and can only be use with policies that set the S3 session variables
        # No input or output parameters. This microservice only uses
        # the internal rei data structure.
        # Returns zero on success
        # Output from running the example is:
        #  Username is rods
        ON (msiCheckOwner==0)
        {
           writeLine("stdout","Username is $userNameClient");
        }
}
```

4.65   Core :: Data Object :: msiCollRsync

Example rule: iRODS/clients/icommands/test/rules4.0/rulemsiCollRsync.r

```
msiCollRsync    (        msParam_t *      inpParam1,
                         msParam_t *      inpParam2,
                         msParam_t *      inpParam3,
                         msParam_t *      inpParam4,
                         msParam_t *      outParam          )
```

Parameters:
[in]	inpParam1	- a STR_MS_T which specifies the source collection path.
[in]	inpParam2	- a STR_MS_T which specifies the target collection path.
[in]	inpParam3	- Optional - a STR_MS_T which specifies the target resource.
[in]	inpParam4	- Optional - a STR_MS_T which specifies the rsync mode (RSYNC_MODE_KW). Valid mode is IRODS_TO_IRODS.
[out]	outParam	- a INT_MS_T containing the status.

Note that optional parameters take the value "null" when not being used.

Description:
This microservice recursively syncs a source collection to a target collection.

Example Usage:

```
myTestRule
{
        # Input parameters are:
        #  Source collection path
```

# Target collection path
# Optional target resource
# Optional synchronization mode: IRODS_TO_IRODS
# Output parameter is:
# Status of the operation
# Output from running the example is:
# Synchronized collection /$rodsZoneClient/home/$userNameClient/sub1 with collection /$rodsZoneClient/home/$userNameClient/sub2
msiCollRsync(*srcColl,*destColl,*Resource, "IRODS_TO_IRODS", *Status);
writeLine("stdout","Synchronized collection *srcColl with collection *destColl");
}
INPUT *srcColl="/$rodsZoneClient/home/$userNameClient/sub1",
*destColl="/$rodsZoneClient/home/$userNameClient/sub2", *Resource="demoResc"
OUTPUT ruleExecOut

4.66   Core :: Data Object :: msiDataObjChksum

Example rule: iRODS/clients/icommands/test/rules4.0/rulemsiDataObjChksum.r

msiDataObjChksum (msParam_t *   inpParam1,
                             msParam_t *   msKeyValStr,
                             msParam_t *   outParam   )

Parameters:
[in]   inpParam1   - A DataObjInp_MS_T or a STR_MS_T which would be taken as
                        dataObj path.
[in]   msKeyValStr   - Optional - a STR_MS_T. This is the special msKeyValStr format
                        of keyWd1=value1++++keyWd2=value2++++keyWd3=value3...
                        If the keyWd is not specified (without the '=' char), the value is
                        assumed to be the target resource ("destRescName") for
                        backward compatibility. Valid keyWds are:
                        "ChksumAll"   - checksum all replicas. This keyWd has no
                                        value. But the '=' character is still needed.
                        "verifyChksum" - verify the chksum value.
                        "forceChksum" - checksum data-objects even if a checksum already
                                        exists in iCAT. This keyWd has no value.
                        "replNum"   - the replica number to checksum. This
                                        keyWd has no value.
[out]   outParam   - a STR_MS_T containing the chksum value.

Description:
This microservice calls rsDataObjChksum to chksum the iput data object as part of a workflow execution.
The example generates checksums for all replicas. Checksums are stored in the iCAT.

Example Usage:

myTestRule {
# Input parameters are:
# Data object path
# Optional flags in form Keyword=value
#   ChksumAll=

```
#    verifyChksum=
#    forceChksum=
#    replNum=
# Output parameters are:
#   Checksum value
# Output from running the example is
#   Collection is /$rodsZoneClient/home/$userNameClient/sub1 and file is foo1
#   Saved checksum for file foo1 is f03e80c9994d137614935e4913e53417, new checksum is
f03e80c9994d137614935e4913e53417
   msiSplitPath(*dataObject,*Coll,*File);
   writeLine("stdout","Collection is *Coll and file is *File");
   *Q1 = select DATA_CHECKSUM where DATA_NAME = '*File' AND COLL_NAME = '*Coll';
   foreach(*R1 in *Q1) {
     *chkSumS = *R1.DATA_CHECKSUM;
     msiDataObjChksum(*dataObject,*Flags,*chkSum);
     writeLine("stdout","Saved checksum for file *File is *chkSumS, new checksum is *chkSum");
   }
}
INPUT *dataObject="/$rodsZoneClient/home/$userNameClient/sub1/foo1", *Flags="forceChksum="
OUTPUT ruleExecOut
```

4.67   Core :: Data Object :: msiDataObjCopy

Example rule: iRODS/clients/icommands/test/rules4.0/rulemsiDataObjCopy.r

msiDataObjCopy	(	msParam_t *	inpParam1,
		msParam_t *	inpParam2,
		msParam_t *	msKeyValStr,
		msParam_t *	outParam)

Parameters:

[in]	inpParam1	- a DataObjCopyInp_MS_T or DataObjInp_MS_T which is the source DataObjInp or STR_MS_T which would be the source object path.
[in]	inpParam2	- Optional - a DataObjInp_MS_T which is the destination DataObjInp or STR_MS_T which would be the destination object path.
[in]	msKeyValStr	- Optional - a STR_MS_T. This is the special msKeyValStr format of keyWd1=value1++++keyWd2=value2++++keyWd3=value3... If the keyWd is not specified (without the '=' char), the value is assumed to be the target resource ("destRescName") for backward compatibility. Valid keyWds are:

"destRescName" - the resource to copy to.

"forceFlag"   - overwrite existing copy. This keyWd has no value. But the '=' character is still needed.

"numThreads"   - the number of threads to use.

"filePath"   - The physical file path of the uploaded file on the server.

"dataType"   - the data type of the file.

"verifyChksum" - verify the transfer using checksum. this keyWd has no value. But the '=' character is still needed.

[out]	outParam	- a INT_MS_T for the status.

Description:
This microservice copies a file from one logical (source) collection to another logical (destination) collection. The destination collection can be put on another storage resource.

Example Usage:

```
myTestRule
{
        # Input parameters are:
        #  Source data object path
        #  Optional destination object path
        #  Optional flags in form keyword=value
        #   destRescName
        #   forceFlag=
        #   numThreads
        #   filePath="Physical file path of the uploaded file on the server"
        #   dataType
        #   verifyChksum=
        # Output parameter is:
        #   Status
        # Output from running the example is
        #  File /$rodsZoneClient/home/$userNameClient/sub1/foo1 copied to
        /$rodsZoneClient/home/$userNameClient/sub2/foo1
        msiDataObjCopy(*SourceFile,*DestFile,"forceFlag=", *Status);
        writeLine("stdout", "File *SourceFile copied to *DestFile");
}
INPUT *SourceFile="/$rodsZoneClient/home/$userNameClient/sub1/foo1",
*DestFile="/$rodsZoneClient/home/$userNameClient/sub2/foo1"
OUTPUT ruleExecOut
```

4.68   Core :: Data Object :: msiDataObjGet

Example rule: iRODS/clients/icommands/test/rules4.0/rulemsiDataObjGet.r

msiDataObjGet (	msParam_t *	inpParam1,
	msParam_t *	msKeyValStr,
	msParam_t *	outParam)

Parameters:
[in]	inpParam1	- A DataObjInp_MS_T or STR_MS_T which would be taken as dataObj path.
[in]	msKeyValStr	- Optional - a STR_MS_T. This is the special msKeyValStr format of keyWd1=value1++++keyWd2=value2++++keyWd3=value3... If the keyWd is not specified (without the '=' char), the value is assumed to be the client's local file path ("localPath") for backward compatibility. Valid keyWds are:

"localPath"   - the client's local file path.
"rescName"   - the resource of the copy to get.
"replNum"   - the replica number of the copy to get.
"numThreads"   - the number of threads to use.

"forceFlag"	- overwrite local copy. This keyWd has no value. But the '=' character is still needed
	"verifyChksum" - verify the transfer using checksum. this keyWd has no value. But the '=' character is still needed.
[out]	outParam	- a INT_MS_T containing the status.

Description:

This microservice gets a data object by requesting the client to call a rcDataObjGet API as part of a workflow execution.

Note:

This call should only be used through the rcExecMyRule (irule) call i.e., rule execution initiated by clients and should not be called internally by the server since it interacts with the client through the normal client/server socket connection. Also, it should never be called through delay since it requires client interaction. The localPath is required on input.

Example Usage:

```
myTestRule
{
        # Input parameters are:
        #  Data object path
        #  Flags in form keyword=value
        #   localPath
        #   rescName
        #   replNum
        #   numThreads
        #   forceFlag
        #   verifyChksum
        # Output parameter is
        #   Status
        # Output from running the example is:
        #  File /$rodsZoneClient/home/$userNameClient/sub1/foo1 is retrieved from the data grid
        msiSplitPath(*SourceFile,*Coll,*File);
        msiDataObjGet(*SourceFile, "localPath=./*File++++forceFlag=", *Status);
        writeLine("stdout", "File *SourceFile is retrieved from the data grid");
}
INPUT *SourceFile="/$rodsZoneClient/home/$userNameClient/sub1/foo1"
OUTPUT ruleExecOut
```

4.69   Core :: Data Object :: msiDataObjPhymv

Example rule: iRODS/clients/icommands/test/rules4.0/rulemsiDataObjPhymv.r

msiDataObjPhymv	(	msParam_t *	inpParam1,
		msParam_t *	inpParam2,
		msParam_t *	inpParam3,
		msParam_t *	inpParam4,
		msParam_t *	inpParam5,
		msParam_t *	outParam	)

Parameters:

[in]	inpParam1	- A DataObjInp_MS_T or STR_MS_T which would be taken as dataObj path.
[in]	inpParam2	- Optional - a STR_MS_T which specifies the dest resourceName.
[in]	inpParam3	- Optional - a STR_MS_T which specifies the src resourceName.
[in]	inpParam4	- Optional - a STR_MS_T which specifies the replNum.
[in]	inpParam5	- Optional - a STR_MS_T which specifies the IRODS_ADMIN_KW, irodsAdmin, for administrator controlled data movement or is "null"
[out]	outParam	- a INT_MS_T containing the status.

Description:
This microservice calls rsDataObjPhymv to physically move the input data object to another resource.

Note:
If the policy acSetRescSchemeForCreate sets a default resource as forced, the physical move will not be done to the requested resource.

Example Usage:

```
myTestRule
{
        # Input parameters are:
        #  Data object path
        #  Optional destination resource name
        #  Optional source resource name
        #  Optional replica number
        #  Optional keyword for IRODS_ADMIN
        # Output parameters are:
        #  Status
        # Output from running the example is:
        #  Replica number 0 of file /$rodsZoneClient/home/$userNameClient/sub1/foo1 is moved from
        resource demoResc to resource testResc
        msiDataObjPhymv(*SourceFile,*DestResource,*SourceResource,*ReplicaNumber, "null", *Status);
        writeLine("stdout","Replica number *ReplicaNumber of file *SourceFile is moved from resource
        *SourceResource to resource *DestResource");
}
INPUT *SourceFile="/$rodsZoneClient/home/$userNameClient/sub1/foo1", *DestResource="testResc",
*SourceResource="demoResc", *ReplicaNumber="0"
OUTPUT ruleExecOut
```

4.70   Core :: Data Object :: msiDataObjPut

Example rule: iRODS/clients/icommands/test/rules4.0/rulemsiDataObjPut.r

msiDataObjPut (	msParam_t *	inpParam1,
	msParam_t *	inpParam2,
	msParam_t *	msKeyValStr,
	msParam_t *	outParam)

Parameters:

[in]	inpParam1	- A DataObjInp_MS_T or STR_MS_T which would be taken as dataObj path.

| [in] | inpParam2 | - Optional - a STR_MS_T which specifies the resource. |
| [in] | msKeyValStr | - Optional - a STR_MS_T. This is the special msKeyValStr format of keyWd1=value1++++keyWd2=value2++++keyWd3=value3... If the keyWd is not specified (without the '=' char), the value is assumed to be the client's local file path ("localPath") for backward compatibility. Valid keyWds are: |

"localPath"   - the client's local file path.
"destRescName" - the target resource - where the object should go.
"all"   - upload to all resources
 "forceFlag"   - overwrite existing copy. This keyWd has
                    no value. But the '=' character is still needed.
"replNum"   - the replica number to overwrite.
 "numThreads" - the number of threads to use.
 "filePath"   - The physical file path of the uploaded file on the server.
 "dataType"   - the data type of the file.
 "verifyChksum" - verify the transfer using checksum. This keyWd has no
                    value. But the '=' character is still needed.

| [out] | outParam | - a INT_MS_T containing the status. |

Description:
This microservice requests the client to call a rcDataObjPut API as part of a workflow execution.

Note:
This call should only be used through the rcExecMyRule (irule) call i.e., rule execution initiated by clients and should not be called internally by the server since it interacts with the client through the normal client/server socket connection. Also, it should never be called through delay since it requires client interaction.

Example Usage:

myTestRule
{
       # Input parameters are:
     # Data object path
     # Optional resource or resource group
     # Optional flags in form keyword=value
     #   localPath
     #   destRescName
     #   all - to upload to all resources within a resource group
     #   forceFlag=
     #   replNum - the replica number to overwrite
     #   numThreads
     #   filePath - the physical file path of the uploaded file on the server
     #   dataType
     #   verifyChksum=
     # Output parameter is:
     #   Status
     # Output from running the example is:
     # File /$rodsZoneClient/home/$userNameClient/sub1/foo1 is written to the data grid as foo1
     msiDataObjPut(*DestFile,*DestResource, "localPath=*LocalFile++++forceFlag=", *Status);
     writeLine("stdout","File *LocalFile is written to the data grid as *DestFile");
}
INPUT *DestFile="/$rodsZoneClient/home/$userNameClient/sub1/foo1", *DestResource="demoResc",
*LocalFile="foo1"
OUTPUT ruleExecOut

4.71   Core :: Data Object :: msiDataObjRename

Example rule: iRODS/clients/icommands/test/rules4.0/rulemsiDataObjRename.r

msiDataObjRename	(	msParam_t *	inpParam1,
		msParam_t *	inpParam2,
		msParam_t *	inpParam3,
		msParam_t *	outParam)

Parameters:

[in]   inpParam1   - A DataObjCopyInp_MS_T or STR_MS_T which would be taken
                    as the src dataObj path.

[in]   inpParam2   - Optional - A DataObjInp_MS_T which is the destination
                    DataObjInp or STR_MS_T which would be the destination object Path.

[in]   inpParam3   - Optional - a INT_MS_T or STR_MS_T which specifies the
                    object type. A 0 means data obj and > 0 means collection.

[out] outParam   - a INT_MS_T containing the status.

Description:
This microservice calls rsDataObjRename to rename the iput data object or collection to another path. The destination path name cannot exist before the call. All replicas are changed to the new name.

Example Usage:

```
myTestRule
{
        # Input parameters are:
        #  Source data object path
        #  Optional destination object path
        #  Optional Object type
        #    0 means data object
        #    1 means collection
        # Output parameter is:
        #   Status
        # Output from running the example is:
        # The name of /$rodsZoneClient/home/$userNameClient/sub1/foo1 is changed to
        /$rodsZoneClient/home/$userNameClient/sub1/foo2
        msiDataObjRename(*SourceFile,*NewFilePath,"0", *Status);
        # To change the name of a collection, set the third input parameter to 1
        writeLine("stdout","The name of *SourceFile is changed to *NewFilePath");
}
INPUT *SourceFile="/$rodsZoneClient/home/$userNameClient/sub1/foo1",
*NewFilePath="/$rodsZoneClient/home/$userNameClient/sub1/foo2"
OUTPUT ruleExecOut
```

4.72   Core :: Data Object :: msiDataObjRepl

Example rule: iRODS/clients/icommands/test/rules4.0/rulemsiDataObjRepl.r

msiDataObjRepl (msParam_t * inpParam1,
msParam_t * msKeyValStr,
msParam_t * outParam)

Parameters:
[in]   inpParam1   - a msParam of type DataObjInp_MS_T or STR_MS_T which
would be the obj Path.
[in]   msKeyValStr   - Optional - a STR_MS_T. This is the special msKeyValStr format
of keyWd1=value1++++keyWd2=value2++++keyWd3=value3...
If the keyWd is not specified (without the '=' char), the value is
assumed to be the target resource ("destRescName") for
backward compatibility. Valid keyWds are:

"destRescName"	- the target resource to replicate to.
"backupRescName"	- the target resource to backup the data. If this keyWd is used, the backup mode will be switched on.
"rescName"	- the resource of the source copy.
"updateRepl"	- update other replicas with the latest copy. This keyWd has no value. But the '=' character is still needed.
"replNum"	- the replica number to use as source.
"numThreads"	- the number of threads to use.
"all"	- replicate to all resources in the resource group. This keyWd has no value.
"irodsAdmin"	- admin user replicate other users' files. This keyWd has no value.
"verifyChksum"	- verify the transfer using checksum. This keyWd has no value.
"rbudpTransfer"	- use RBUDP (datagram) protocol for the data transfer. This keyWd has no value.
"rbudpSendRate"	- Valid only if "rbudpTransfer" is on. This is the send rate in kbits/sec. The default is 600,000.
"rbudpPackSize"	- Valid only if "rbudpTransfer" is on. This is the packet size in bytes. The default is 8192.

[out]   outParam   - a msParam of type INT_MS_T which is the status of the operation.

Description:
This microservice replicates a file in a collection (it assigns a different replica number to the new copy in the iCAT Metadata Catalog).

Note:
Can be called by client through irule. In the example, the replica is physically stored in the "testResc" resource.

Example Usage:

myTestRule
{
        # Input parameters are:
        # Data Object path
        # Optional flags in form keyword=value
        #   destRescName - the target resource for the replica
        #   backupRescName - specifies use of the resource for the backup mode

    #   rescName - the resource holding the source data
    #   updateRepl= - specifies all replicas will be updated
    #   replNum - specifies the replica number to use as the source
    #   numThreads - specifies the number of threads to use for transmission
    #   all - specifies to replicate to all resources in a resource group
    #   irodsAdmin - enables administrator to replicate other users' files
    #   verifyChksum - verify the transfer using checksums
    #   rbudpTransfer - use Reliable Blast UDP for transport
    #   rbudpSendRate - the transmission rate in kbits/sec, default is 600 kbits/sec
    #   rbudpPackSize - the packet size in bytes, default is 8192
    # Output parameter is:
    # Status
    # Output from running the example is:
    # The file /$rodsZoneClient/home/$userNameClient/sub1/foo3 is replicated onto resource testResc
    msiDataObjRepl(*SourceFile, "destRescName=*Resource", *Status);
    writeLine("stdout","The file *SourceFile is replicated onto resource *Resource");
}
INPUT *SourceFile="/$rodsZoneClient/home/$userNameClient/sub1/foo3", *Resource="testResc"
OUTPUT ruleExecOut

4.73   Core :: Data Object :: msiDataObjRsync

Example rule: iRODS/clients/icommands/test/rules4.0/rulemsiDataObjRsync.r

msiDataObjRsync	(	msParam_t *	inpParam1,	
		msParam_t *	inpParam2,	
		msParam_t *	inpParam3,	
		msParam_t *	inpParam4,	
		msParam_t *	outParam	)

Parameters:

[in]	inpParam1	- A DataObjInp_MS_T or STR_MS_T which would be taken as dataObj path.
[in]	inpParam2	- Optional - a STR_MS_T which specifies the rsync mode. Valid mode is IRODS_TO_IRODS and IRODS_TO_COLLECTION.
[in]	inpParam3	- Optional - a STR_MS_T which specifies the resource name.
[in]	inpParam4	- Optional - a STR_MS_T which specifies the RSYNC_DEST_PATH_KW, rsyncDestPath. For IRODS_TO_IRODS, this is the target path. For IRODS_TO_COLLECTION, this is the top level target collection. e.g., if dataObj (inpParam1) is /$rodsZoneClient/home/$userNameClient/foo and the target collection (inpParam4) is /tempZone/archive, then the target path is /tempZone/archive/home/$userNameClient/foo.
[out]	outParam	- a INT_MS_T containing the status.

Description:
This microservice synchronizes a data object with the data grid by requesting the client to call a rcDataObjRsync API as part of a workflow execution.

Note:
For now, this microservice should only be used for IRODS_TO_IRODS mode because of the logistic difficulty with the microservice getting the checksum values of the local file.

Example Usage:

myTestRule
{
       # Input parameters are:
       # Data object path
       # Optional flag for mode
       #   IRODS_TO_IRODS
       #   IRODS_TO_COLLECTION
       # Optional storage resource
       # Optional target collection
       # Output parameters are:
       # Status
       # Output from running the example is:
       # The file /$rodsZoneClient/home/$userNameClient/sub1/foo2 is synchronized onto the logical data object path /$rodsZoneClient/home/$userNameClient/rules
       msiDataObjRsync(*SourceFile, "IRODS_TO_IRODS", *DestResource,*DestPathName,*Status);
       writeLine("stdout","The file *SourceFile is synchronized onto the logical data object path *DestPathName");
}
INPUT *SourceFile="/$rodsZoneClient/home/$userNameClient/sub1/foo2", *DestResource="testResc", *DestPathName="/$rodsZoneClient/home/$userNameClient/rules"
OUTPUT ruleExecOut

4.74   Core :: Data Object :: msiDataObjTrim

Example rule: iRODS/clients/icommands/test/rules4.0/rulemsiDataObjTrim.r

msiDataObjTrim	(	msParam_t *	inpParam1,
		msParam_t *	inpParam2,
		msParam_t *	inpParam3,
		msParam_t *	inpParam4,
		msParam_t *	inpParam5,
		msParam_t *	outParam)

Parameters:

[in]	inpParam1	- A DataObjInp_MS_T or STR_MS_T which would be taken as dataObj path.
[in]	inpParam2	- Optional - a STR_MS_T which specifies the resourceName.
[in]	inpParam3	- Optional - a STR_MS_T which specifies the replNum.
[in]	inpParam4	- Optional - a STR_MS_T which specifies the minimum number of copies to keep. A value of 1 means no replicas will be kept.
[in]	inpParam5	- Optional - a STR_MS_T which specifies administrator controlled trimming of replicas irodsAdmin – flag to indicate actions by an administrator
[out]	outParam	- a INT_MS_T containing the status.

Description:
This microservice calls rsDataObjTrim to trim down the number of replicas of a data object.

Example Usage:

myTestRule
{
       # Input parameters are:
       # Data object path
       # Optional storage resource name
       # Optional replica number
       # Optional number of replicas to keep
       # Optional administrator flag irodsAdmin, to enable administrator to trim replicas
       # Output parameter is:
       # Status
       # Output from running the example is:
       # The replicas of File /$rodsZoneClient/home/$userNameClient/sub1/foo2 are deleted
       msiDataObjTrim(*SourceFile, "null", "null", "1", "null", *Status);
       writeLine("stdout","The replicas of file *SourceFile are deleted");
}
INPUT *SourceFile="/$rodsZoneClient/home/$userNameClient/sub1/foo2"
OUTPUT ruleExecOut

4.75   Core :: Data Object :: msiDataObjUnlink

Example rule: iRODS/clients/icommands/test/rules4.0/rulemsiDataObjUnlink.r

msiDataObjUnlink	(	msParam_t *	inpParam,	
		msParam_t *	outParam	)

Parameters:

[in]   inpParam   - a msParam of type DataObjInp_MS_T or STR_MS_T which would be taken as msKeyValStr. msKeyValStr - This is the special msKeyValStr format of keyWd1=value1++++keyWd2=value2++++keyWd3=value3... If the keyWd is not specified (without the '=' char), the value is assumed to be the path of the data object("objPath") for backward compatibility. Valid keyWds are:

                     "objPath"   - the path of the data object to remove.
                     "replNum"   - the replica number of the copy to remove.
                     "forceFlag="   - Remove the data object instead of putting it in trash. This keyWd has no value. But the '=' character is still needed.
                     "irodsAdminRmTrash=" - Admin rm trash. This keyWd has no value.
                     "irodsRmTrash="   - rm trash. This keyWd has no value.

[out]   outParam   - a msParam of type INT_MS_T for the status.

Description:
This microservice deletes an existing data object.

Note:

Can be called by client through irule. When used with irodsRmTrash, the objPath must specify a file within the trash.

The msiDataObjUnlink microservice will not delete a collection.

Example Usage:

```
myTestRule
{
        # Input parameter is:
        # Flags in form keyword=value
        #   objPath - the data object path to remove
        #   replNum - the replica number to be removed
        #   forceFlag= - flag to remove file without transferring to trash
        #   irodsAdminRmTrash - flag to allow administrator to remove trash
        #   irodsRmTrash - flag for user to remove trash
        # Output parameter is:
        #   Status
        # Output from running the example is:
        # Replica number 1 of file /$rodsZoneClient/home/$userNameClient/sub1/foo3 is removed
        msiDataObjUnlink("objPath=*SourceFile++++replNum=1", *Status);
        writeLine("stdout","Replica number 1 of file *SourceFile is removed");
}
INPUT *SourceFile="/$rodsZoneClient/home/$userNameClient/sub1/foo3"
OUTPUT ruleExecOut
```

4.76   Core :: Data Object :: msiGetObjType

Example rule: iRODS/clients/icommands/test/rules4.0/rulemsiGetObjType.r

msiGetObjType (msParam_t *   objParam,
                         msParam_t *   typeParam   )

Parameters:
[in]   objParam   - a msParam of type STR_MS_T, the path of the iRODS object
[out]   typeParam   - a msParam of type STR_MS_T, output value of the object type

Description:
This microservice gets an object's type from the iCAT to specify whether file, collection resource, or user.

Note:
Valid object types are:
-d	file
-c	collection
-r	resource
-g	resource group
-u	user
-m	metadata
-t	token

Example Usage:

myTestRule
{
    # Input parameter is:
    # Object name
    # Output parameter is:
    # Type
    # Output from running the example is:
    # The type of object /$rodsZoneClient/home/$userNameClient/sub1/foo3 is -d
    # The type of object demoResc is -r
    msiGetObjType(*SourceFile,*Type);
    writeLine("stdout","The type of object *SourceFile is *Type");
    msiGetObjType(*Resource,*Type1);
    writeLine("stdout","The type of object *Resource is *Type1");
}
INPUT *SourceFile="/$rodsZoneClient/home/$userNameClient/sub1/foo3", *Resource="demoResc"
OUTPUT ruleExecOut

4.77   Core :: Data Object :: msiObjStat

Example rule: iRODS/clients/icommands/test/rules4.0/rulemsiObjStat.r

msiObjStat   (msParam_t *   inpParam1,
                            msParam_t *   outParam   )

Parameters:
[in]   inpParam1   - A DataObjInp_MS_T or STR_MS_T which would be taken as
                            dataObj path.
[out]   outParam   - a RodsObjStat_PI structure containing an integer with value
                            COLL_OBJ_T (collection or DATA_OBJ_T (data object).

Description:
This microservice calls rsObjStat to get the stat of an iRODS path as part of a workflow execution.

Example Usage:

myTestRule
{
    # Input parameter is:
    # Data object path
    # Output parameter is:
    # Type of object is written into a RodsObjStat_PI structure
    msiSplitPath(*SourceFile,*Coll,*File);
    msiObjStat(*SourceFile,*Stat);
    msiObjStat(*Coll,*Stat1);
    writeLine("stdout","Type of object is written into a RodsObjStat_PI structure");
}
INPUT *SourceFile="/$rodsZoneClient/home/$userNameClient/sub1/foo3"
OUTPUT ruleExecOut

4.78   Core :: Data Object :: msiPhyPathReg

Example rule: iRODS/clients/icommands/test/rules4.0/rulemsiPhyPathReg.r

msiPhyPathReg   (msParam_t *   inpParam1,
                                          msParam_t *   inpParam2,
                                          msParam_t *   inpParam3,
                                          msParam_t *   inpParam4,
                                          msParam_t *   outParam   )

Parameters:
[in]   inpParam1   - A DataObjInp_MS_T or STR_MS_T which would be taken as
                             object path. The path can be a data object or a collection path.
[in]   inpParam2   - Optional - a STR_MS_T which specifies the dest resourceName.
[in]   inpParam3   - Optional - a STR_MS_T which specifies the physical path to be
                             registered.
[in]   inpParam4   - Optional - a STR_MS_T which specifies whether the path to be
                             registered is a directory. A keyword string "collection" indicates
                             the path is a directory. A "null" string indicates the path is a file.
                             A keyword string "mountPoint" (MOUNT_POINT_STR) means mount the
                             file directory given in inpParam3. A keyword string "linkPoint"
                             (LINK_POINT_STR) means soft link the collection given in
                             inpParam3.
[out]   outParam   - a INT_MS_T containing the status.

Description:
This microservice calls rsPhyPathReg to register a physical path with the iCAT.

Note:
The data object path in iRODS must be created before the registration is done.

Example Usage:

myTestRule
{
        # Input parameters are:
        # Data object path
        # Optional destination resource
        # Optional physical path to register
        # Optional flag for type of
        #   collection - specifies the path is a directory
        #   null   - specifies the path is a file
        #   mountPoint - specifies to mount the physical path
        #   linkPoint   - specifies soft link the physical path
        # Output parameter is:
        # Status
        # Output from running the example is:
        # The local collection /home/reagan/irods-scripts/ruletest is mounted under the logical collection
        /$rodsZoneClient/home/$userNameClient/irods-rules
         msiPhyPathReg(*DestCollection,*Resource,*SourceDirectory, "mountPoint", *Stat);
         writeLine("stdout","The local collection *SourceDirectory is mounted under the logical collection
        *DestCollection");

}
INPUT *DestCollection="/$rodsZoneClient/home/$userNameClient/irods-rules",
*SourceDirectory="/home/reagan/irods-scripts/ruletest", *Resource="demoResc"
OUTPUT ruleExecOut

4.79   Core :: Data Object :: msiSetReplComment

Example rule: iRODS/clients/icommands/test/rules4.0/rulemsiSetReplComment.r

msiSetReplComment   (msParam_t *   inpParam1,
                                        msParam_t *   inpParam2,
                                        msParam_t *   inpParam3,
                                        msParam_t *   inpParam4   )

Parameters:
[in]   inpParam1   - a INT with the id of the object (can be null if unknown, the next
                          param will then be used)
[in]   inpParam2   - a msParam of type DataObjInp_MS_T or a STR_MS_T which
                          would be taken as dataObj path
[in]   inpParam3   - a INT which gives the replica number
[in]   inpParam4   - a STR_MS_T containing the comment

Description:
This microservice sets the data_comments attribute of a data object.

Note:
Can be called by client through irule

Example Usage:

myTestRule {
#Input parameters are:
Object ID if known
Data object path
Replica number
Comment to be added
#Output parameter is:
Status
#Output from running the example is:
# The comment added to file /$rodsZoneClient/home/$userNameClient/sub1/foo3 is "New comment"
# The comment retrieved from iCAT is "New comment"
  msiSetReplComment("null",*SourceFile,0,*Comment);
  writeLine("stdout","The comment added to file *SourceFile is *Comment");
  msiSplitPath(*SourceFile,*Coll,*File);
  *Q1 = select DATA_COMMENTS where DATA_NAME = '*File' AND COLL_NAME = '*Coll';
  foreach(*R1 in *Q1) {
   *com = *R1.DATA_COMMENTS;
   writeLine("stdout","The comment retrieved from iCAT is *com");
  }
}
INPUT *SourceFile="/$rodsZoneClient/home/$userNameClient/sub1/foo3", *Comment="New comment"
OUTPUT ruleExecOut

4.80   Core :: Helper :: msiAddKeyValToMspStr

Example rule: iRODS/clients/icommands/test/rules4.0/rulemsiAddKeyValToMspStr.r

msiAddKeyValToMspStr   (msParam_t *   keyStr,
                                         msParam_t *   valStr,
                                         msParam_t *   msKeyValStr   )

Parameters:
[in]   keyStr   - a STR_MS_T key to be added to msKeyValStr.
[in]   valStr   - a STR_MS_T value to be added to msKeyValStr.
[out]   msKeyValStr   - a msKeyValStr to hold the new keyVal pair.

Description:
Adds a key and value to existing msKeyValStr which is a special kind of STR_MS_T that has the format - keyWd1=value1++++keyWd2=value2++++keyWd3=value3...

Note:
none

Example Usage:

```
myTestRule
{
        # Input parameters are:
        #  Attribute name
        #  Attribute value
        # Output from running the example is:
        #  The string now contains
        #  destRescName=demoResc
        msiAddKeyValToMspStr(*AttrName,*AttrValue,*KeyValStr);
        writeLine("stdout","The string now contains");
        writeLine("stdout","*KeyValStr");
}
INPUT *AttrName="destRescName", *AttrValue="demoResc"
OUTPUT ruleExecOut
```

4.81   Core :: Helper :: msiExit

Example rule: iRODS/clients/icommands/test/rules4.0/rulemsiExit.r

msiExit   (msParam_t *   inpParam1,
                            msParam_t *   inpParam2   )

Parameters:

| [in] | inpParam1 | - A STR_MS_T which specifies the status error to add to the error stack. |
| [in] | inpParam2 | - A STR_MS_T which specifies the error explanation to add to the error stack. |

Description:
Add a user error explanation to the error stack.

Note:
This call should only be used through the rcExecMyRule (irule) call i.e., rule execution initiated by clients and should not be called internally by the server since it interacts with the client through the normal client/server socket connection.

Example Usage:

```
myTestRule
{
        # Input parameters are:
        #  Status error to add to the error stack
        #  Message to add to the error stack
        # Output from running the example is:
        #  Error number 200 and message Test Error
        writeLine("stdout","Error number *Error and message *Message");
        msiExit(*Error,*Message);
}
INPUT *Error="200", *Message="Test Error"
OUTPUT ruleExecOut
```

4.82   Core :: Helper :: msiGetSessionVarValue

Example rule: iRODS/clients/icommands/test/rules4.0/rulemsiGetSessionVarValue.r

| **msiGetSessionVarValue** | (| msParam_t * | inpVar, |
| | | msParam_t * | outputMode   ) |

Parameters:

| [in] | inpVar | - A STR_MS_T which specifies the name of the session variable to output. The input session variable should NOT start with the "$" character. An input value of "all" means output all valid session variables. |
| [in] | outputMode | - A STR_MS_T which specifies the output mode. Valid modes are |

"server"   - log the output to the server log
"client"   - send the output to the client specified in rError structure
                       (screen if running interactively)
"all"   - send to both client and server

Description:
Gets the value of a session variable from the rei structure in memory

Note:
none

Example Usage:

```
myTestRule
{
        # Input parameters are:
        #  Session variable
        #    Session variable without the $ sign
        #    all    - output all of the defined variables
        #  Output mode flag:
        #    server  - log the output to the server log
        #    client  - send the output to the client specified in rError structure
        #    all    - send the output to both client and server
        # Output from running the example is:
        #  Variables are written to the log file
        # Output in irods/server/log/rodsLog.2011.6.1 log file is:
        #  msiGetSessionVarValue: userNameClient=rods
        msiGetSessionVarValue(*A, "server");
        writeLine("stdout","Variables are written to the log file");
}
INPUT *A="userNameClient"
OUTPUT ruleExecOut
```

4.83   Core :: Helper :: msiGetStderrInExecCmdOut

Example rule: iRODS/clients/icommands/test/rules4.0/rulemsiGetStderrInExecCmdOut.r

msiGetStderrInExecCmdOut (msParam_t *   inpExecCmdOut,
                                       msParam_t *   outStr   )

Parameters:
[in]   inpExecCmdOut - a ExecCmdOut_MS_T containing the status of the command
                              execution and the stdout/stderr output.
[out]   outStr   - a STR_MS_T to hold the retrieved stderr buffer.

Description:
Gets stderr buffer from ExecCmdOut into buffer.

Note:
none

Example Usage:

```
myTestRule
{
        # Only executables stored within irods/server/bin/cmd can be run
        # Input parameter is:
        #  Output buffer from the exec command which holds the status, output, and error messages
        # Output parameter is:
        #  String to hold the retrieved error message
        # Output from running the example is:
        #  Error message is
        msiExecCmd(*Cmd,*ARG," ", "", "", *HELLO_OUT);
```

# *HELLO_OUT holds the status, output and error messages
msiGetStderrInExecCmdOut(*HELLO_OUT,*ErrorOut);
writeLine("stdout","Error message is *ErrorOut");
}
INPUT *Cmd="hello", *ARG="iRODS"
OUTPUT ruleExecOut

4.84   Core :: Helper :: msiGetStdoutInExecCmdOut

Example rule: iRODS/clients/icommands/test/rules4.0/rulemsiGetStdoutInExecCmdOut.r

msiGetStdoutInExecCmdOut   (msParam_t *   inpExecCmdOut,
                                             msParam_t *   outStr   )

Parameters:
[in]   inpExecCmdOut - a ExecCmdOut_MS_T containing the status of the command
                                      execution and the stdout/stderr output.
[out]   outStr   - a STR_MS_T to hold the retrieved stdout buffer.

Description:
Gets stdout buffer from ExecCmdOut into string buffer.

Note:
none

Example Usage:

myTestRule
{
        # Input parameter is:
        # Buffer holding the status, output and error messages from the command execution
        # Output parameter is:
        # String holding the output message
        # Output from executing the command is
        # Output message is Hello World iRODS from irods
        msiExecCmd("hello", *ARG," ", "", "", *HELLO_OUT);

        # *HELLO_OUT holds the status, output and error messages
        msiGetStdoutInExecCmdOut(*HELLO_OUT,*Out);
        writeLine("stdout","Output message is *Out");
}
INPUT *ARG="iRODS"
OUTPUT ruleExecOut

4.85   Core :: Helper :: msiSplitPath

Example rule: iRODS/clients/icommands/test/rules4.0/rulemsiSplitPath.r

msiSplitPath	(	msParam_t *	inpPath,
		msParam_t *	outParentColl,
		msParam_t *	outChildName	)

Parameters:
[in]   inpPath   - a STR_MS_T which specifies the pathname to split.
[out]   outParentColl   - a STR_MS_T to hold the returned parent path.
[out]   outChildName   - a STR_MS_T to hold the returned child value.

Description:
Splits a pathname into parent collection and file values.

Note:

Example Usage:

```
myTestRule
{
        # Input parameter is:
        #   Data object path
        # Output parameters are:
        #  Collection name
        #  File name
        # Output from running the example is:
        #  Object is /$rodsZoneClient/home/$userNameClient/sub1/foo1
        #  Collection is /$rodsZoneClient/home/$userNameClient/sub1 and file is foo1
        writeLine("stdout","Object is *dataObject");
        msiSplitPath(*dataObject,*Coll,*File);
        writeLine("stdout","Collection is *Coll and file is *File");
}
INPUT *dataObject="/$rodsZoneClient/home/$userNameClient/sub1/foo1"
OUTPUT ruleExecOut
```

4.86   Core :: Helper :: msiStrCat – included in 4.0.1+

Example rule: iRODS/clients/icommands/test/rules4.0/rulemsiStrCat.r

msiStrCat	(	msParam_t *	targParam,
		msParam_t *	srcParam	)

Parameters:
[in,out] targParam   - A STR_MS_T which specifies the string that will be extended.
[in]   srcParam   - A STR_MS_T which specifies the string that will be added.

Description:
Concatenate a source string onto the end of a target string.

Note:

The concatenation operator "++" can also be used to do string concatentation.

Example Usage:

```
mytestrule{
#rule to concatenate two strings using  msiStrCat
 *str1 = "Start of string";
 *str2 = " end of string";
 writeLine("stdout", "Concatenate \"*str1\" with \"*str2\"");
 msiStrCat(*str1, *str2);
 writeLine("stdout", "Result is \"*str1\"");
}
INPUT null
OUTPUT ruleExecOut
```

4.87   Core :: Helper :: msiWriteRodsLog

Example rule: iRODS/clients/icommands/test/rules4.0/rulemsiWriteRodsLog.r

msiWriteRodsLog   (msParam_t *   inpParam1,
                                        msParam_t *   outParam   )

Parameters:
[in]   inpParam1   - A STR_MS_T which specifies the message to log.
[out]   outParam   - An INT_MS_T containing the status.

Description:
Writes a message into iRODS/server/log/rodsLog.

Note:
This call should only be used through the rcExecMyRule (irule) call i.e., rule execution initiated by clients and should not be called internally by the server since it interacts with the client through the normal client/server socket connection.

Example Usage:

```
myTestRule
{
        # Input parameter is:
        #  Message to send to iRODS server log file
        # Output parameter is:
        #  Status
        # Output from running the example is:
        #  Message is Test message for irods/server/log/rodsLog
        # Output written to log file is:
        #  msiWriteRodsLog message: Test message for irods/server/log/rodsLog
        writeLine("stdout","Message is *Message");
        msiWriteRodsLog(*Message,*Status);
}
INPUT *Message="Test message for irods/server/log/rodsLog"
```

4.88   Core :: Proxy Command :: msiExecCmd

Example rule: iRODS/clients/icommands/test/rules4.0/rulemsiExecCmd.r

msiExecCmd	(	msParam_t *	inpParam1,
		msParam_t *	inpParam2,
		msParam_t *	inpParam3,
		msParam_t *	inpParam4,
		msParam_t *	inpParam5,
		msParam_t *	outParam)

Parameters:

[in]   inpParam1   - a ExecCmd_MS_T or a STR_MS_T which specifies the command (cmd) to execute.

[in]   inpParam2   - Optional - a STR_MS_T which specifies the argv (cmdArgv) of the command

[in]   inpParam3   - Optional - a STR_MS_T which specifies the host address (execAddr) to execute the command.

[in]   inpParam4   - Optional - a STR_MS_T which specifies an iRODS file path (hintPath). The command will be executed on the host where this file is stored.

[in]   inpParam5   - Optional - A INT_MS_T or a STR_MS_T. If it is greater than zero, the resolved physical path from the logical hintPath (inpParam4) will be used as the first argument in the command.

[out]   outParam   - a ExecCmdOut_MS_T containing the status of the command execution and the stdout/stderr output.

Description:
This microservice requests the client to call a rcExecCmd API to fork and execute a command that resides in the iRODS/server/bin/cmd directory.

Note:
This call does not require client interaction, which means it can be used through rcExecMyRule (irule) or internally by the server. Only commands that are in the irods/server/bin/cmd directory can be run.

Example Usage:

```
myTestRule
{
        # Input parameters are:
        #  Command to be executed located in directory irods/server/bin/cmd
        #  Optional command argument
        #  Optional host address for command execution
        #  Optional hint for remote data object path, command is executed on host where the file is stored
        #  Optional flag. If > 0, use the resolved physical data object path as first argument
        # Output parameter is:
        #  Structure holding status, stdout, and stderr from command execution
        # Output from running the example is:
```

```
        #  Command result is
        #  Hello world written from irods
        msiExecCmd(*Cmd,*Arg, "null", "null", "null", *Result);
        msiGetStdoutInExecCmdOut(*Result,*Out);
        writeLine("stdout","Command result is");
        writeLine("stdout","*Out");
}
INPUT *Cmd="hello", *Arg="written"
OUTPUT ruleExecOut
```

4.89   Core :: Rule Engine :: msiAdmAddAppRuleStruct

Example rule: iRODS/clients/icommands/test/rules4.0/rulemsiAdmAddAppRuleStruct.r

msiAdmAddAppRuleStruct	(	msParam_t *	reFilesParam,
		msParam_t *	dvmFilesParam,
		msParam_t *	fnmFilesParam)

Parameters:

[in]   reFilesParam   - a msParam of type STR_MS_T, which is an application Rules file name without the .re extension.

[in]   dvmFilesParam   - a msParam of type STR_MS_T, which is a variable name mapping file without the .dvm extension.

[in]   fnmFilesParam   - a msParam of type STR_MS_T, which is an application microservice mapping file name without the .fnm extension.

Description:
This is a microservice that reads the specified files in the configuration directory 'server/config/reConfigs' and adds them to the in-memory structures being used by the Rule Engine. These rules are loaded before the rules from the "core.re" file, and hence can be used to override the core rules from the "core.re" file (i.e., it adds application level rules and DVM and FNM mappings to the rule engine).

Note:
This microservice requires iRODS administration privileges and adds the given rules (re) file, $-variable mapping (dvm) and microservice logical name mapping (fnm) files to the working memory of the rule engine. Any subsequent rule or microservices will also use the newly prepended rules and mappings

Rules are maintained in three locations:
   •   A "core.re" file that is the current set of rules.
   •   An In-Memory Rule Base (App Rule Struct) that holds the rules used during a session. This has three parts: rules from the "core.re" file, application rules loaded by **msiAdmAddAppRuleStruct**, and rules executed from the irule command.
   •   An iCAT database table that manages persistent versions of rules.

Example Usage:

```
myTestRule
{
        #  Examples are in irods/server/config/reConfigs
        #  Input parameters are:
```

105

```
    # Rule file without the .re extension
    # Session variable file name mapping file without the .dvm extension
    # Application microservice mapping file without the .fnm extension
    # Output from running the example is:
    # List of the rules in the In-memory Rule Base
    msiAdmAddAppRuleStruct("*File", "", "");
    msiAdmShowIRB();
}
INPUT *File="core3"
OUTPUT ruleExecOut
```

4.90   Core :: Rule Engine :: msiAdmClearAppRuleStruct

Example rule: iRODS/clients/icommands/test/rules4.0/rulemsiAdmClearAppRuleStruct.r

msiAdmClearAppRuleStruct   (   )

Parameters:
N/A.

Description:
This is a microservice that clears the application level Rules and DVM and FNM mappings that were loaded into the rule engine's working memory.

Note:
This microservice needs iRODS administration privileges to perform this function.
Clears the application structures in the working memory of the rule engine holding the rules, $-variable mappings and microservice name mappings.

Rules are maintained in three locations:
- A "core.re file" that is the current set of rules
- An In-Memory Rule Base (App Rule Struct) that holds the rules used during a session. This has three parts: rules from the "core.re" file, application rules loaded by **msiAdmAddAppRuleStruct**, and rules executed from the irule command
- An iCAT database table that manages persistent versions of rules

Example Usage:

```
myTestRule
{
    # No Input parameter
    # Output from running the example:
    # List of rules after adding rule and after clearing rules
    msiAdmAddAppRuleStruct(*A," ", "");
    msiAdmShowIRB();
    msiAdmClearAppRuleStruct;
    msiAdmShowIRB();
}
INPUT *A="nara"
OUTPUT ruleExecOut
```

4.91   Core :: Rule Engine :: msiAdmShowCoreRE

Example rule:
iRODS/clients/icommands/test/rules4.0/rulemsiAdmShowCoreRE.r

msiAdmShowCoreRE (   )

Parameters:
none

Description:
This is a microservice that prints the "/etc/irods/core.re" file.

Note:
Rules are maintained in three locations:
- A "core.re" file that is the current set of rules.
- An In-Memory Rule Base (App Rule Struct) that holds the rules used during a session. This has three parts: rules from the "core.re" file, application rules loaded by **msiAdmAddAppRuleStruct**, and rules executed from the irule command.
- An iCAT database table that manages persistent versions of rules.

Example Usage:

```
myTestRule
{
        # Input parameter is:
        # none
        # Output from running the example is:
        # Listing of the core.re file
        msiAdmShowCoreRE();
}
INPUT null
OUTPUT ruleExecOut
```

4.92   Core :: Rule Engine :: msiAdmShowDVM

Example rule:
iRODS/clients/icommands/test/rules4.0/rulemsiAdmShowDVM.r

msiAdmShowDVM (msParam_t *   bufParam   )

Parameters:

[in]   bufParam   - is a msParam (not used for anything, a dummy parameter)

Description:
This is a microservice that reads the data-value-mapping data structure in the Rule Engine and pretty-prints that structure to the stdout buffer.

Note:
This microservice uses a dummy parameter.
Lists the currently loaded dollar variable mappings from the rule engine memory. The list is written to stdout in ruleExecOut.

Example Usage:

myTestRule
{
        # Dummy input argument
        # Output from running the example:
        # List of Session variable mappings from the rule engine memory
        msiAdmShowDVM(*A);
}
INPUT *A="null"
OUTPUT ruleExecOut

4.93   Core :: Rule Engine :: msiAdmShowFNM

Example rule:
iRODS/clients/icommands/test/rules4.0/rulemsiAdmShowFNM.r

msiAdmShowFNM   (msParam_t *   bufParam   )

Parameters:
[in]   bufParam   - is a msParam (not used for anything, a dummy parameter)

Description:
This is a microservice that reads the function-name-mapping data structure in the rule engine and pretty-prints that structure to the stdout buffer.

Note:
This microservice has a dummy parameter.
This microservice lists the currently loaded microservices and action name mappings from the rule engine memory. The list is written to stdout in ruleExecOut.

Example Usage:

myTestRule
{
        # Dummy input parameter
        # Output from running the example is a list of the microservice and action name mappings from the rule engine memory

```
        msiAdmShowFNM(*A);
}
INPUT *A="null"
OUTPUT ruleExecOut
```

4.94   Core :: Rule Engine :: msiAdmShowIRB

Example rule:
iRODS/clients/icommands/test/rules4.0/rulemsiAdmShowIRB.r

msiAdmShowIRB   (   )

Parameters:
None

Description:
This is a microservice that reads the data structure in the rule engine, which holds the current set of Rules, and pretty-prints that structure to the stdout buffer.

Note:
The IRB term refers to the In-memory Rule Base, to differentiate from the "core.re" file that is read each time a new session is started.

Rules are maintained in three locations:
- A "core.re" file that is the current set of rules
- An In-Memory Rule Base (App Rule Struct) that holds the rules used during a session. This has three parts: rules from the "core.re" file, application rules loaded by **msiAdmAddAppRuleStruct**, and rules executed from the irule command
- An iCAT database table that manages persistent versions of rules

Example Usage:

```
myTestRule
{
        # Dummy input parameter
        # Output from running the example is:
        #  List of rules from the rule engine memory
        msiAdmShowIRB();
}
INPUT *B="null"
OUTPUT ruleExecOut
```

4.95   Core :: String Manipulation :: split

Example rule:
iRODS/clients/icommands/test/rules4.0/split.r

String split operator

Description:
Split a string into its constituent words. The rule example is in
iRODS/clients/icommands/test/rules4.0/split.r.

Example Usage:

```
mytestrule{
#rule to split a string into its constituent words
 *B=split(*A, ", ");
 writeLine("stdout", "Split of input \"*A\" is \"*B\"");
}
INPUT *A="true, false"
OUTPUT ruleExecOut
```


4.96   Core :: String Manipulation :: msiStrlen

Example rule:
iRODS/clients/icommands/test/rules4.0/rulemsiStrlen.r

msiStrlen   (msParam_t *   stringIn,
                              msParam_t *   lengthOut   )

Parameters:
[in]   stringIn   - a STR_MS_T which specifies the input string.
[out]   lengthOut   - a STR_MS_T to hold the returned string length.

Description:
Returns the length of a given string.

Note:
none

Example Usage:

```
myTestRule
{
        # Input parameter is:
        #  String
        # Output parameter is:
        #  Length of string
        # Output from running the example is:
        #  The String: /$rodsZoneClient/home/$userNameClient/sub1/foo1 has length 29
        msiStrlen(*StringIn,*Length);
```

```
            writeLine("stdout","The string: *StringIn has length *Length");
}
INPUT *StringIn="/$rodsZoneClient/home/$userNameClient/sub1/foo1"
OUTPUT ruleExecOut
```

4.97   Core :: String Manipulation :: msiStrchop

Example rule:
iRODS/clients/icommands/test/rules4.0/rulemsiStrchop.r

msiStrchop   (msParam_t *   stringIn,
                             msParam_t *   stringOut   )

Parameters:
[in]   stringIn   - a STR_MS_T which specifies the input string.
[out]   stringOut   - a STR_MS_T to hold the string without the last char.

Description:
Removes the last character of a given string.

Note:
none

Example Usage:

```
myTestRule
{
        # Input parameter is:
        #  String
        # Output parameter is:
        #  String without the last character
        # Output from running the example is:
        #  The input string is:  /$rodsZoneClient/home/$userNameClient/sub1/foo1/
        #  The output string is: /$rodsZoneClient/home/$userNameClient/sub1/foo1
        msiStrchop(*StringIn,*StringOut);
        writeLine("stdout","The input string is:  *StringIn");
        writeLine("stdout","The output string is: *StringOut");
}
INPUT *StringIn="/$rodsZoneClient/home/$userNameClient/sub1/foo1/"
OUTPUT ruleExecOut
```

4.98   Core :: String Manipulation :: msiSubstr

Example rule:

iRODS/clients/icommands/test/rules4.0/rulemsiSubstr.r

msiSubstr   (msParam_t *   stringIn,
                            msParam_t *   offset,
                            msParam_t *   length,
                            msParam_t *   stringOut   )

Parameters:

[in]   stringIn   - a STR_MS_T which specifies the input string.

[in]   offset   - a STR_MS_T which specifies the position of the beginning of the substring (0 is first character). If negative, then offset specifies the position from the end of the string (-1 is the last character).

[in]   length   - a STR_MS_T which specifies the length of substring to return. If length is not specified, too large, negative, or "null", then return the substring from the offset to the end of stringIn.

[out]   stringOut   - a STR_MS_T to hold the resulting substring.

Description:
Returns a substring of the given string.

Note:
none

Example Usage:

```
myTestRule
{
        # Input parameters are:
        #  String
        #  Offset from start counting from 0.  If negative, count from end
        #  Length of the substring
        # Output parameter is:
        #  Substring
        # Output from running the example is:
        #  The input string is: /$rodsZoneClient/home/$userNameClient/sub1/foo1/
        #  The offset is 10 and the length is 4
        #  The output string is: home
        msiSubstr(*StringIn,*Offset,*Length,*StringOut);
        writeLine("stdout","The input string is:  *StringIn");
        writeLine("stdout","The offset is *Offset and the length is *Length");
        writeLine("stdout","The output string is: *StringOut");
}
INPUT *StringIn="/$rodsZoneClient/home/$userNameClient/sub1/foo1/", *Offset="10", *Length="4"
OUTPUT ruleExecOut
```

4.99   Core :: Workflow :: assign

Example rule:
iRODS/clients/icommands/test/rules4.0/assign.r

assign (msParam_t * var,
msParam_t * value)

Parameters:
[in] var - var is a msParam of type STR_MS_T which is a variable name or a Dollar Variable.
[in] value - value is a msParam of type STR_MS_T that is computed and value assigned to variable.

Description:
This microservice assigns a value to a variable.

Note:
This microservice is deprecated. In versions 3.0-4.0, algebraic equations are used instead. Type checking is done to ensure consistency. Functions are provided to convert between data types, including:

str   convert integer to string variable
int   convert string to an integer
double   convert string to a double
bool   convert string to a Boolean variable

The rule example is in iRODS/clients/icommands/test/rules4.0/assign.r.

Example Usage:

```
myTestRule
{
        # Workflow command to assign a value to a variable
        # The assign microservice has been replaced with direct algebraic equations
        # Output from running the example is:
        #  Value assigned is assign
        #
        #   deprecated use:
        #      assign(*A,*B);
        #
        *A = *B;
        writeLine("stdout", "Value assigned is *A");
}
INPUT *B="assign"
OUTPUT ruleExecOut
```

4.100   Core :: Workflow :: break

Example rule:
iRODS/clients/icommands/test/rules4.0/break.r

break ( )

Parameters:
N/A.

Description:
This microservice is used to break while, for and forEach loops.

Note:
This microservice is similar to a break statement in the C language. The rule example is in iRODS/clients/icommands/test/rules4.0/break.r.

Example Usage:

```
myTestRule
{
        # Workflow command to break out of a loop
        # Output from running the example is:
        # abc
        *A = list("a", "b", "c", "d");
        *B = "";
        foreach(*A)
        {
           if(*A=="d") then
           {
                   break;
           }
           *B = *B ++ *A;
        }
        writeLine("stdout", *B);
}
INPUT null
OUTPUT ruleExecOut
```

4.101   Core :: Workflow :: cut

Example rule:
iRODS/clients/icommands/test/rules4.0/cut.r

cut   (   )

Parameters:
N/A.

Description:
This tells the rule engine to not retry any other applicable rules for this action.

Note:

The example invokes a "print" rule with two versions. The cut statement specifies that the second version will not be tried after the first version is explicitly failed. The rule example is in iRODS/clients/icommands/test/rules4.0/cut.r.

Example:

```
myTestRule
{
        # Workflow operator to specify that no other versions of the rule will be tried
        # Output from running the example is:
        #  ERROR: rcExecMyRule error.  status = -1089000 CUT_ACTION_PROCESSED_ERR
        #  Level 0: DEBUG:
        print;
}

print
{
        or
        {
                writeLine("serverLog", "print 1");
                cut;
                fail;
        }
        or
        {
                writeLine("serverLog", "print 2");
                succeed;
        }
}

INPUT null
OUTPUT ruleExecOut
```

4.102   Core :: Workflow :: delay

Example rule:
iRODS/clients/icommands/test/rules4.0/delay.r

delay   (msParam_t *   mPA)   {workflow ::: recovery}

Parameters:
[in]   mPA   - mPA is a msParam of type STR_MS_T which is a delay Condition about
                     when to execute the body. These following tags are used:
                 EA   - execAddress - host where the delayed execution needs to
                                      be performed
                 ET   - execTime - absolute time when it needs to be performed.
                 PLUSET   - relExeTime - relative to current time when it needs to
                                      execute
                 EF   - execFreq - frequency (in time widths) it needs to be

performed. The format for EF is quite rich:

The EF value is of the format:

nnnnU <directive>   where nnnn is a number, and U is the unit of the number (s-sec, m-min, h-hour, d-day, y-year).

The <directive> can be for the form: <empty-directive> - equal to

REPEAT FOR EVER

REPEAT UNTIL SUCCESS

REPEAT nnnn TIMES   - where nnnn is an integer

REPEAT UNTIL <time> - where <time> is of the time format supported by checkDateFormat function below.

REPEAT UNTIL SUCCESS OR UNTIL <time>

REPEAT UNTIL SUCCESS OR nnnn TIMES

DOUBLE FOR EVER

DOUBLE UNTIL SUCCESS   - delay is doubled every time.

DOUBLE nnnn TIMES

DOUBLE UNTIL <time>

DOUBLE UNTIL SUCCESS OR UNTIL <time>

DOUBLE UNTIL SUCCESS OR nnnn TIMES

DOUBLE UNTIL SUCCESS UPTO <time>

Description:

Execute a set of operations later when certain conditions are met. Can be used to perform periodic operations also. The set of operations are encapsulated in Brackets following the delay command.

        <PLUSET>1m</PLUSET><EF>10m<///EF>

        means start after 1 minute and repeat every 10 minutes

Note:

This microservice is a set of statements that will be delayed in execution until delayCondition is true. The condition also supports repeating of the body until success or until some other condition is satisfied. This microservice takes the delayCondition as the delay argument. The workflow is encapsulated in brackets, with the recovery microservice inserted after the symbols " ::: " for each workflow microservice. The delayCondition is given as a tagged condition. In the example, there are two conditions that are specified, one to specify execution after 30 seconds, and a second to repeat after 30 seconds. The iqstat command and iqdel commands can be used to delete the rule from the queue.

The command delayExec is deprecated. The microservice "delayExec" is now equivalent to "delay". Both are interpreted using the new rule language syntax, with the workflow specified within brackets.

The rule example is in iRODS/clients/icommands/test/rules4.0/delay.r.

Example Usage:

myTestRule
{
       # Workflow operator to execute a given workflow at a delayed specification
       # Input parameters are:
       # Delay condition composed from tags
       #   EA   - host where the execution if performed
       #   ET   - Absolute time when execution is done
       #   PLUSET - Relative time for execution
       #   EF   - Execution frequency
       #   Workflow specified within brackets
       # Output from running the example is:

```
# exec
# Output written to the iRODS/server/log/reLog log file:
# writeLine: inString = Delayed exec
delay("<PLUSET>30s</PLUSET>")
{
        writeLine("serverLog", "Delayed exec");
}
writeLine("stdout","exec");
}
INPUT null
OUTPUT ruleExecOut
```

4.103   Core :: Workflow :: errorcode

Example rule:
iRODS/clients/icommands/test/rules4.0/rulemsiErrorCode.r

errorcode (microservice)

Parameters:
The argument is a microservice that is being executed.

Description:
The error return is trapped, allowing the rule to implement conditional processing of errors without having to invoke a recovery microservice. The rule example is in iRODS/clients/icommands/test/rules4.0/ rulemsiErrorCode.r

Example Usage:

```
myTestRule
{
        # Workflow operator to trap an error code of passed command
        # Input parameter is:
        #  microservice whose error code will be trapped
        # Output parameter is:
        #  none
        if (errorcode( msiExecCmd(*Cmd, *Arg, "null", "null", "null", *Result)) < 0 )
        {
                writeLine("stdout","Microservice execution had an error");
        }
        else
        {
                writeLine("stdout","Microservice executed successfully");
        }
}
INPUT *Cmd="hello", *ARG="iRODS"
OUTPUT ruleExecOut
```

4.104 Core :: Workflow :: errormsg

Example rule:
iRODS/clients/icommands/test/rules4.0/rulemsiErrorMsg.r

Error message handling

Description:
Error messages can be trapped and processed. Use:

                \<errorcode\> = errormsg(\<expression\>, \<errormsg\>)

where \<expression\> is an input expression to be executed, usually a microservice call, \<errormsg\> is an output variable containing the error message generated from that expression, and \<errorcode\> is the error code generated from that expression. This prevents the error message from being output to stderr. The rule example is in iRODS/clients/icommands/test/rules4.0/ rulemsiErrorMsg.r.

Example Usage:

```
mytestrule{
# rule to test errormsg
# usage is <errorcode> = errormsg(<expression>, <errormsg>)
  *out=errormsg(msiGetSystemTime(*Start,"human"),*msg);
  writeLine("stdout", "errorcode = *out, errormsg = *msg");
}
INPUT null
OUTPUT ruleExecOut
```

4.105 Core :: Workflow :: fail

Example rule:
iRODS/clients/icommands/test/rules4.0/fail.r

fail ( )

Parameters:
N/A.

Description:
Fail immediately - recovery and retries are possible. The rule example is in iRODS/clients/icommands/test/rules4.0/fail.r.

Example Usage:

```
myTestRule
{
        # Workflow function to cause immediate failure
        # Output from running the example is:
        #  ERROR: rcExecMyRule error.  status = -1091000 FAIL_ACTION_ENCOUNTERED_ERR
        if(*A=="fail")
        {
                    fail;
        }
}
INPUT *A="fail"
OUTPUT ruleExecOut
```

4.106   Core :: Workflow :: foreach

Example rule:
iRODS/clients/icommands/test/rules4.0/foreach.r

foreach (msParam_t *   inlist   )   {workflow ::: recovery}

Parameters:
[in]   inlist   - a msParam of type STR_MS_T which is a comma separated string or
                                StrArray_MS_T which is an array of strings or
                                IntArray_MS_T which is an array of integers or
                                GenQueryOut_MS_T which is an iCAT query result.

Description:
Performs a loop over a list of items given in different forms.

Note:
This executes a "for" loop in C-type language looping over a list. It takes a table (or list of strings, or comma-separated string list), and for each item in the list, executes the corresponding body of the for-loop. The first parameter specifies the variable that has the list (the same variable name is used in the body of the loop to denote an item of the list!). The workflow is a sequence of microservices that is encapsulated in brackets, with the recovery procedure specified on each line after the " ::: " symbol.

The microservice "forEachExec" is deprecated. It is replaced with "foreach".

The rule example is in iRODS/clients/icommands/test/rules4.0/foreach.r.

Example Usage:

```
myTestRule
{
        # Workflow operator to iterate over a list
        # Input parameter is:
        # List
        # Workflow executed within brackets
```

```
            # Output from running the example is:
            #  abcd
            *A = list("a", "b", "c", "d");
            *B = "";
            foreach(*A)
            {
                  *B = *B ++ *A;
            }
            writeLine("stdout", *B);
}
INPUT null
OUTPUT ruleExecOut
```

4.107   Core :: Workflow :: for

Example rule: iRODS/clients/icommands/test/rules4.0/for.r

for	(	msParam_t *	initial,	
		msParam_t *	condition,	
		msParam_t *	step)	{ workflow ::: recovery }

Parameters:

[in]	initial	- a msParam of type STR_MS_T which is an initial assignment statement for the loop variable.
[in]	condition	- a msParam of type STR_MS_T which is a logical expression checking a condition.
[in]	step	- a msParam of type STR_MS_T which is an increment/decrement of loop variable.

Description:
It is a for loop in the rule language.

Note:
This microservice loops over an integer *-variable until a condition is met.
Similar to the "for" construct in C.

The microservice "forExec" is deprecated and replaced with "for".

The rule example is in iRODS/clients/icommands/test/rules4.0/for.r.

Example Usage:

```
myTestRule
{
            # Input parameters are:
            #  Loop initiation
            #  Loop termination
            #  Loop increment
            #  Workflow in brackets
            # Output from running the example is:
            #  abcd
```

```
            *A = list("a", "b", "c", "d");
            *B = "";
            for(*I=0;*I<4;*I=*I+1)
            {
                  *B = *B ++ elem(*A, *I);
            }
            writeLine("stdout", *B);
}
INPUT null
OUTPUT ruleExecOut
```

4.108   Core :: Workflow :: if

Example rule: iRODS/clients/icommands/test/rules4.0/if.r

if   (msParam_t *   condition)   {workflow ::: recovery }
          else
          {workflow ::: recovery }

Parameters:
[in]   condition   - a msParam of type STR_MS_T which is a logical expression
                              computing to TRUE or FALSE.

Description:
This is an if-then-else construct in the rule language for conditional tests. If the logical expression is true, the specified workflow is executed. If the logical expression is false, the workflow after the "else" statement is executed.

Note:
The argument is a conditional check. If the check is successful (TRUE), the microservice sequence in the workflow will be executed. If the check fails, then the microservice sequence after the "else" statement will be executed.

The microservice "ifExec" is deprecated and replaced with "if".

The rule example is in iRODS/clients/icommands/test/rules4.0/if.r

Example Usage:

```
myTestRule
{
          # Workflow operator to evaluate conditional expression
          # Input parameters are:
          #  Logical expression that computes to TRUE or FALSE
          #  Workflow to be executed defined within brackets
          #  Else clause defined within brackets
          # Output from running the example is:
          #  0
          if(*A=="0")
          {
```

```
                    writeLine("stdout", "0");
            }
            else
            {
                    writeLine("stdout", "not 0");
            }
}
INPUT *A="0"
OUTPUT ruleExecOut
```

4.109   Core :: Workflow :: applyAllRules

Example rule: iRODS/clients/icommands/test/rules4.0/ruleApplyAllRules.r

applyAllRules   (msParam_t *   actionParam,
                                msParam_t *   reiSaveFlagParam,
                                msParam_t *   allRuleExecFlagParam   )

Parameters:
[in]   actionParam   - a msParam of type STR_MS_T which is the name
                                   of an action to be executed.
[in]   reiSaveFlagParam   - a msParam of type STR_MS_T which is 0 or 1. The value is used to
                                   check if the rei structure needs to be saved at every rule invocation
                                   inside the execution. This helps to save time if the rei structure is
                                   known not to be changed when executing the underlying rules.
[in]   allRuleExecFlagParam   - allRuleExecFlagParam is a msParam of type STR_MS_T which is 0
                                   or 1 specifies whether the "apply all rule" condition applies only to the
                                   actionParam invocation or is recursively done at all levels of
                                   invocation of every rule inside the execution.

Description:
This microservice executes all applicable rules for a given action name.

Note:
Normal operations of the rule engine is to stop after a rule (one of the alternate actions) completes
successfully. But in some cases, one may want the rule engine to try all alternatives and succeed in as
many as possible. Then by firing that rule under this microservice all alternatives are tried.

The actionParam name should not be quoted in the microservice invocation.

The rule example is in iRODS/clients/icommands/test/rules4.0/ruleApplyAllRules.r.

Example Usage:

```
myTestRule
{
        # Input parameters are:
        #  Action to perform
        #  Flag for whether to save REI structure, 1 is yes
        #  Flag for whether to apply recursively, 1 is yes
        #  Output from executing the example is:
```

```
        #  print 1
        #  print 2
        applyAllRules(print, *SaveREI, *All);
}
print
{
        or
        {
                writeLine("stdout", "print 1");
        }
        or
        {
                writeLine("stdout", "print 2");
        }
}
INPUT *All="1", *SaveREI="0"
OUTPUT ruleExecOut
```

4.110   Core :: Workflow :: msiGoodFailure

Example rule: iRODS/clients/icommands/test/rules4.0/rulemsiGoodFailure.r

msiGoodFailure (   )

Parameters:
N/A.

Description:
This microservice performs no operations but fails the current rule application immediately even if the body still has some more microservices to execute. Other definitions of the rule are not retried upon this failure. It is useful when you want to fail and ensure no recovery is initiated.

Note:
Useful when you want to fail a rule without retries. The rule example is in iRODS/clients/icommands/test/rules4.0/rulemsiGoodFailure.r.

Example Usage:

```
myTestRule
{
        # Workflow function to fail immediately with no recovery
        # Output from running the example is:
        #  ERROR: rcExecMyRule error.  status = -1088000 RETRY_WITHOUT_RECOVERY_ERR
        msiGoodFailure;
}
INPUT null
OUTPUT null
```

4.111 Core :: Workflow :: msiSleep

Example rule: iRODS/clients/icommands/test/rules4.0/rulemsiSleep.r

msiSleep (msParam_t * secPtr,
msParam_t * microsecPtr)

Parameters:
[in]   secPtr   - secPtr is a msParam of type STR_MS_T which is seconds
[in]   microsecPtr   - microsecPrt is a msParam of type STR_MS_T which is microseconds

Description:
Sleep for some amount of time

Note:
Similar to sleep in C.. The rule example is in iRODS/clients/icommands/test/rules4.0/rulemsiSleep.r.

Example Usage:

```
myTestRule
{
        # Input parameters are:
        #  Number of seconds to sleep
        #  Number of micro-seconds to sleep
        # Output from running the example is:
        #  Jun 01 2011 17:04:59
        #  Jun 01 2011 17:05:09
        writeLine("stdout", timestr(time()));
        msiSleep(*Sec, *MicroSec);
        writeLine("stdout", timestr(time()));
}
INPUT *Sec="10", *MicroSec="0"
OUTPUT ruleExecOut
```

4.112 Core :: Workflow :: nop, null

Example rule: iRODS/clients/icommands/test/rules4.0/nop.r

nop, null - No action

Parameters:
N/A.

Description:

Executes "no action" or "no operation". The rule example is in
iRODS/clients/icommands/test/rules4.0/nop.r.

Example usage:

```
myTestRule
{
        # Workflow function for no operation
        # Output from running the example is:
        #  nop
         nop;
        writeLine("stdout", "nop");
}
INPUT null
OUTPUT ruleExecOut
```

4.113   Core :: Workflow :: print_hello

Example rule: iRODS/clients/icommands/test/rules4.0/print_hello.r

Print_hello   ( )

Parameters:
None

Description:
Prints out the string "Hello" to stdout.

Note:
This executes the "hello" command stored in the server/bin/cmd directory. A recovery microservice is
available called "recover_print_hello". The rule example is in
iRODS/clients/icommands/test/rules4.0/print_hello.r.

Example usage:

```
myTestRule
{
        #  Output string is written to stdout
        writeLine("stdout","Execute command to print out hello");
        print_hello;
}
INPUT null
OUTPUT ruleExecOut
```

4.114   Core :: Workflow :: remote

Example rule: iRODS/clients/icommands/test/rules4.0/remote.r

Remote (msParam_t *   mPD
              msParam_t *   mPA   )   {workflow ::: recovery}

Parameters:
[in]   mPD   - a msParam of type STR_MS_T which is a host name of the server where
               the body needs to be executed.
[in]   mPA   - a msParam of type STR_MS_T which is a delayCondition about when to
               execute the body.

Description:
Manages the execution of a set of microservices at a remote location.

Note:
This microservice takes a set of microservices that need to be executed at a remote iRODS server. The execution is done immediately and synchronously with the result returned back from the call.

The microservice "remoteExec" is deprecated and replaced with "remote".

The rule example is in iRODS/clients/icommands/test/rules4.0/remote.r.

Example Usage:

```
myTestRule
{
        # Workflow operation to execute microservices at a remote location
        # Input parameters are:
        #  Host name where workflow is executed
        #  Delaycondition for executing the workflow
        #  Workflow ::: recovery-workflow  that will be executed, listed in brackets
        # Output from running the example written to server log:
        #  writeLine: inString = local exec
        #  writeLine: inString = remote exec
        # Output from running the example written to standard out:
        #  local exec
        writeLine("serverLog", "local exec");
        remote("localhost", "null")
        {
            writeLine("serverLog", "remote exec");
        }
        writeLine("stdout", "local exec");
}
INPUT null
OUTPUT ruleExecOut
```

4.115   Core :: Workflow :: succeed

Example rule: iRODS/clients/icommands/test/rules4.0/succeed.r

succeed - Succeed immediately

Parameters:
N/A.

Description:
Succeed immediately. The rule example is in iRODS/clients/icommands/test/rules4.0/succeed.r.

Example usage:

```
myTestRule
{
        # Workflow operation to cause rule to immediately succeed
        # Output from running the example is:
        #  succeed
        if(*A == "succeed")
        {
            writeLine("stdout", "succeed");
            succeed;
        }
        else
        {
            fail;
        }
}
INPUT *A="succeed"
OUTPUT ruleExecOut
```

4.116   Core :: Workflow :: while

Example rule: iRODS/clients/icommands/test/rules4.0/while.r

while   (msParam_t *   condition   )   {workflow ::: recovery }

Parameters:
[in]   condition   - a msParam of type STR_MS_T which is a logical
                                                         expression computing to TRUE or FALSE.

Description:
This is a while loop in the rule language.

Note:
The first argument is a condition that will be checked on each loop iteration. The body of the while loop, given as a sequence of microservices ::: recovery-microservice, is listed in brackets.

The microservice "whileExec" is deprecated and replaced with "while".

The rule example is in iRODS/clients/icommands/test/rules4.0/while.r.

Example Usage:

```
myTestRule {
# Workflow operation to loop until condition is false
# Input parameter is
#  Logical expression which evaluates to TRUE or FALSE
#  Workflow that is executed, defined within brackets
# Output from running the example is:
#  abcd
  *A = list("a", "b", "c", "d");
  *B = "";
  *I=0;
  while(*I < 4) {
    *B = *B ++ elem(*A, *I);
    *I = *I + 1;
  }
  writeLine("stdout", *B);
}
INPUT null
OUTPUT ruleExecOut
```

4.117   Core :: Workflow :: writeLine

Example rule: iRODS/clients/icommands/test/rules4.0/writeLine.r

| **writeLine** | (| msParam_t * | where, |
| | | msParam_t * | inString) |

Parameters:

| [in] | where | - a msParam of type STR_MS_T which is the buffer name in ruleExecOut. Currently stdout, stderr, serverLog, and a user variable can be used. |
| [in] | inString | - a msParam of type STR_MS_T which is a string to be written into a buffer. |

Description:
This microservice writes a given string followed by a new-line character into the target buffer in ruleExecOut Parameter.

Note:
This microservice takes a given buffer string and appends it to the back of the buffer (either stdout or stderr or serverLog in ruleExecOut parameter) followed by a new line character. In the OUTPUT line, the ruleExecOut is a system MS-parameter (*variable) that is automatically available.

Example Usage:

```
myTestRule {
# Input parameters are:
#  Name of output buffer
#   stdout
#   stderr
```

```
#   serverLog
#   user-defined buffer
#   String to write
# Output from running the example is:
#  line
     writeLine(*Where, *StringIn);
}
INPUT *Where="stdout", *StringIn="line"
OUTPUT ruleExecOut
```

4.118   Core :: Workflow :: writePosInt

Example rule: iRODS/clients/icommands/test/rules4.0/writePosInt.r

| **writePosInt** | (| msParam_t * | where, |
| | | msParam_t * | inString) |

Parameters:

| [in] | where | - a msParam of type STR_MS_T which is the buffer name in ruleExecOut. Currently stdout, stderr, serverLog, and a user variable can be used. |
| [in] | inString | - a msParam of type STR_MS_T which is a string to be written into a buffer. |

Description:
This microservice writes a positive integer into the target buffer in ruleExecOut Parameter.

Note:
This microservice takes a given positive integer, converst to ascii, and appends it to the back of the buffer (either stdout or stderr or serverLog in ruleExecOut parameter). In the OUTPUT line, the ruleExecOut is a system MS-parameter (*variable) that is automatically available and listed to the screen.

Example Usage:

```
myTestRule {
#Input parameters are:
#  Location (stdout, stderr)
#  Integer
  *A = 1;
  writeLine("stdout","Wrote an integer");
  writePosInt("stdout",*A);
  writeLine("stdout","");
}
INPUT null
OUTPUT ruleExecOut
```

4.119   Core :: Workflow :: writeString

Example rule: iRODS/clients/icommands/test/rules4.0/writeString.r

writeString   (msParam_t *   where,
                             msParam_t *   inString)

Parameters:
[in]   where   - where is a msParam of type STR_MS_T which is the buffer name
                                  in ruleExecOut. Currently stdout and stderr.
[in]   inString   - inString is a msParam of type STR_MS_T which is a string to be
                                  written into the buffer

Description:
This microservice writes a given string into the target buffer in ruleExecOut parameter.

Note:
This microservice takes a given buffer string and appends it to the back of the buffer (either stdout or stderr
or serverLog). In the OUTPUT line, the ruleExecOut is a system MS-parameter (*variable) that is
automatically available that specifies copying of the "stdout" buffer to the client.

Example Usage:

myTestRule {
# Input parameters are:
# Buffer where the string is written
#   stdout
#   stderr
#   serverLog
# String that is written
# Output from running the example is:
# string
   writeString(*Where, *StringIn);
   writeLine(*Where, "cheese");
}
INPUT *Where="stdout", *StringIn="string"
OUTPUT ruleExecOut

4.120   Core :: Framework Services System :: msiCheckHostAccessControl

Example rule: iRODS/clients/icommands/test/rules4.0/acmsiCheckHostAccessControl.r

msiCheckHostAccessControl   (   )

Parameters:
None

Description:
This microservice sets the access control policy. It checks the access control by user and group from a given host based on the policy given in the HostAccessControl file.

Note:
The policy is implemented in the core.re file.

This microservice controls access to the iRODS service based on the information in the host based access configuration file: iRODS/server/config/HostAccessControl. This is a column-based file that identifies who is allowed to connect if the acChkHostAccessControl policy is turned on.

The first column specifies a user that is allowed to connect to this iRODS server. An entry of "all" means all users are allowed.

The second column specifies the group name. An entry of "all" means, all groups are allowed.

The third and fourth columns specify the address and the address mask. Together, they define the client IP addresses/domains that are permitted to connect to the iRODS server. The address column specifies the IP address and the Mask column specifies which bits will be ignored, i.e., after those bits are taken out, the connection address must match the address in the address column.

<name>	<group>	<address>	<mask>
all	all	127.0.0.1	255.255.255.255

The rule example is in iRODS/clients/icommands/test/rules4.0/acmsiCheckHostAccessControl.r.

Example Usage:

```
acChkHostAccessControl {
# No arguments
#  The file iRODS/server/config/HOST_ACCESS_CONTROL_FILE
#  is read to identify hosts that can access iRODS.
  msiCheckHostAccessControl;
}
```

4.121   Core :: Framework Services System :: msiDeleteDisallowed

Example rule: iRODS/clients/icommands/test/rules4.0/acmsiDeleteDisallowed.r

msiDeleteDisallowed   (   )

Parameters:
None

Description:
This microservice sets the policy for specifying that certain data cannot be deleted.

Note:
The policy is implemented in the core.re file. An acDataDeletePolicy rule condition is used to decide which collections to protect. The output that is generated when you try to delete a protected file is:
ERROR: rmUtil: rm error for /$rodsZoneClient/home/$userNameClient/sub1/foo3, status = -1097000
status = -1097000 NO_RULE_OR_MSI_FUNCTION_FOUND_ERR

The rule example is in iRODS/clients/icommands/test/rules4.0/acmsiDeleteDisallowed.r.

Example Usage:

```
acDataDeletePolicy {
# Output when try to delete a file:
#  ERROR: rmUtil: rm error for /$rodsZoneClient/home/$userNameClient/sub1/foo3, status = -1097000
status = -1097000 NO_RULE_OR_MSI_FUNCTION_FOUND_ERR
#  Rule condition is used to choose which collections to protect
  ON($objPath like "/$rodsZoneClient/home/$userNameClient/*") {
    msiDeleteDisallowed;
  }
}
```

4.122   Core :: Framework Services System :: msiDigestMonStat

Example rule: iRODS/clients/icommands/test/rules4.0/rulemsiDigestMonStat.r

msiDigestMonStat	(	msParam_t *	cpu_wght,
		msParam_t *	mem_wght,
		msParam_t *	swap_wght,
		msParam_t *	runq_wght,
		msParam_t *	disk_wght,
		msParam_t *	netin_wght,
		msParam_t *	netout_wght)

Parameters:
[in]	cpu_wght	- Required - a msParam of type STR_MS_T defining relative CPU weighting.
[in]	mem_wght	- Required - a msParam of type STR_MS_T defining relative memory weighting
[in]	swap_wght	- Required - a msParam of type STR_MS_T defining relative swap weighting
[in]	runq_wght	- Required - a msParam of type STR_MS_T defining relative run queue weighting
[in]	disk_wght	- Required - a msParam of type STR_MS_T defining relative disk space weighting
[in]	netin_wght	- Required - a msParam of type STR_MS_T defining relative inbound network weighting
[in]	netout_wght	- Required - a msParam of type STR_MS_T defining relative

outbound network weighting

Description:
This microservice calculates and stores a load factor for each connected resource based on the weighting values passed in as parameters.

Note:
The following values are loaded from R_LOAD_SERVER:

> cpu_used
> mem_used
> swap_used
> runq_load
> disk_space
> net_input
> net_output

The stored load factor is calculated as such:
load_factor = cpu_wght*cpu_used + mem_wght*mem_used + swap_wght*swap_used + runq_wght*runq_load + disk_wght*disk_space + netin_wght*net_input + netout_wght*net_output

The digest of the load factor can be retrieved by the iquest query:

> iquest "SELECT SLD_RESC_NAME,SLD_LOAD_FACTOR"

See also: https://wiki.irods.org/index.php/Resource_Monitoring_System

Example Usage:

```
myTestRule {
#Input parameters are:
#  CPU weight
#  Memory weight
#  Swap weight
#  Run queue weight
#  Disk weight
#  Network transfer in weight
#  Network transfer out weight
#Output from running the example is:
#  CPU weight is 1, Memory weight is 1, Swap weight is 0, Run queue weight is 0
#  Disk weight is 0, Network transfer in rate is 1, Network transfer out rate is 1
#  List of resources and the computed load factor digest
  msiDigestMonStat(*Cpuw, *Memw, *Swapw, *Runw, *Diskw, *Netinw, *Netow);
  writeLine("stdout","CPU weight is *Cpuw, Memory weight is *Memw, Swap weight is *Swapw, Run
queue weight is *Runw");
  writeLine("stdout","Disk weight is *Diskw, Network transfer in rate is *Netinw, Network transfer out rate
is *Netow");
  *Q1 = select SLD_RESC_NAME, SLD_LOAD_FACTOR;
  foreach(*R1 in *Q1) {
    msiPrintKeyValPair("stdout",*R1);
  }
}
INPUT *Cpuw="1", *Memw="1", *Swapw="0", *Runw="0", *Diskw="0", *Netinw="1", *Netow="1"
OUTPUT ruleExecOut
```

4.123   Core :: Framework Services System :: msiFlushMonStat

Example rule: iRODS/clients/icommands/test/rules4.0/rulemsiFlushMonStat.r

msiFlushMonStat   (msParam_t *   inpParam1,
                                      msParam_t *   inpParam2   )

Parameters:
[in]   inpParam1   - Required - a msParam of type STR_MS_T defining the timespan
                            in hours. "default" is equal to 24 hours.
[in]   inpParam2   - Required - a msParam of type STR_MS_T defining the
                            tablename to be flushed. Currently must be either "serverload" or
                            "serverloaddigest".

Description:
This microservice flushes the servers' monitoring statistics.

Note:
This microservice removes the servers' metrics older than the number of hours in "timespan".
See also: https://wiki.irods.org/index.php/Resource_Monitoring_System

Example Usage:

myTestRule {
#Input parameters are:
Timespan before which stats are deleted (in hours)
Table to be flushed
serverload
serverloaddigest
#Output from running the example is a list of load factors per resource
  msiFlushMonStat(*Time, *Table);
  msiDigestMonStat(*Cpuw, *Memw, *Swapw, *Runw, *Diskw, *Netinw, *Netow);
  *Q1 = select SLD_RESC_NAME, SLD_LOAD_FACTOR;
  foreach(*R1 in *Q1) {
    msiPrintKeyValPair("stdout",*R1); }
  }
}
INPUT *Time="24", *Table="serverload", *Cpuw="1", *Memw="1", *Swapw="0", *Runw="0",
*Diskw="0", *Netinw="1", *Netow="1"
OUTPUT ruleExecOut

4.124   Core :: Framework Services System :: msiListEnabledMS

Example rule: iRODS/clients/icommands/test/rules4.0/listMS.r

msiListEnabledMS (msParam_t * outKVPairs)

Parameters:
[out] outKVPairs - A KeyValPair_MS_T containing the results.

Description:
Returns the list of compiled microservices on the local iRODS server

Note:
This microservice looks at /var/lib/irods/iRODS/server/re/include/reAction.hpp and returns the list of compiled microservices on the local iRODS server. The results are written to a KeyValPair_MS_T. For each pair the keyword is the MS name while the value is the module where the microservice belongs. Standard non-module microservices are listed as "core".

Example Usage:

```
myTestRule {
# Output
#  Buffer holding list of microservices in form Key=Value
# Output from running the example is:
#   List of microservices that are enabled
  msiListEnabledMS(*Buf);
  writeKeyValPairs("stdout", *Buf,":");
}
INPUT null
OUTPUT ruleExecOut
```

4.125   Core :: Framework Services System :: msiSysMetaModify

Example rule: iRODS/clients/icommands/test/rules4.0/acmsiSysMetaModify.r

msiSysMetaModify (msParam_t * sysMetadata,
                       msParam_t * value)

Parameters:
[in] sysMetadata - A STR_MS_T which specifies the system metadata to be modified. Allowed values are: "datatype", "comment", "time".
[in] value - A STR_MS_T which specifies the value to be given to the system metadata.

Description:
Modify system metadata.

Note:

This call should only be used within a core.re rule, as it requires that the rei structure be initialized for file manipulation. The rule example is in iRODS/clients/icommands/test/rules4.0/acmsiSysMetaModify.r and illustrates this service called by the core.re rule acPostProcForPut.

Example Usage:

```
acPostProcForPut {
 ON($filePath like "\*.txt") {
  msiSysMetaModify("datatype", "text");
 }
}
```

4.126   Core :: Framework Services System :: msiNoTrashCan

Example rule: iRODS/clients/icommands/test/rules4.0/acmsiNoTrashCan.r

msiNoTrashCan (   )

Parameters:
None

Description:
This microservice sets the policy to no trash can.

Note:
The default policy is that a trash can will be used. When a file is deleted from iRODS, it is actually moved to the trash can located in a corresponding path under /data-grid/trash. With no trash can, instead the file is deleted directly. Moving the file to the trash can is normally much faster, but then the trash can should be periodically emptied. The rule example is in iRODS/clients/icommands/test/rules4.0/acmsiNoTrashCan.r.

Example Usage:

```
acTrashPolicy {
# System control
 msiNoTrashCan;
}
```

4.127   Core :: Framework Services System :: msiOprDisallowed

Example rule: iRODS/clients/icommands/test/rules4.0/acmsiOprDisallowed.r

msiOprDisallowed (   )

Parameters:
None

Description:
This generic microservice sets the policy for determining that the desired action is not allowed. To be called by a rule in core.re.

Note:
The msiOprDisallowed microservice can be used by all the rules to disallow the execution of specific actions. The rule example is in iRODS/clients/icommands/test/rules4.0/acmsiOprDisallowed.r.

Example Usage:

```
acSetRescSchemeForCreate {
  ON ($objPath like "\*foo*") {
   msiOprDisallowed;
  }
}
```

4.128   Core :: Framework Services System :: msiServerMonPerf

Example rule: iRODS/clients/icommands/test/rules4.0/rulemsiServerMonPerf.r

msiServerMonPerf   (msParam_t *   verb,
                                     msParam_t *   ptime   )

Parameters:
[in]   verb   - a msParam of type STR_MS_T defining verbose mode:
                      "default" - not verbose
                      "verbose" - verbose mode
[in]   ptime   - a msParam of type STR_MS_T defining probe time in seconds. "default"
                      is equal to 10 seconds.

Description:
This microservice monitors the servers' activity and performance.

Note:
This microservice monitors the servers' activity and performance for CPU, network, memory and more. It retrieves the list of servers to monitor from the MON_CFG_FILE if it exists, or the iCAT if the configuration file does not exist.
The MON_PERF_SCRIPT is executed on each host. The result is put in the OUTPUT_MON_PERF file and in the iCAT catalog.

The digest of the load factor can be retrieved by the iquest query:
        iquest "SELECT SLD_RESC_NAME,SLD_LOAD_FACTOR"

Example Usage:

acServerMonPerf {

```
# This microservice invokes a command in iRODS/server/bin/cmd
#    irodsServerMonPerf    - a perl script to get monitoring information
 delay("<PLUSET>30s</PLUSET>< EF>1h</EF>") {
   msiServerMonPerf("default", "default");
 }
}
INPUT null
OUTPUT ruleExecOut
```

4.129   Core :: Framework Services System :: msiSetBulkPutPostProcPolicy

Example rule: iRODS/clients/icommands/test/rules4.0/acmsiSetBulkPutPostProcPolicy**.r**

msiSetBulkPutPostProcPolicy   (msParam_t *   xflag   )

Parameters:
[in]   xflag   - Required - a msParam of type STR_MS_T.
                      "on" - enable execution of acPostProcForPut.
                      "off" - disable execution of acPostProcForPut.

Description:
This microservice sets whether the post processing "put" rule (acPostProcForPut) should be run (on or off) for the bulk put operation. Setting the policy to "off" improves performance, as no post processing is done when uploading using the bulk option.

Note:
The policy is implemented by default in the core.re file. The rule example is in iRODS/clients/icommands/test/rules4.0/acmsiSetBulkPutPostProcPolicy.r.

Example Usage:

acBulkPutPostProcPolicy {msiSetBulkPutPostProcPolicy("off");}

4.130   Core :: Framework Services System :: msiSetChkFilePathPerm

Example rule: iRODS/clients/icommands/test/rules4.0/acmsiSetChkFilePathPerm**.r**

msiSetChkFilePathPerm (msParam_t *   xchkType   )

Parameters:
[in]   - xchkType   - Required - a msParam of type STR_MS_T which defines the check type to set.

Description:
This microservice sets the policy for checking the file path permission when registering a physical file path using commands such as ireg and imcoll. For now, the only safe setting is the default, msiSetChkFilePathPerm("disallowPathReg"), which prevents non-admin users from using imcoll and ireg. You can experiment with the other settings, but we do not recommend them for production at this time. This rule also sets the policy for checking the file path when unregistering a data object without deleting the physical file. Normally, a normal user cannot unregister a data object if the physical file is located in a resource vault. Setting the chkType input of msiSetChkFilePathPerm to "noChkPathPerm" allows this check to be bypassed.

> Valid values for chkType are:
> - "disallowPathReg" - Disallow registration of iRODS path using ireg and imcoll by a non-privileged user.
> - "noChkPathPerm" - Do not check file path permission when registering a file. WARNING - This setting can create a security problem if used.
> - "doChkPathPerm" - Check UNIX ownership of physical files before registering. Registration of a path inside an iRODS resource vault path is not allowed.
> - "chkNonVaultPathPerm" - Check UNIX ownership of physical files before registering. Registration of a path inside an iRODS resource vault path is allowed if the vault path belongs to the user.

Note:
This microservice is used in the core.re file in the policy acSetChkFilePathPerm.

Example Usage:

acSetChkFilePathPerm {msiSetChkFilePathPerm("doChkPathPerm"); }

acSetChkFilePathPerm {msiSetChkFilePathPerm("disallowPathReg"); }

4.131   Core :: Framework Services System :: msiSetDataObjAvoidResc

---

Example rule: iRODS/clients/icommands/test/rules4.0/acmsiSetDataObjAvoidResc.**r**

msiSetDataObjAvoidResc   (msParam_t *   xavoidResc   )

Parameters:
[in]   xavoidResc   - a msParam of type STR_MS_T - the name of the resource to avoid

Description:
This microservice specifies the resource to avoid when opening a file in the data grid. The copy stored in the specified resource will not be picked unless it is the only copy

Note:
The policy is implemented in the core.re file. The rule example is in iRODS/clients/icommands/test/rules4.0/acmsiSetDataObjAvoidResc.r.

Example Usage:

acPreprocForDataObjOpen {msiSetDataObjAvoidResc("demoResc");}

4.132   Core :: Framework Services System :: msiSetDataObjPreferredResc

Example rule: iRODS/clients/icommands/test/rules4.0/acmsiSetDataObjPreferredResc.r

msiSetDataObjPreferredResc   (msParam_t *   xpreferredRescList   )

Parameters:
[in]   xpreferredRescList   - a msParam of type STR_MS_T, percent-delimited list of resources

Description:
If the data object has multiple copies, this microservice specifies the preferred resource for the opened object.

Note:
The copy stored in this preferred resource will be picked if it exists. More than one resource can be input using the character "%" as separator. e.g., resc1%resc2%resc3. The most preferred resource should be at the beginning of the list. The rule example is in iRODS/clients/icommands/test/rules4.0/acmsiSetDataObjPreferredResc.r.

Example Usage:

acPreprocForDataObjOpen {msiSetDataObjPreferredResc("demoResc%testResc");}

4.133   Core :: Framework Services System :: msiSetDataTypeFromExt

Example rule: iRODS/clients/icommands/test/rules4.0/acmsiSetDataTypeFromExt.r

msiSetDataTypeFromExt   (   )

Parameters:
None

Description:
This microservice checks if the filename has an extension (string following a period (.)) and if so, checks if the iCAT has a matching entry for it, and if so sets the dataObj data_type.

Note:
Always returns success since it is only doing an attempt; that is, failure is common and not really a failure. The types of data recognized by iRODS are:

AIX DLL	DICOM image	Mac Executable	SGI DLL
AIX Executable	directory shadow object	Mac OSX Executable	SGI Executable
ascii compressed Huffman	DLL	Movie	SGML File

ascii compressed Lempel-Ziv	Document	MP3 - MPEG Audio	shadow object
ascii text	DVI format	MPEG	Slide
audio streams	ebcdic compressed Huffman	MPEG 3 Movie	Solaris DLL
AVI	ebcdic compressed Lempel-Ziv	MPEG Movie	Solaris Executable
binary file	ebcdic text	MSWord Document	Spread Sheet
BMP -Bit Map	email	NSF Award Abstracts	SQL script
C code	Excel Spread Sheet	NT DLL	streams
C include file	Executable	NT Executable	tar bundle
compressed file	fig image	object code	tar file
compressed mmCIF file	FITS image	orb data	tcl script
compressed PDB file	fortran code	pbm image	text
compressed tar file	☐generic	PDF Document	tiff image
Cray DLL	gif image	perl script	Troff format
Cray Executable	html	PNG-Portable Network Graphics	URL
CSS-Cascading Style Sheet	image	Postscript format	uuencoded tiff
data file	java code	Power Point Slide	video streams
database	jpeg image	print-format	Wave Audio
database object	LaTeX format	program code	WMV-Windows Media Video
database shadow object	library code	Quicktime Movie	Word format
datascope data	link code	realAudio	xml
DICOM header	Mac DLL	realVideo	XML Schema

The rule example is in iRODS/clients/icommands/test/rules4.0/acmsiSetDataTypeFromExt.r.

Example Usage:

acPostProcForPut {msiSetDataTypeFromExt;}

4.134   Core :: Framework Services System :: msiSetDefaultResc

---

msiSetDefaultResc	(	msParam_t *	xdefaultRescList,
		msParam_t *	xoptionStr	)

Parameters:

[in]   xdefaultRescList   - Required - a msParam of type STR_MS_T which is a list of %delimited resource Names. It is the resource that is used if no resource is input. A "null" means there is no defaultResc.

[in]   xoptionStr   - a msParam of type STR_MS_T which is an option (preferred, forced, null) with null as default. A "forced" input means the defaultResc will be used

regardless of the user input. The forced action only applies to users with normal privilege.

Description:
This microservice specifies the resource to use if no resource is input.

Note:
A "null" means there is no default resource. More than one resource can be input using the character "%" as separator. If it is used, it should be executed right after the screening function msiSetNoDirectRescInp. The rule example is in iRODS/clients/icommands/test/rules4.0/acmsiSetDefaultResc.r.

Example Usage:

```
acSetRescSchemeForCreate {
  msiSetNoDirectRescInp("testResc");
  msiSetDefaultResc("demoResc", "preferred");
  msiSetRescSortScheme("default");
}
```

4.135   Core :: Framework Services System :: msiSetGraftPathScheme

msiSetGraftPathScheme (msParam_t *   xaddUserName,
                                  msParam_t *   xtrimDirCnt   )

Parameters:
[in]   xaddUserName   - This msParam specifies whether the userName should be added to the physical path. e.g. $vaultPath/$userName/$logicalPath. "xaddUserName" can have two values - yes or no.
[in]   xtrimDirCnt   - This msParam specifies the number of leading directory elements of the logical path to trim. Sometimes it may not be desirable to graft the entire logical path. e.g., for a logicalPath /myZone/home/me/foo/bar, it may be desirable to graft just the part "home/me/foo/bar" to the vaultPath. "xtrimDirCnt" should be set to 1 in this case. The default value is 1.

Description:
This microservice sets the VaultPath scheme to GRAFT_PATH. It grafts (adds) the logical path to the vault path of the resource when generating the physical path for a data object.

Note:
The policy is implemented in the core.re file. The default is addUserName == yes and trimDirCnt == 1. If trimDirCnt is greater than 1, the home or trash entry will be taken out. The rule example is in iRODS/clients/icommands/test/rules4.0/acmsiSetGraftPathScheme.r.

Example Usage:

```
acSetVaultPathPolicy {msiSetGraftPathScheme("no", "1");}
```

4.136   Core :: Framework Services System :: msiSetMultiReplPerResc

msiSetMultiReplPerResc (   )

Parameters:
None.

Description:
By default, the system allows one copy per resource.
This microservice sets the number of copies per resource to unlimited.

Note:
When multiple replicas are enabled on the same resource, the way the physical file name is specified is modified. If the first copy is stored on:

      /Vault/home/$userNameClient/sub1

the second copy will be stored on

      /Vault/replica/home/$userNameClient/sub1

The rule example is in iRODS/clients/icommands/test/rules4.0/acmsiSetMultiReplPerResc.r.

Example Usage:

acSetMultiReplPerResc {msiSetMultiReplPerResc();}

4.137   Core :: Framework Services System :: msiSetNoDirectRescInp

---

msiSetNoDirectRescInp (msParam_t *   xrescList,   )

Parameters:
[in]   xrescList   - InpParam is a xrescList of type STR_MS_T which is a list of %-
      delimited resource names e.g., resc1%resc2%resc3.

Description:
This microservice sets a list of resources that cannot be used by a normal user directly. It checks a given list of taboo-resources against the user provided resource name and disallows if the resource is in the list of taboo-resources.

Note:
This microservice is optional, but if used, should be the first function to execute because it screens the resource input. The rule example is in iRODS/clients/icommands/test/rules4.0/acmsiSetNoDirectRescInp.r.

Session Variables Used:
rei->doinp->condInput   - user set resource list
rei->rsComm->proxyUser.authInfo.authFlag

Example Usage:

acSetRescSchemeForCreate {
 msiSetNoDirectRescInp("testResc");
 msiSetDefaultResc("demoResc", "random");
 msiSetRescSortScheme("byRescType");
}

4.138   Core :: Framework Services System :: msiSetNumThreads

msiSetNumThreads   (msParam_t *   xsizePerThrInMbStr,
                              msParam_t *   xmaxNumThrStr,
                              msParam_t *   xwindowSizeStr   )

Parameters:
[in]   xsizePerThrInMbStr   - The number of threads is computed using: numThreads = fileSizeInMb / sizePerThrInMb + 1 where sizePerThrInMb is an integer value in MBytes. It also accepts the word "default" which sets sizePerThrInMb to a default value of 32.
[in]   xmaxNumThrStr   - The maximum number of threads to use. It accepts an integer value up to 16. It also accepts the word "default" which sets maxNumThr to a default value of 4.
[in]   xwindowSizeStr   - The TCP window size in Bytes for the parallel transfer. A value of 0 or "default" means a default size of 1,048,576 bytes.

Description:
This microservice specifies the parameters for determining the number of threads to use for data transfer. It sets the number of threads and the TCP window size.

Note:
The msiSetNumThreads function must be present or no threads will be used for all transfers. The acSetNumThreads rule supports conditions based on $rescName so that different policies can be set for different resources. For a network bandwidth of 350 MB/sec and a round-trip latency of 100 milliseconds, the xwindowSizeStr should be set to 35 Mbytes to fill the network pipe. If the window size is smaller, multiple I/O streams will be needed. The rule example is in iRODS/clients/icommands/test/rules4.0/acmsiSetNumThreads.r.

Example Usage:

acSetNumThreads {msiSetNumThreads("32", "8", "default");}

4.139   Core :: Framework Services System :: msiSetPublicUserOpr

msiSetPublicUserOpr   (msParam_t *   xoprList)

Parameters:
[in]   xoprList   - Only 2 operations are allowed - "read" - read files; "query" – browse some system level metadata. More than one operation can be input using the character "%" as separator. e.g., read%query.

Description:
This microservice sets a list of operations that can be performed by the user "public".

Note:

The rule example is in iRODS/clients/icommands/test/rules4.0/acmsiSetPublicUserOpr.r.

Session Variables Used:
rei->rsComm->clientUser.authInfo.authFlag

Example Usage:

acSetPublicUserPolicy {msiSetPublicUserOpr("read%query");}

4.140   Core :: Framework Services System :: msiSetRandomScheme

msiSetRandomScheme   (   )

Parameters:
None

Description:
This microservice sets the scheme for composing the physical path in the vault to RANDOM. A randomly generated path is appended to the vaultPath when generating the physical path. e.g., $vaultPath/$userName/$randomPath. The advantage with the RANDOM scheme is renaming operations (imv, irm) are much faster because there is no need to rename the corresponding physical path.

Note:
The rule example is in iRODS/clients/icommands/test/rules4.0/acmsiSetRandomScheme.r.

Example Usage:

acSetVaultPathPolicy {msiSetRandomScheme;}

4.141   Core :: Framework Services System :: msiSetRescQuotaPolicy

msiSetRescQuotaPolicy   (msParam_t *   xflag   )

Parameters:
[in]   xflag   - Required - a msParam of type STR_MS_T.
                "on" - enable Resource Quota enforcement
                "off" - disable Resource Quota enforcement (default)

Description:
This microservice sets the resource quota to on or off.

Note:
The rule example is in iRODS/clients/icommands/test/rules4.0/acmsiSetRescQuotaPolicy.r.

Example Usage:

acRescQuotaPolicy {msiSetRescQuotaPolicy("on");}

4.142   Core :: Framework Services System :: msiSetRescSortScheme

msiSetRescSortScheme   (msParam_t *   xsortScheme   )

Parameters:
[in]   xsortScheme   - The sorting scheme. Valid schemes are "default", "random",
                                "byLoad" and "byRescClass". The "byRescClass" scheme will
                                put the cache class of resource on the top of the list. The
                                "byLoad" scheme will put the least loaded resource on the top of
                                the list. This requires that the resource monitoring system be
                                switched on in order to pick up the load information for each
                                server in the resource group list. The scheme "random" and
                                "byRescClass" can be applied in sequence.

Description:
This microservice sets the scheme for selecting the best resource to use when creating a data object.

Note:
The rule example is in iRODS/clients/icommands/test/rules4.0/acmsiSetRescSortScheme.r.

Example Usage:

```
acSetRescSchemeForCreate {
 msiSetDefaultResc("demoResc", "null");
 msiSetRescSortScheme("random");
 msiSetRescSortScheme("byRescClass");
}
```

4.143   Core :: Framework Services System :: msiSetReServerNumProc

msiSetReServerNumProc   (msParam_t *   xnumProc   )

Parameters:
[in]   xnumProc   - a STR_MS_T representing number of processes.
                             This value can be "default" or an integer

Description:
Sets the number of processes to use when running jobs in the irodsReServer. The irodsReServer supports
multi-tasking such that one or two long-running jobs will not block the execution of other jobs.

Note:
The allowed range is 0-4. A value of 0 means that no forking will be done. The default value is 1. The
rule example is in iRODS/clients/icommands/test/rules4.0/acmsiSetReServerNumProc.r.

Example Usage:

```
acSetReServerNumProc {msiSetReServerNumProc("4");}
```

4.144   Core :: Framework Services System :: msiSetResource

msiSetResource (msParam_t *   xrescName   **)**

Parameters:
[in]   xrescName   - is a msParam of type STR_MS_T

Description:
This microservice sets the resource as part of a workflow execution.

Note:
The rule example is in iRODS/clients/icommands/test/rules4.0/acmsiSetResource.r.

Example Usage:

```
acRegisterData {
  ON($objPath like "/home/collections.nvo/2mass/fits-images/*") {
    acCheckDataType("fits image");
    msiSetResource("testResc");
    msiRegisterData;
  }
}
```

4.145   Core :: Framework Services System :: msiSortDataObj

msiSortDataObj (msParam_t *   xsortScheme   **)**

Parameters:
[in]   xsortScheme   - input sorting scheme

Description:
This microservice sorts the copies of the data object using a sorting scheme.

Note:
Currently, "random" and "byRescClass" sorting schemes are supported. If "byRescClass" is set, data objects in the "cache" resources will be used ahead of those in the "archive" resources. The sorting schemes can be chained. Thus msiSortDataObj("random"); msiSortDataObj("byRescClass"); means that the data objects will be sorted randomly first and then separated by class. The rule example is in iRODS/clients/icommands/test/rules4.0/acmsiSortDataObj.r.

Example Usage:

```
acPreprocForDataObjOpen {
  msiSortDataObj("byRescClass");
  msiStageDataObj("demoResc");
}
```

4.146   Core :: Framework Services System :: msiStageDataObj

msiStageDataObj   (msParam_t *   xcacheResc   )

Parameters:
[in]   xcacheResc   - The resource name in which to cache the object

Description:
This microservice stages the data object to the specified resource before operation. It stages a copy of the data object in the cacheResc before opening the data object.

Note:
This is typically used to make a copy on a local storage resource. The $writeFlag session variable has been created to be used as a condition for differentiating between open for read ($writeFlag == 0) and open for write ($writeFlag == 1). e.g. :

acPreprocForDataObjOpen {ON($writeFlag == "0") {msiStageDataObj("demoResc");}}

acPreprocForDataObjOpen {ON($writeFlag == "1") { } }

```
acPreprocForDataObjOpen {
  msiSortDataObj("random");
  msiSetDataObjPreferredResc("xyz%demoResc8%abc");
  msiStageDataObj("demoResc8");
}
```

The rule example is in iRODS/clients/icommands/test/rules4.0/acmsiStageDataObj.r

Example Usage:

```
acPreprocForDataObjOpen {
  msiSortDataObj("byRescClass");
  msiStageDataObj("demoResc");
}
```

4.147   Core :: Framework Services System :: msiSysChksumDataObj

msiSysChksumDataObj (   )

Parameters:
None

Description:
This microservice performs a checksum on the just uploaded or copied data object.

Note:
The checksum is done at the remote storage location. The rule example is in
iRODS/clients/icommands/test/rules4.0/acmsiSysChksumDataObj.r.

Example Usage:

acPostProcForPut {msiSysChksumDataObj; }

4.148   Core :: Framework Services System :: msiSysReplDataObj

---

msiSysReplDataObj   (msParam_t *   xcacheResc,
                                        msParam_t *   xflag   )

Parameters:
[in]   xcacheResc   - storage resource for replica
[in]   xflag   - flag controlling replication
              all   – a copy will be made on all resources in a resource group
              null   – only a single copy will be made within the resource group
              updateRepl   – existing stale copies are updated to the latest copy
              rbudpTransfer   – use the Reliable Blast UDP protocol for the transfer

Description:
This microservice replicates a data object. It can be used to replicate a copy of the just uploaded or copied data object to the specified replResc.

Note:
The "all" flag is only meaningful if the replResc is a resource group. In this case, setting xflag to "all" means a copy will be made on all of the resources in the resource group. A "null" input means a single copy will be made in one of the resources in the resource group. More than one flag value can be set using the %" character as a separator. e.g., "all%updateRepl". Here the "all" flag means replicate to all resources in a resource group and update all stale copies since the "updateRepl" flag is also set.

It may be desirable to do replication only if the dataObject is stored in a resource group. For example, the following rule can be used:

acPostProcForPut {ON($rescGroupName != "") {msiSysReplDataObj($rescGroupName,"all");}}

The rule example is in iRODS/clients/icommands/test/rules4.0/acmsiSysReplDataObj.r.

Example Usage:

acPostProcForPut {
 ON($rescGroupName != "") {
  msiSysReplDataObj($rescGroupName,"all");
 }
}

4.149   Core :: iCAT System Services :: msiAclPolicy

---

msiAclPolicy (msParam_t* msParam   )

Parameters:

[in]   msParam   - a msParam of type STR_MS_T – can have value 'STRICT'

Description:
        Limits display of information about files owned by a user.
Note:
Should not be used outside of the rules defined in core.re. Once set STRICT, strict mode remains in force
(users cannot call it in another rule to change the mode back to non-strict). See core.re.

If not called or called with an argument other than STRICT, the STANDARD setting is in effect, which is
fine for many sites. By default, users are allowed to see certain metadata, for example the data-object and
sub-collection names in each other's collections. When made STRICT by calling msiAclPolicy(STRICT),
the General Query Access Control is applied on collections and data object metadata which means that ils,
etc., will need 'read' access or better to the collection to see a list of the collection contents (name of data-
objects, sub-collections, etc.). Formerly this was controlled at build-time via a GEN_QUERY_AC flag in
config.mk. Default is the normal, non-strict level, allowing users to see other collections. In all cases,
access control to the data-objects is enforced. When "STRICT" is set, the user will only be able to see
their home collection. They will not be able to view the start of the directory path, "/datagrid-name/home",
or "/datagrid-name/trash".

Even with STRICT access control, the admin user is not restricted so various microservices and queries
will still be able to evaluate system-wide information.

Since iRODS 2.5, $userNameClient is available although this is only secure in a iRODS-password
environment (not GSI), but you can then have rules for specific users:

        acAclPolicy {ON($userNameClient == "quickshare") { } }
        acAclPolicy {msiAclPolicy("STRICT"); }

The rule example is in iRODS/clients/icommands/test/rules4.0/acmsiAclPolicy.r.

Example Usage:

acAclPolicy { msiAclPolicy("STRICT"); }

4.150   Core :: iCAT System Services :: msiAddConditionToGenQuery

---

msiAddConditionToGenQuery   (msParam_t *   attribute,
                                            msParam_t *   operator,
                                            msParam_t *   value,
                                            msParam_t *   queryInput   )

Parameters:
[in]   attribute   - Required - A STR_MS_T with the iCAT attribute name (see
                               wiki.irods.org/index.php/icatAttributes).
[in]   operator   - Required - A STR_MS_T with the operator.
[in]   value   - Required - A STR_MS_T with the value.
[in,out]   queryInput   - Required - A GenQueryInp_MS_T.

Description:
Adds a condition to a genQueryInp_t structure.

Note:

This microservice adds a condition to an existing genQueryInp_t, based on three parameters. The first is an iCAT attribute index given without its 'COL_' prefix. The second one is the SQL operator. The third one is the value and may contain wildcards. Normally used with msiAddSelectFieldToGenQuery and msiExecGenQuery to build queries from the results of other microservices or actions within an iRODS rule.

Example Usage:

```
myTestRule {
# Input parameters are:
#  Attribute name
#  Operator
#  Value
#  Input/Output
#  General query structure
#  Output from running the example is:
#  List of files in collection /$rodsZoneClient/home/rods

 # initial condition for query corresponds to "COLL_NAME like
'/$rodsZoneClient/home/$userNameClient/%%'"
 msiMakeGenQuery(*Select, "COLL_NAME like '/$rodsZoneClient/home/$userNameClient/%%'",
*GenQInp);

 # adding condition to query "DATA_NAME like rule%%"
 msiAddConditionToGenQuery(*Attribute,*Operator,*Value,*GenQInp);
 msiExecGenQuery(*GenQInp,*GenQOut);
 foreach(*GenQOut)
 {
  msiGetValByKey(*GenQOut, "DATA_NAME", *DataFile);
  msiGetValByKey(*GenQOut, "COLL_NAME", *Coll);
  writeLine("stdout","*Coll/*DataFile");
 }
}
INPUT *Select="DATA_NAME, COLL_NAME", *Attribute="DATA_NAME", *Operator=" like ",
*Value="rule%%"
OUTPUT ruleExecOut
```

4.151   Core :: iCAT System Services :: msiAddSelectFieldToGenQuery

---

msiAddSelectFieldToGenQuery (msParam_t *   select,

                                        msParam_t *   function,

                                        msParam_t *   queryInput   **)**

Parameters:

[in]   select   - Required - A STR_MS_T with the select field.
[in]   function   - Optional - A STR_MS_T with the function. Valid values are
                        [MIN|MAX|SUM|AVG|COUNT]
[in,out] queryInput   - Optional - A GenQueryInp_MS_T structure.

Description:

Sets a select field in a genQueryInp_t structure.

Note:
This microservice sets a select field in a genQueryInp_t structure from two parameters. The first is an iCAT attribute index given without its 'COL_' prefix. The second one is the optional SQL operator. A new genQueryInp_t is created if queryInput is NULL. The msiAddSelectFieldToGenQuery microservice typically follows msiMakeGenQuery to build and extend queries within a rule.

Example Usage:

```
myTestRule {
# Input parameters are:
#  Select field
#  Function to apply to attribute
# Input/Output parameter:
#  GenQuery structure
# Output from running the example is:
#  List of sizes of collections in /$rodsZoneClient/home/rods

  # initial select is on COLL_NAME
  msiMakeGenQuery(*Select, "COLL_NAME like '/$rodsZoneClient/home/$userNameClient/%%'",
*GenQInp);

  # add select on sum(DATA_SIZE)
  msiAddSelectFieldToGenQuery(*SelectAdd,*Function,*GenQInp);
  msiExecGenQuery(*GenQInp,*GenQOut);
  foreach(*GenQOut)
  {
    msiGetValByKey(*GenQOut, "DATA_SIZE", *Size);
    msiGetValByKey(*GenQOut, "COLL_NAME", *Coll);
    writeLine("stdout","For collection *Coll, the size of the files is *Size");
  }
}
INPUT *Select="COLL_NAME", *SelectAdd="DATA_SIZE", *Function="SUM"
OUTPUT ruleExecOut
```

4.152   Core :: iCAT System Services :: msiAddUserToGroup

msiAddUserToGroup   (msParam_t *   msParam   )

Parameters:
[in]   msParam   - a msParam of type STR_MS_T, the name of the group

Description:
This microservice adds a user to a group.

Note:
Should not be used outside of the rules defined in core.re. This is called via an 'iadmin' command. The rule example is in iRODS/clients/icommands/test/rules4.0/acmsiAddUserToGroup.r.

Example Usage:

```
acCreateUserF1 {
```

```
# this should only be executed within the core.re file
   msiCreateUser              :::   msiRollback;
   acCreateDefaultCollections :::   msiRollback;
   msiAddUserToGroup("public") :::   msiRollback;
   msiCommit;
}
```

4.153   Core :: iCAT System Services :: msiCloseGenQuery

---

msiCloseGenQuery   (msParam_t *   genQueryInp_msp,
                                          msParam_t *   genQueryOut_msp   )

Parameters:
[in]   genQueryInp_msp   - Required - a GenQueryInp_MS_T containing the query parameters
                                     and conditions.
[in]   genQueryOut_msp   - Required - a GenQueryOut_MS_T to write results to. If its
                                     continuation index is 0 the query will be closed.

Description:
This microservice closes an unfinished query. This is based on the code from #msiGetMoreRows.

Note:

Example Usage:

```
mytestrule{
#rule to create a query and then close the associated buffer using msiCloseGenQuery
# Input
#   Query input buffer
#   Query result buffer
  *Coll = "/$rodsZoneClient/home/$userNameClient" ++ "%";
  msiMakeGenQuery("count(DATA_NAME), sum(DATA_SIZE)", "COLL_NAME like '*Coll'",
*GenQInp2);
#========= this counts files in a collection =============
  msiExecGenQuery(*GenQInp2, *GenQOut2);
  foreach(*Row in *GenQOut2) {
   *num = *Row.DATA_NAME;
   *sizetotal = *Row.DATA_SIZE;
  } # end of retrieval of number and size
  msiCloseGenQuery(*GenQInp2, *GenQOut2);
  writeLine("stdout", "Number of files is *num and total size is *sizetotal");
}
INPUT null
OUTPUT ruleExecOut
```

4.154   Core :: iCAT System Services :: msiCommit

---

msiCommit   (   )

Parameters:
None

Description:
This microservice commits pending database transactions, registering the new state information into the iCAT.

Note:
This is used to commit changes (if any) into the iCAT database as part of a rule and microservice chain. See core.re for examples. In other cases, iCAT updates and inserts are automatically committed into the iCAT Database as part of the normal operations (in the 'C' code). The rule example is in iRODS/clients/icommands/test/rules4.0/acmsiCommit.r.

Example Usage:

```
acCreateUserF1 {
# This is the acCreateUserF1 policy in the core.re file
 ON ($otherUserName == "anonymous")
 {
  msiCreateUser ::: msiRollback;
  msiCommit;
 }
}
```

4.155   Core :: iCAT System Services :: msiCreateCollByAdmin

msiCreateCollByAdmin (msParam_t *   xparColl,
                                    msParam_t *   xchildName   )

Parameters:
[in]   xparColl   - a msParam of type STR_MS_T for parent collection
[in]   xchildName   - a msParam of type STR_MS_T for child collection

Description:
This microservice creates a collection by an administrator executed command.

Note:
Should not be used outside of the rules defined in core.re. This is called via an 'iadmin' command, and can only be executed by a person with a rodsadmin role. The rule example is in iRODS/clients/icommands/test/rules4.0/acmsiCreateCollByAdmin.r.

Example Usage:

```
acCreateCollByAdmin(*parColl,*childColl) {
 msiCreateCollByAdmin(*parColl,*childColl);
}
```

4.156   Core :: iCAT System Services :: msiCreateUser

msiCreateUser ( )

Parameters:
None

Description:
This microservice creates a new user.

Note:
Should not be used outside of the rules defined in core.re. This is called via an 'iadmin' command. The rule example is in iRODS/clients/icommands/test/rules4.0/acmsiCreateUser.r.

Example Usage:

```
acCreateUserF1 {
# This is the acCreateUserF1 policy in the core.re file
 msiCreateUser          ::: msiRollback;
 acCreateDefaultCollections ::: msiRollback;
 msiAddUserToGroup("public")  ::: msiRollback;
 msiCommit;
}
```

4.157   Core :: iCAT System Services :: msiDeleteCollByAdmin

msiDeleteCollByAdmin (msParam_t *   xparColl,
                               msParam_t *   xchildName   )

Parameters:
[in]   xparColl   - a msParam of type STR_MS_T for the parent collection
[in]   xchildName   - a msParam of type STR_MS_T for the child collection

Description:
This microservice deletes a collection by an administrator executed command.

Note:
Should not be used outside of the rules defined in core.re. This is called via an 'iadmin' command. This microservice can only be executed by a person with a rodsadmin role. The rule example is in iRODS/clients/icommands/test/rules4.0/acmsiDeleteCollByAdmin.r.

Session Variables Used:
rei->rsComm->clientUser.authFlag (must be admin)

Example Usage:

```
acDeleteCollByAdmin(*parColl,*childColl) {
 msiDeleteCollByAdmin(*parColl,*childColl);
}
```

4.158   Core :: iCAT System Services :: msiDeleteUnusedAVUs

msiDeleteUnusedAVUs (   )

Parameters:
None

Description:
This function deletes unused AVUs from the iCAT. See 'iadmin rum'. This requires execution by a person with a rodsadmin role.

Note:
This causes the unused AVUs to be removed from the ICAT.

Session Variables Used:
rei->rsComm->clientUser.authFlag (must be admin)

Example Usage:

```
myTestRule {
  delay (*arg1) {
    msiDeleteUnusedAVUs;
  }
}
INPUT *arg1="<PLUSET>1m</PLUSET><EF>24h</EF>"
OUTPUT ruleExecOut
```

4.159   Core :: iCAT System Services :: msiDeleteUser

msiDeleteUser (   )

Parameters:
None

Description:
This microservice deletes a user.

Note:
Should not be used outside of the rules defined in core.re. This is called via an 'iadmin' command by a person with a rodsadmin role.

When a user is deleted, decisions should also be made about deletion of the data, the files they may have in trash, and the files they may have in bundle and replica directories. The rule example is in iRODS/clients/icommands/test/rules4.0/acmsiDeleteUser.r.

Session Variables Used:
rei->rsComm->clientUser.authFlag (must be admin)

Example Usage:

```
acDeleteUserF1 {
# This is the acDeleteUserF1 policy in the core.re file
  acDeleteDefaultCollections ::: msiRollback;
  msiDeleteUser          ::: msiRollback;
  msiCommit;
}
```

4.160   Core :: iCAT System Services :: msiExecGenQuery

---

msiExecGenQuery   (msParam_t *   genQueryInParam,
                                     msParam_t *   genQueryOutParam   )

Parameters:
[in]   genQueryInParam   - a msParam of type GenQueryInp_MS_T structure holding the query
[out]   genQueryOutParam   - a msParam of type GenQueryOut_MS_T structure holding the result

Description:
This function executes a given general query structure and returns the first 256 rows of the result.

Note:
Takes a SQL-like iRODS query (no FROM clause) and returns a table structure. Use a loop over msiGetMoreRows to get all rows. The example loops over all files in a collection for arbitrarily large collections by working with the continuation index. The processing is done in sets of 256 records at a time. To return more row values, modify MAX_SQL_ROWS in iRODS/ lib/core/include/rodsGenQuery.h.

Example Usage:

```
myTestRule {
# Input parameters are:
#  Structure holding the query
# Output parameter is:
#  Structure holding the query result
# Output from running the example is:
#  List of the number of files and size of files in collection /$rodsZoneClient/home/$userNameClient/large-
coll
  *ContInxOld = 1;
  *Count = 0;
  *Size = 0;
  msiMakeGenQuery("DATA_ID, DATA_SIZE", *Condition,*GenQInp);
  msiExecGenQuery(*GenQInp, *GenQOut);
  msiGetContInxFromGenQueryOut(*GenQOut,*ContInxNew);
  while(*ContInxOld > 0) {
   foreach(*GenQOut) {
     msiGetValByKey(*GenQOut, "DATA_SIZE", *Fsize);
     *Size = *Size + double(*Fsize);
     *Count = *Count + 1;
   }
   *ContInxOld = *ContInxNew;
   if(*ContInxOld > 0) {msiGetMoreRows(*GenQInp,*GenQOut,*ContInxNew);}
```

```
}
 writeLine("stdout","Number of files in *Coll is *Count and total size is *Size");
}
INPUT *Coll = "/$rodsZoneClient/home/$userNameClient/large-coll", *Condition="COLL_NAME like
'*Coll'"
OUTPUT ruleExecOut
```

4.161   Core :: iCAT System Services :: msiExecStrCondQuery

msiExecStrCondQuery (msParam_t *   queryParam,
                                    msParam_t *   genQueryOutParam   )

Parameters:
[in]   queryParam   - a msParam of type GenQueryInp_MS_T
[out]   genQueryOutParam   - a msParam of type GenQueryOut_MS_T

Description:
This function takes a given query string, creates an iCAT query, executes it, and returns the values. This
example returns up to 256 rows from the query. To get more results, iterate over msiGetMoreRows as in
the example for rulemsiExecGenQuery.r.

Note:
The query string can also be generated by msiMakeQuery.

Example Usage:

```
myTestRule {
# Input parameters are:
#  String with conditional query
# Output parameter is:
#  Result string
 msiExecStrCondQuery(*Select,*QOut);
 foreach(*QOut) {
  msiPrintKeyValPair("stdout", *QOut)
 }
}
INPUT *Select="SELECT DATA_NAME where DATA_NAME like 'rule%%'"
OUTPUT ruleExecOut
```

4.162   Core :: iCAT System Services :: msiGetContInxFromGenQueryOut

msiGetContInxFromGenQueryOut   (msParam_t *   genQueryOutParam,
                                                   msParam_t *   continueInx   )

Parameters:
[in]   genQueryOutParam   - Required - of type GenQueryOut_MS_T which holds the query result.
[out]   continueInx   - a INT_MS_T containing the new continuation index. A value greater
                                   than 1 indicates additional rows are available.

Description:
This microservice gets the continuation index value from genQueryOut generated by msiExecGenQuery.

Note:
The output result continueInx can be used to determine whether there are remaining rows to retrieve from the generated query. The example loops over queries to the iCAT catalog to get additional rows. The microservices within the foreach loop are executed for each row returned from the iCAT query.

Example Usage:

```
myTestRule {
# Input parameters are:
#  Structure holding the query
# Output parameter is:
#  Continuation index, non-zero when additional rows are available
# Output from running the example is:
#  List of the number of files and size of files in collection /$rodsZoneClient/home/rods
  *ContInxOld = 1;
  *Count = 0;
  *Size = 0;
  msiMakeGenQuery("DATA_ID, DATA_SIZE", *Condition,*GenQInp);
  msiExecGenQuery(*GenQInp, *GenQOut);
  msiGetContInxFromGenQueryOut(*GenQOut,*ContInxNew);
  while(*ContInxOld > 0) {
   if(*ContInxNew == 0) { *ContInxOld = 0; }
   foreach(*GenQOut) {
     msiGetValByKey(*GenQOut, "DATA_SIZE", *Fsize);
     *Size = *Size + double(*Fsize);
     *Count = *Count + 1;
   }
   if(*ContInxOld > 0) {msiGetMoreRows(*GenQInp,*GenQOut,*ContInxNew);}
  }
  writeLine("stdout","Number of files in *Coll is *Count and total size is *Size");
}
INPUT *Coll = "/$rodsZoneClient/home/$userNameClient/%%", *Condition="COLL_NAME like '*Coll'"
OUTPUT ruleExecOut
```

4.163   Core :: iCAT System Services :: msiGetMoreRows

msiGetMoreRows	(	msParam_t *	genQueryInp_msp,	
		msParam_t *	genQueryOut_msp,	
		msParam_t *	continueInx	)

Parameters:

[in]	genQueryInp_msp	- Required - a GenQueryInp_MS_T containing the query parameters and conditions.
[in]	genQueryOut_msp	- Required - a GenQueryOut_MS_T to write results to. If its continuation index is 0 the query will be closed.
[out]	continueInx	- a INT_MS_T containing the new continuation index (after the query).

Description:
This microservice continues an unfinished query by returning the next set of 256 rows.

Note:
This microservice gets the next batch of rows for an open iCAT query. This is used after initial msiMakeGenQuery and msiExecGenQuery microservice calls that have more than 256 rows in the response.

Example Usage:

```
myTestRule {
# Input parameters are:
#  Structure holding the query
#  Structure holding the query result
# Output parameter is:
#  Continuation index, greater than zero is additional rows can be retrieved
# Output from running the example is:
#  List of the number of files and size of files in collection /$rodsZoneClient/home/rods
  *ContInxOld = 1;
  *Count = 0;
  *Size = 0;
  msiMakeGenQuery("DATA_ID, DATA_SIZE", *Condition,*GenQInp);
  msiExecGenQuery(*GenQInp, *GenQOut);
  msiGetContInxFromGenQueryOut(*GenQOut,*ContInxNew);
  while(*ContInxOld > 0) {
   foreach(*GenQOut) {
     msiGetValByKey(*GenQOut, "DATA_SIZE", *Fsize);
     *Size = *Size + double(*Fsize);
     *Count = *Count + 1;
   }
   *ContInxOld = *ContInxNew;
   if(*ContInxOld > 0) {msiGetMoreRows(*GenQInp,*GenQOut,*ContInxNew);}
  }
  writeLine("stdout","Number of files in *Coll is *Count and total size is *Size");
}
INPUT *Coll = "/$rodsZoneClient/home/$userNameClient/%%", *Condition="COLL_NAME like '*Coll'"
OUTPUT ruleExecOut
```

4.164   Core :: iCAT System Services :: msiMakeGenQuery

msiMakeGenQuery   (msParam_t *   selectListStr,
                                     msParam_t *   condStr,
                                     msParam_t *   genQueryInpParam   )

Parameters:
[in]   selectListStr   - Required - a STR_MS_T containing the parameters.
[in]   condStr   - Required - a STR_MS_T containing the conditions
[out]   genQueryInpParam   - a GenQueryInp_MS_T containing the parameters and
                                conditions.

Description:

This microservice constructs an SQL string that can be issued to the iCAT catalog by a subsequent call to msiExecGenQuery. The SQL string is contained in a GenQueryInp_MS_T structure.

Note:
This microservice sets up a genQueryInp_t data structure needed by calls to rsGenQuery(). It is typically executed before calls to msiExecGenQuery and msiGetMoreRows.

Example Usage:

```
myTestRule {
# Input parameters are:
#  Selected attribute list
#  Condition for selecting files
# Output parameter is:
#  Structure holding the query
# Output from running the example is:
#  List of the number of files and size of files in collection /$rodsZoneClient/home/rods
 *ContInxOld = 1;
 *Count = 0;
 *Size = 0;
 msiMakeGenQuery("DATA_ID, DATA_SIZE", *Condition,*GenQInp);
 msiExecGenQuery(*GenQInp, *GenQOut);
 msiGetContInxFromGenQueryOut(*GenQOut,*ContInxNew);
 while(*ContInxOld > 0) {
  if(*ContInxNew == 0) { *ContInxOld = 0; }
  foreach(*GenQOut) {
    msiGetValByKey(*GenQOut, "DATA_SIZE", *Fsize);
    *Size = *Size + double(*Fsize);
    *Count = *Count + 1;
  }
  if(*ContInxOld > 0) {msiGetMoreRows(*GenQInp,*GenQOut,*ContInxNew);}
 }
 writeLine("stdout","Number of files in *Coll is *Count and total size is *Size");
}
INPUT *Coll = "/$rodsZoneClient/home/$userNameClient/%%", *Condition="COLL_NAME like '*Coll'"
OUTPUT ruleExecOut
```

4.165   Core :: iCAT System Services :: msiMakeQuery

msiMakeQuery	(	msParam_t *	selectListParam,	
		msParam_t *	conditionsParam,	
		msParam_t *	queryOutParam	)

Parameters:
[in]   selectListParam - a STR_MS_T containing the parameters that are selected in the query.
[in]   conditionsParam - a STR_MS_T containing the condition for the query.
[out]   queryOutParam   - a STR_MS_T containing the parameters and conditions as sql.

Description:
Creates an sql query from a parameter list and condition.

Note:

This microservice creates a sql query string from the input parameter list (select statement) and condition.

Example Usage:

myTestRule {
# Input parameters are:
# Attribute list
# Condition for selecting files
# Output parameter is:
# SQL execution string
# Output from running the example is:
# List of all files that start with rule
  msiMakeQuery(*Select,*Condition,*Query);
  msiExecStrCondQuery(*Query, *GenQOut);
  foreach(*GenQOut) {msiPrintKeyValPair("stdout", *GenQOut);}
}
INPUT *Select="DATA_NAME, COLL_NAME, DATA_RESC_NAME, DATA_REPL_NUM, DATA_SIZE", *Condition="DATA_NAME like 'rule%%'"
OUTPUT ruleExecOut

4.166   Core :: iCAT System Services :: msiPrintGenQueryInp

msiPrintGenQueryInp   (msParam_t *   where,
                                      msParam_t *   genQueryInpParam   )

Parameters:
[in]   where   - Required - a STR_MS_T specifying the output buffer.
[in]   genQueryInpParam   - Required - a GenQueryInp_MS_T containing the
                                       parameters and conditions.

Description:
This microservice prints the given GenQueryInp_MS_T structure to the given target buffer. This provides a way to list the contents of a query that is being issued to the iCAT metadata catalog.

Note:
The target buffer can be "stdout", "stderr", "serverLog", or an internal buffer.

Example Usage:

myTestRule {
# Input parameter is:
# Buffer where string will be written
# GenQueryInp string
# Output from running the example is:
# Selected Column 501 With Option 1
# Selected Column 407 With Option 4
# Condition Column 501 like '/$rodsZoneClient/home/$userNameClient/%%'

  msiMakeGenQuery(*Select, "COLL_NAME like '/$rodsZoneClient/home/$userNameClient/%%'", *GenQInp);

  # add select on sum(DATA_SIZE)

```
msiAddSelectFieldToGenQuery(*SelectAdd,*Function,*GenQInp);
msiPrintGenQueryInp("stdout", *GenQInp);
}
INPUT *Select="COLL_NAME", *SelectAdd="DATA_SIZE", *Function="SUM"
OUTPUT *GenQInp, ruleExecOut
```

4.167   Core :: iCAT System Services :: msiPrintGenQueryOutToBuffer

---

msiPrintGenQueryOutToBuffer	(	msParam_t *	queryOut,	
		msParam_t *	format,	
		msParam_t *	buffer	)

Parameters:

[in]	queryOut	- Required - A GenQueryOut_MS_T structure holding the query result.
[in]	format	- Optional - A STR_MS_T with a C-style format string, similar to the iquest icommand format.
[out]	buffer	- A BUF_LEN_MS_T structure for the result.

Description:
Writes the contents of the output results from a query contained in a GenQueryOut_MS_T structure into a buffer.

Note:
The results can be formatted with an optional C-style format string the same way it is done in iquest. The format string specifies how the selected attributes will be printed. The format string:
    " %-5.5s access has been given to user %-6.6s for the file %s"
will map the attributes in the SELECT statement to the "%" variables in the format string
        SELECT DATA_ACCESS_NAME, USER_NAME, DATA_NAME
in the order they are listed. Thus DATA_ACCESS_NAME replaces the first "%" and is listed as a string of 5 characters, USER_NAME replaces the second "%" and is listed as a string of 6 characters, and DATA_NAME replaces the third "%" and is listed as a string or arbitrary length.

Example Usage:

```
myTestRule {
# Input parameters are:
#  GenQueryOut structure
#  C-style format string
# Output parameter is:
#  Buffer for result
  msiMakeGenQuery("DATA_ID, DATA_SIZE", *Condition,*GenQInp);
  msiExecGenQuery(*GenQInp, *GenQOut);
  msiPrintGenQueryOutToBuffer(*GenQOut,*Form,*Buf);
  writeBytesBuf("stdout", *Buf);
}
INPUT *Coll = "/$rodsZoneClient/home/$userNameClient/%%", *Condition="COLL_NAME like
'*Coll'", *Form="For data-ID %-6.6s the data size is %-8.8s"
OUTPUT ruleExecOut
```

4.168   Core :: iCAT System Services :: msiQuota

msiQuota   (   )

Parameters:
None

Description:
Calculates storage usage and checks quota values (over/under/how-much-used).

Note:
Causes the ICAT quota tables to be updated. This must be executed by a person with a rodsadmin role.

Session Variables Used:
rei->rsComm->clientUser.authFlag (must be admin)

Example Usage:

```
myTestRule {
# Administrator command to cause update to iCAT quota tables
  delay("<PLUSET>30s</PLUSET><EF>24h</EF>") {
    msiQuota;
    writeLine("serverLog", "Updated quota check");
  }
}
INPUT null
OUTPUT ruleExecOut
```

4.169   Core :: iCAT System Services :: msiSetQuota

msiQuota   (msParam_t   *type,
                              msParam_t   *name,
                              msParam_t   *resource,
                              msParam_t   *value   )

Parameters:
[in] type   - a STR_MS_T - Can be either "user" or "group"
[in] name   - a STR_MS_T with the name of the user or group
[in] resource   - Optional - a STR_MS_T with the name of the resource where the
                            quota will apply, or "total" for the quota to be system-wide.
[in] value   - an INT_MST_T or DOUBLE_MS_T or STR_MS_T with the
                            quota value (in bytes)

Description:
This microservice sets a storage quota for a given user or group of users for either a specific storage system or for total storage.

Note:

If no resource name is provided, the quota will apply across all resources. The microservice requires rodsadmin privileges.

Example Usage:

```
myTestRule {
# Input parameters are:
#  Type of quota (user or group)
#  User or group name
#  Optional resource on which the quota applies (or total for all resources)
#  Quota value in bytes
  msiSetQuota(*Type, *Name, *Resource, *Value);
  writeLine("stdout","Set quota on *Name for resource *Resource to *Value bytes");
}
INPUT *Type="user", *Name="rods", *Resource="demoResc", *Value="1000000000"
OUTPUT ruleExecOut
```

4.170   Core :: iCAT System Services :: msiRenameCollection

msiRenameCollection   (msParam_t *   oldName,
                                       msParam_t *   newName   )

Parameters:
| [in] | oldName | - a msParam of type STR_MS_T with the old collection name. |
| [in] | newName | - a msParam of type STR_MS_T with the new name for the collection. |

Description:
This function renames a collection and is used via a rule with msiRenameLocalZone.

Note:
Should not be used outside of the rules defined in core.re. This is called via an 'iadmin' command. The rule example is in iRODS/clients/icommands/test/rules4.0/acmsiRenameCollection.r.

Example Usage:

```
acRenameLocalZone(*oldZone,*newZone){
   msiRenameCollection("/" ++ str(*oldZone) ++ "", *newZone) ::: msiRollback;
   msiRenameLocalZone(*oldZone,*newZone) ::: msiRollback;
   msiCommit;
}
```

4.171   Core :: iCAT System Services :: msiRenameLocalZone

msiRenameLocalZone   (msParam_t *   oldName,
                                     msParam_t *   newName   )

Parameters:
[in]   oldName   - a msParam of type STR_MS_T

[in]   newName   - a msParam of type STR_MS_T

Description:
This microservice renames the LOCALZone by updating multiple tables in iCAT. This can only be executed by a person with the rodsadmin role.

Note:
Should not be used outside of the rules defined in core.re. This is called via an 'iadmin' command. The rule example is in iRODS/clients/icommands/test/rules4.0/acmsiRenameLocalZone.r.

Example Usage:

```
acRenameLocalZone(*oldZone,*newZone){
    msiRenameCollection("/" ++ str(*oldZone) ++ "", *newZone) ::: msiRollback;
    msiRenameLocalZone(*oldZone,*newZone) ::: msiRollback;
    msiCommit;
}
```

4.172   Core :: iCAT System Services :: msiRollback

msiRollback   (   )

Parameters:
None

Description:
This function deletes user and collection information from the iCAT by rolling back the database transaction.

Note:
This is used to reverse changes to the iCAT database as part of a rule and microservice recovery chain. See core.re for examples. In other cases, iCAT updates and inserts are automatically rolled-back as part of the normal operations (from within the 'C' code of a microservice). The rule example is in iRODS/clients/icommands/test/rules4.0/acmsiRollback.r.

Example Usage:

```
acRenameLocalZone(*oldZone,*newZone){
    msiRenameCollection("/" ++ str(*oldZone) ++ "", *newZone) ::: msiRollback;
    msiRenameLocalZone(*oldZone,*newZone) ::: msiRollback;
    msiCommit;
}
```

4.173   Core :: iCAT System Services :: msiServerBackup

msiServerBackup   (msParam_t   *options,
                           msParam_t   *keyValOut   )

Parameters:

[in]	options	- Optional - a STR_MS_T that contains one of more options in the format keyWd1=value1++++keyWd2=value2++++keyWd3=value3... Currently no options have been defined. This is a place holder for future options.
[out]	keyValOut	- a KeyValPair_MS_T with the number of files and bytes written.

Description:

Copies iRODS server files to the local resource

Note:

Copies server files to the local vault and registers them into iCAT. Object (.o) files and binaries are not included.

Example Usage:

```
myTestRule {
# Input parameter is:
#  Options - currently none are specified for controlling server backup
# Output parameter is:
#  Result - a keyvalpair structure holding number of files and size
#
#  This will take a while to run.
#  Backup files are stored in a directory as hostname_timestamp:
#
#  $ ils system_backups
#  /$rodsZoneClient/home/$userNameClient/system_backups:
#    C- /$rodsZoneClient/home/$userNameClient/system_backups/localhost_2011-08-19.16:00:29
#
#
  msiServerBackup(*Opt,*Result);
  writeKeyValPairs("stdout", *Result, " : ");
}
INPUT *Opt=""
OUTPUT ruleExecOut
```

4.174   Core :: iCAT System Services :: msiSetACL

---

msiSetACL	(	msParam_t *	recursiveFlag,	
		msParam_t *	accessLevel,	
		msParam_t *	userName,	
		msParam_t *	pathname	)

Parameters:

[in]	recursiveFlag	- a STR_MS_T, either "default" or "recursive". "recursive" is only relevant if set with accessLevel set to "inherit".
[in]	accessLevel	- a STR_MS_T containing one of the following permissions: null read write own inherit

| [in] | userName | - a STR_MS_T, the user name or group name who will have ACL changed. For user names in a federated data grid, use user_name#zone_name |
| [in] | pathName | - a STR_MS_T, the collection or data object that will have its ACL changed. |

Description:
This microservice changes the ACL for a given pathname, either a collection or a data object.

Note:
For collections, the modification can be recursive and the inheritance bit can be changed as well. The list of access controls is arranged from lowest level to highest level. When an access control is set, all lower level access controls are also enabled. Only a single access control is saved per person. The new access permissions are only those set by the application of the microservice.

Example Usage:

```
myTestRule {
# Input parameters are:
# Recursion flag
#   default
#   recursive - valid if access level is set to inherit
# Access Level
#   null
#   read
#   write
#   own
#   inherit
# User name or group name who will have ACL changed
# Path or file that will have ACL changed
  msiSetACL("default", *Acl,*User,*Path);
  writeLine("stdout","Set owner access for *User on file *Path");
}
INPUT *User="testuser", *Path="/$rodsZoneClient/home/$userNameClient/sub1/foo3", *Acl = "write"
OUTPUT ruleExecOut
```

4.175   Core :: iCAT System Services :: msiVacuum

msiVacuum   (   )

Parameters:
None

Description:
Postgres vacuum, done periodically to optimize indices and performance.

Note:
The effect of this is that the iCAT database gets optimized. This microservice works with PostgreSQL only. The rule example is in iRODS/clients/icommands/test/rules4.0/acmsiVacuum.r.

Example Usage:

```
acVacuum(*Delay) {
  delay(*Delay) {msiVacuum;}
```

}

4.176   Core :: Email Microservices :: msiSendMail

Example rule: iRODS/clients/icommands/test/rules4.0/rulemsiSendMail.r

msiSendMail   (msParam_t *   xtoAddr,
                               msParam_t *   xsubjectLine,
                               msParam_t *   xbody   )

Parameters:
[in]   xtoAddr   - a msParam of type STR_MS_T which is an address of the receiver.
[in]   xsubjectLine   - a msParam of type STR_MS_T which is a subject of the message.
[in]   xbody   - a msParam of type STR_MS_T which is a body of the message.

Description:
Sends email.

Note:
This microservice sends e-mail using the mail command in the unix system. The first argument is the e-mail address of the receiver. The second argument is the subject string and the third argument is the body of the e-mail. No attachments are supported. The sender of the e-mail is the unix userid running the irodsServer.

Example Usage:

myTestRule {
# Input parameters are:
# Address
# Subject of e-mail
# Message body
  msiSendMail(*Address,*Subject,*Body);
  writeLine("stdout","Sent e-mail to *Address about *Subject");
}
INPUT *Address="irod-chat@googlegroups.com", *Subject="Test message", *Body="Testing the msiSendMail microservice"
OUTPUT ruleExecOut

4.177   Core :: Email Microservices :: msiSendStdoutAsEmail

Example rule: iRODS/clients/icommands/test/rules4.0/rulemsiSendStdoutAsEmail.r

msiSendStdoutAsEmail (msParam_t *   xtoAddr,
                                    msParam_t *   xsubjectLine   )

Parameters:
[in]   xtoAddr   - a msParam of type STR_MS_T which is the address of the receiver.
[in]   xsubjectLine   - a msParam of type STR_MS_T which is the subject of the message.

Description:
Sends the current buffer content in rei->ruleExecOut->stdoutBuf.buf as email.

Note:
This microservice, given a xtoAddr parameter (an e-mail address) and a xsubjectLine parameter, sends out the stdout buffer as the body of the e-mail.

Example Usage:

myTestRule {
# Input parameters are:
# Address
# Subject
  writeLine("stdout","Message from stdout buffer");
  msiSendStdoutAsEmail(*Address,*Subject);
  writeLine("stdout","Sent e-mail to *Address about *Subject");
}
INPUT *Address="irod-chat@googlegroups.com", *Subject="Test message"
OUTPUT ruleExecOut

4.178   Core :: Key-Value (Attr-Value) :: msiAddKeyVal

Example rule: iRODS/clients/icommands/test/rules4.0/rulemsiAddKeyValToMspStr.r

msiAddKeyVal (msParam_t *   inKeyValPair,
                         msParam_t *   key,
                         msParam_t *   value   )

Parameters:
[in,out] inKeyValPair   - Optional - a KeyValPair_MS_T
[in]   key   - Required - A STR_MS_T containing the key
[in]   value   - Optional - A STR_MS_T containing the value

Description:
Adds a new key and value to a keyValPair_t structure.

Note:
A new keyValPair_t structure is created if inKeyValPair is NULL.

Example Usage:

myTestRule {
# Input parameters are:
# Key-value buffer (may be empty)
# Key

```
# Value
 msiGetSystemTime(*Time, "human");
 msiAddKeyVal(*Keyval,*Key,*Time);
 msiAssociateKeyValuePairsToObj(*Keyval,*Coll,"-C");
 msiGetCollectionPSmeta(*Coll,*Buf);
 writeBytesBuf("stdout", *Buf);
}
INPUT *Coll="/$rodsZoneClient/home/$userNameClient/sub1", *Key="TimeStamp"
OUTPUT ruleExecOut
```

4.179   Core :: Key-Value (Attr-Value) :: msiAssociateKeyValuePairsToObj

---

Example rule: iRODS/clients/icommands/test/rules4.0/rulemsiAssociateKeyValuePairsToObj.r

msiAssociateKeyValuePairsToObj	(	msParam_t *	metadataParam,	
		msParam_t *	objParam,	
		msParam_t *	typeParam	)

Parameters:
[in]   metadataParam   - a msParam of type KeyValPair_MS_T holding the key-value structure.
[in]   objParam   - a msParam of type STR_MS_T that specifies the object to which the metadata will be added.
[in]   typeParam   - a msParam of type STR_MS_T that defines the type of object.

Description:
This microservice associates <key, value> pairs from a given keyValPair_t structure with an object.

Note:
The object type is also needed:
        -d for data object
        -R for resource
        -G for resource group
        -C for collection
        -u for user

The check for success uses the microservice msiGetCollectionPSmeta to retrieve the attribute values that were loaded..

Example Usage:

```
myTestRule {
# Input parameters are:
# Key-value buffer (may be empty)
# Key
# Value
 msiGetSystemTime(*Time, "human");
 msiAddKeyVal(*Keyval, "TimeStamp", *Time);
 msiAssociateKeyValuePairsToObj(*Keyval,*Coll,"-C");
 msiGetCollectionPSmeta(*Coll,*Buf);
```

```
    writeBytesBuf("stdout", *Buf);
}
INPUT *Coll="/$rodsZoneClient/home/$userNameClient/sub1"
OUTPUT ruleExecOut
```

4.180   Core :: Key-Value (Attr-Value) :: msiGetValByKey

Example rule: iRODS/clients/icommands/test/rules4.0/rulemsiGetValByKey.r

msiGetValByKey	(	msParam_t *	inKVPair,
		msParam_t *	inKey,
		msParam_t *	outVal)

Parameters:

[in]	inKVPair	- This msParam is of type KeyValPair_PI which is a KeyValPair List.
[in]	inKey	- This msParam is of type STR_MS_T which is a key.
[out]	outVal	- This msParam is of type STR_MS_T which is a value corresponding to key.

Description:
Given a list of KVPairs and a Key, this microservice gets the corresponding value.

Note:
This is used to extract metadata from a query into a variable for use by subsequent microservices. The dot operator may also be used within a foreach(*Row in *Query) loop to extract values from KVPairs.

Example Usage:

```
myTestRule {
# Input parameters are:
#  Key-value pair list
#  Key
# Output parameter is:
#  Value
# Output from running the example is:
#  List of file in the collection
  writeLine("stdout","List files in collection *Coll");
  msiExecStrCondQuery("SELECT DATA_NAME where COLL_NAME = '*Coll'", *QOut);
  foreach (*QOut) {
    msiGetValByKey(*QOut, "DATA_NAME", *File);
    writeLine("stdout","*File");
  }
}
INPUT *Coll="/$rodsZoneClient/home/$userNameClient/sub1"
OUTPUT ruleExecOut
```

4.181   Core :: Key-Value (Attr-Value) :: msiPrintKeyValPair

Example rule: iRODS/clients/icommands/test/rules4.0/printKeyValPair.r

msiPrintKeyValPair (msParam_t * where,
                         msParam_t * inkvpair)

Parameters:
[in]   where   - a msParam of type STR_MS_T which is either stderr or stdout.
[in]   inkvpair   - a msParam of type KeyValPair_PI which is a KeyValPair list (structure).

Description:
Prints out a row of the key-value structure to the stdout buffer.

Note:
It takes a row-structure from GenQueryOut_MS_T and prints it as a ColumnName=Value pair. The rule uses the result (tabular structure) from execution of an iCAT query. In the example, the microservice msiExecStrCondQuery is used to run the query: SELECT DATA_TYPE_NAME WHERE COLL_NAME = "/$rodsZoneClient/home/$userNameClient/sub1". The result is printed using the msiPrintKeyValPair microservice, which prints each row as an attribute-value pair. A separator line is printed after each row.

Example Usage:

myTestRule {
#Input parameters are:
Location where data are written
stdout
stderr
Structure holding key-value pairs
#Example lists metadata for an input file path
  msiSplitPath(*Path,*Coll,*File);
  *Q1 = select DATA_TYPE_NAME where COLL_NAME = '*Coll' and DATA_NAME = '*File';
  foreach(*R1 in *Q1) {
    msiPrintKeyValPair("stdout",*R1);
  }
}
INPUT *Path="/$rodsZoneClient/home/$userNameClient/sub1/foo1"
OUTPUT ruleExecOut

4.182   Core :: Key-Value (Attr-Value) :: msiRemoveKeyValuePairsFromObj

Example rule: iRODS/clients/icommands/test/rules4.0/rulemsiRemoveKeyValuePairsFromObj.r

msiRemoveKeyValuePairsFromObj (msParam_t * metadataParam,
                                    msParam_t * objParam,
                                    msParam_t * typeParam)

Parameters:
[in]   metadataParam   - a msParam of type KeyValPair_MS_T with the attributes to be removed

| [in] | objParam | - a msParam of type STR_MS_T defining the object from which the attributes will be removed |
| [in] | typeParam | - a msParam of type STR_MS_T defining the type of object |

Description:
This microservice removes <key, value> pairs from an iRODS object.

Note:
The object type is also needed:
> -d for data object
> -R for resource
> -G for resource group
> -C for collection
> -u for user

Example Usage:

```
myTestRule {
# Input parameters are:
#  Key-value pair list
#  Path to object
#  Type of object (-d, -C)
# Output from running the example is:
#  Add metadata

  msiString2KeyValPair(*Str,*Keyval);
  msiAssociateKeyValuePairsToObj(*Keyval,*Path,"-d");

  #  List metadata
  writeLine("stdout","List metadata on file");
  msiGetDataObjPSmeta(*Path,*Buf);
  writeBytesBuf("stdout", *Buf);

  #  Remove metadata
  msiRemoveKeyValuePairsFromObj(*Keyval,*Path,"-d");

  #  List metadata remaining on file
  writeLine("stdout","list metadata after removing *Str");
  msiGetDataObjPSmeta(*Path,*Buf);
  writeBytesBuf("stdout", *Buf);
}
INPUT *Path="/$rodsZoneClient/home/$userNameClient/sub1/foo3", *Str="Testmeta=deletetest"
OUTPUT ruleExecOut
```

4.183   Core :: Key-Value (Attr-Value) :: msiStrArray2String

Example rule: iRODS/clients/icommands/test/rules4.0/rulemsiString2StrArray.r

| **msiStrArray2String** | (| msParam_t * | inSAParam, | |
| | | msParam_t * | outStr |) |

Parameters:
[in]   inSAParam   - a msParam of type strArr_MS_T which is an array of strings.
[out]   outStr   - a msParam of type STR_MS_T which a string with %-separators.

Description:
An array of strings is converted to a string separated by %-signs.

Note:
In the example, a string of %-separated key-value strings is converted to key-value pairs. The string is also converted to a string array, which is then converted back to a string and printed.

Example Usage:

```
myTestRule {
# Input parameter is:
#  Input string - %-separated key=value strings
# Output parameter is:
#  String array buffer
  writeLine("stdout","Input string is *Str");
  msiString2KeyValPair(*Str,*Keyval);
  writeKeyValPairs("stdout", *Keyval," : ");
  msiString2StrArray(*Str,*Stray);
  msiStrArray2String(*Stray, *Str2);
  writeLine("stdout","After conversion to array and back, string is");
  writeLine("stdout", *Str2);
}
INPUT *Str="key1=value1%key2=value2%key3=value3"
OUTPUT ruleExecOut
```

4.184   Core :: Key-Value (Attr-Value) :: msiString2KeyValPair

Example rule: iRODS/clients/icommands/test/rules4.0/rulemsiString2KeyValPair.r

msiString2KeyValPair   (msParam_t *   inBufferP,
                                        msParam_t *   outKeyValPairP)

Parameters:
[in]   inBufferP   - a msParam of type STR_MS_T which is key=value pairs separated by %-sign.
[out]   outKeyValPairP   - a msParam of type KeyValPair_MS_T which is a keyValuePair structure.

Description:
This microservice converts a %-separated key=value pair of strings into a keyValPair structure.

Example Usage:

```
string2KeyValRule {
#
#  Convert a %-separated key=value string of pairs to a keyValPair structure
#
# Input parameter:
```

String with %-separated key=value strings
#
Output parameter:
Key-value structure
#
  writeLine("stdout","See metadata as a Key-Value structure");
  msiString2KeyValPair(*Str,*Keyval);
  writeKeyValPairs("stdout",*Keyval,*Status);
}
INPUT *Str="Tester=rods%Event=document%Home=/$rodsZoneClient/home/$userNameClient"
OUTPUT ruleExecOut

4.185   Core :: Key-Value (Attr-Value) :: msiString2StrArray

Example rule: iRODS/clients/icommands/test/rules4.0/rulemsiString2StrArray.r

| **msiString2StrArray** | (| msParam_t * | inStr , | |
| | | msParam_t * | outSAParam |) |

Parameters:
[in]   inStr   - a msParam of type STR_MS_T which a string with %-separators.
[out]   outSAParam   - a msParam of type strArr_MS_T which is an array of strings.

Description:
A string separated by %-signs is converted to a string array.

Note:
In the example, a string is converted to a string array, and then converted back to a %-separated string and printed.

Example Usage:

myTestRule {
# Input parameter is:
# Input string - %-separated key=value strings
# Output parameter is:
# String array buffer
  writeLine("stdout","Input string is *Str");
  msiString2KeyValPair(*Str,*Keyval);
  writeKeyValPairs("stdout", *Keyval," : ");
  msiString2StrArray(*Str,*Stray);
  msiStrArray2String(*Stray, *Str2);
  writeLine("stdout","After conversion to array and back, string is");
  writeLine("stdout", *Str2);
}
INPUT *Str="key1=value1%key2=value2%key3=value3"
OUTPUT ruleExecOut

4.186   Core :: Key-Value (Attr-Value) :: writeKeyValPairs

Example rule: iRODS/clients/icommands/test/rules4.0/writeKeyValPairs.r

writeKeyValPairs	(	msParam_t *	where,	
		msParam_t *	inKVPair,	
		msParam_t *	separator	)

Parameters:

[in]	where	- a msParam of type STR_MS_T which is the buffer name in ruleExecOut. It can be stdout or stderr.
[in]	inKVPair	- a msParam of type KeyValPair_MS_T
[in]	separator	- Optional - a msParam of type STR_MS_T, the desired parameter

Description:
This microservice writes keyword value pairs to stdout or stderr, using the given separator.

Note:
The writeLine microservice treats the "%" sign as a comment, and does not print the end of the input string after the "%" sign. The rest of the rule works correctly.

Example Usage:

```
myTestRule {
# Input parameters are:
#  String with %-separated key=value pair strings
# Output parameter is:
#  Key-value structure
  writeLine("stdout","Add metadata string *Str to *Path");
  msiString2KeyValPair(*Str,*Keyval);
  writeKeyValPairs("stdout", *Keyval,*Status);
  msiAssociateKeyValuePairsToObj(*Keyval,*Path,"-d");
  msiGetDataObjPSmeta(*Path,*Buf);
  writeBytesBuf("stdout", *Buf);
}
INPUT *Str="Tester=rods%Event=document",
*Path="/$rodsZoneClient/home/$userNameClient/sub1/foo1"
OUTPUT ruleExecOut
```

4.187   Core :: Other User :: msiExtractTemplateMDFromBuf

Example rule: iRODS/clients/icommands/test/rules4.0/rulemsiExtractTemplateMDFromBuf.r

msiExtractTemplateMDFromBuf(	msParam_t *	bufParam,
	msParam_t *	tagParam,
	msParam_t *	metadataParam)

Parameters:

[in]   bufParam   - a msParam of type BUF_MS_T
[in]   tagParam   - a msParam of type TagStruct_MS_T
[out] metadataParam - a msParam of type KeyValPair_MS_T

Description:
This microservice uses a template to parse a buffer containing metadata and create a Key-Value Pairs structure.

Note:
The template defines triplets <pre-string-regexp, keyword, post-string-regexp>. The triplets are read into memory, and used to search a metadata buffer. For each set of pre and post regular expressions, the string between them is associated with the specified keyword. All<key, value> pairs found are stored in a keyValPair_t structure.

In the example, the tag file has the format:
          <PRETAG>X-Mailer: </PRETAG>Mailer User<POSTTAG>
          </POSTTAG>
          <PRETAG>Date: </PRETAG>Sent Date<POSTTAG>
          </POSTTAG>
          <PRETAG>From: </PRETAG>Sender<POSTTAG>
          </POSTTAG>
          <PRETAG>To: </PRETAG>Primary Recipient<POSTTAG>
          </POSTTAG>
          <PRETAG>Cc: </PRETAG>Other Recipient<POSTTAG>
          </POSTTAG>
          <PRETAG>Subject: </PRETAG>Subject<POSTTAG>
          </POSTTAG>
          <PRETAG>Content-Type: </PRETAG>Content Type<POSTTAG>
          </POSTTAG>
The end tag is actually a "return" for unix systems, or a "carriage-return/line-feed" for Windows systems.

Example Usage:

```
myTestRule {
# Input parameters are:
#  Buffer
#  Tag structure
# Output parameter is:
#  Keyval pair buffer

 #Read in 10,000 bytes of the file
 msiDataObjOpen(*Pathfile,*F_desc);
 msiDataObjRead(*F_desc,*Len,*File_buf);
 msiDataObjClose(*F_desc,*Status);

 #Read in the tag template file
 msiDataObjOpen(*Tag,*T_desc);
 msiDataObjRead(*T_desc, 10000, *Tag_buf);
      TemplateIntoTagStruct(*Tag_buf,*Tags);
 msiDataObjClose(*T_desc,*Status);

 #Extract metadata from file using the tag template file
 msiExtractTemplateMDFromBuf(*File_buf,*Tags,*Keyval);
```

```
#Write out extracted metadata
writeKeyValPairs("stdout", *Keyval," : ");
msiGetObjType(*Outfile,*Otype);

#Add metadata to the object
msiAssociateKeyValuePairsToObj(*Keyval,*Outfile,*Otype);
}
INPUT *Tag="/$rodsZoneClient/home/$userNameClient/test/email.tag",
*Pathfile="/$rodsZoneClient/home/$userNameClient/test/sample.email",
*Outfile="/$rodsZoneClient/home/$userNameClient/test/sample.email", *Len=10000
OUTPUT ruleExecOut
```

4.188   Core :: Other User :: msiFreeBuffer

Example rule: iRODS/clients/icommands/test/rules4.0/rulemsiFreeBuffer.r

msiFreeBuffer   (msParam_t *   memoryParam   )

Parameters:
[in]   memoryParam   - the buffer to free

Description:
This microservice frees a named buffer, including stdout and stderr

Note:
Can be used to free a buffer that was previously allocated.

Example Usage:

```
myTestRule {
# Input parameter is:
#  Buffer to free (can be variable buffer or stdout or stderr)
 msiDataObjOpen(*Flags,*F_desc);
 msiDataObjRead(*F_desc,*Len,*Buf);
 msiDataObjClose(*F_desc,*Status);
 msiFreeBuffer(*Buf);
 writeLine("stdout","Freed buffer");
}
INPUT *Flags="objPath=/$rodsZoneClient/home/$userNameClient/sub1/foo1", *Len="100"
OUTPUT ruleExecOut
```

4.189   Core :: Other User :: msiGetDiffTime

Example rule: iRODS/clients/icommands/test/rules4.0/rulemsiGetDiffTime.r

msiGetDiffTime (msParam_t *   inpParam1,

```
                              msParam_t *      inpParam2,
                              msParam_t *      inpParam3,
                              msParam_t *      outParam              )
```

Parameters:
[in]   inpParam1   - a STR_MS_T containing the start date (system time in seconds)
[in]   inpParam2   - a STR_MS_T containing the end date (system time in seconds)
[in]   inpParam3   - Optional - a STR_MS_T containing the desired output format (human)
[out]   outParam   - a STR_MS_T containing the time elapsed between the two dates

Description:
This microservice returns the difference between two system times

Note:
The default output format is in seconds. Use "human" as the third input parameter for human readable
format that converts to days, hours, minutes, and seconds.

Example Usage:

```
myTestRule {
# Input parameters are:
#  Start date in system time in seconds
#  End date in system time in seconds
#  Optional format (human)
# Output parameter is:
#  Duration
  msiGetIcatTime(*Start, "unix");
  msiSleep("10", "");
  msiGetIcatTime(*End, "unix");
  writeLine("stdout","Start time is *Start");
  msiGetDiffTime(*Start,*End,"", *Dur);
  writeLine("stdout","End time is *End");
  writeLine("stdout","Duration is *Dur");
}
INPUT null
OUTPUT ruleExecOut
```

4.190   Core :: Other User :: msiGetIcatTime

Example rule: iRODS/clients/icommands/test/rules4.0/rulemsiGetIcatTime.r

```
msiGetIcatTime (          msParam_t *      timeOutParam,
                          msParam_t *      typeInParam                )
```

Parameters:
[out]   timeOutParam   - a msParam of type STR_MS_T with the system time
[in]   typeInParam   - a msParam of type STR_MS_T for type of output
                                  "icat" or "unix" will return seconds since epoch
                                  otherwise, human friendly

Description:

This function returns the system time for the iCAT server

Note:
This function returns the system time for the iCAT server in either seconds since the epoch, or in a format that specifies year-month-day.hour:minute:second.

Example Usage:

```
myTestRule {
# Input parameters are:
#  Time type (icat/unix or human) in seconds
# Output parameter is:
#  Time value
  msiGetIcatTime(*Start, "unix");
  msiGetIcatTime(*End, "human");
  writeLine("stdout","Time in seconds is *Start");
  writeLine("stdout","Time human readable is *End");
}
INPUT null
OUTPUT ruleExecOut
```

4.191   Core :: Other User :: msiGetSystemTime

Example rule: iRODS/clients/icommands/test/rules4.0/rulemsiGetSystemTime.r

msiGetSystemTime	(	msParam_t *	outParam,	
		msParam_t *	inpParam	)

Parameters:
[out]	outParam	- a STR_MS_T containing the time
[in]	inpParam	- Optional - a STR_MS_T containing the desired output format (human)

Description:
This microservice returns the local system time of the iRODS server.

Note:
Default output format is system time in seconds, use "human" as input parameter for human readable format in year-month-day.hour:minute:second.

Example Usage:

```
myTestRule {
# Input parameters are:
#  Time type "icat" or "unix" returns time in seconds
#       "human" returns date in Year-Month-Day.Hour:Minute:Second
# Output parameter is:
#  Time value for local system
  msiGetSystemTime(*Start, "unix");
  msiGetSystemTime(*End, "human");
  writeLine("stdout","Time in seconds is *Start");
  writeLine("stdout","Time human readable is *End");
```

}
INPUT null
OUTPUT ruleExecOut

4.192   Core :: Other User :: msiGetTaggedValueFromString

Example rule: iRODS/clients/icommands/test/rules4.0/rulemsiGetTaggedValueFromString.r

msiGetTaggedValueFromString (msParam_t *   inTagParam,
                                                                      msParam_t *   inStrParam,
                                                                      msParam_t *   outValueParam   )

Parameters:
[in]   inTagParam   - a msParam of type STR_MS_T
[in]   inStrParam   - a msParam of type STR_MS_T
[out]   outValueParam   - a msParam of type INT_MS_T

Description:
This microservice gets a tagged value from a string. When given a tag-name, this microservice gets the value from a file in tagged-format (pseudo-XML).

Note:
This performs some regular expression matching. Given a regular expression as a tag-value "t", it identifies the corresponding string in the match string with a string that matches a sub-string value: "<t>.*</t>". The service is used for processing a tagged structure. In this example, "IP-address" is successfully parsed from the tagged string:

        [in]   Tag   Mail
        [in]   String   <Mail>IP-address</Mail>
        [out]   Value   IP-address

Example Usage:

myTestRule {
# Input parameters are:
# Tag string
# Input string
# Output parameter is:
# Value associated with tag
  writeLine("stdout","String that is tested is");
  writeLine("stdout","*Str");
  msiGetTaggedValueFromString(*Tag,*Str,*Val);
  writeLine("stdout","Found value is *Val");
}
INPUT *Tag="Mail", *Str="<Mail>IP-address</Mail>"
OUTPUT ruleExecOut

4.193   Core :: Other User :: msiHumanToSystemTime

Example rule: iRODS/clients/icommands/test/rules4.0/rulemsiHumanToSystemTime.r

msiHumanToSystemTime   (msParam_t *   inpParam,

                                         msParam_t *   outParam   )

Parameters:
[in]   inpParam   - a STR_MS_T containing the input date
[out]   outParam   - a STR_MS_T containing the timestamp

Description:
Converts a human readable date to a system timestamp.

Note:
Expects an input date in the form: YYYY-MM-DD.hh:mm:ss

Example Usage:

myTestRule {
# Input parameter is:
# Date in human readable form
# Output parameter is:
# Time stamp in seconds since epoch
  msiGetSystemTime(*Date, "human");
  msiHumanToSystemTime(*Date,*Time);
  writeLine("stdout","Input date is *Date");
  writeLine("stdout","Time in unix seconds is *Time");
}
INPUT null
OUTPUT ruleExecOut

4.194   Core :: Other User :: msiReadMDTemplateIntoTagStruct

Example rule: iRODS/clients/icommands/test/rules4.0/rulemsiReadMDTemplateIntoTagStruct.r

msiReadMDTemplateIntoTagStruct   (msParam_t *   bufParam,

                                                   msParam_t *   tagParam   )

Parameters:
[in]   bufParam   - a msParam of type BUF_LEN_MS_T
[out]   tagParam   - a return msParam of type TagStruct_MS_T

Description:
This microservice parses a buffer containing a template-style file and stores the tags in a tag structure.

Note:
The template buffer should contain triplets of the form:

            <PRETAG>re1</PRETAG>kw<POSTTAG>re2</POSTTAG>

"re1" identifies the pre-string. "re2" identifies the post-string and any value between re1 and re2 in a metadata buffer will be associated with the keyword "kw".

Example Usage:

myTestRule {
# Input parameter is:
# Tag buffer
# Output parameter is:
# Tag structure

  # Read in first 10,000 bytes of file
  msiDataObjOpen(*Pathfile,*F_desc);
  msiDataObjRead(*F_desc,*Len,*File_buf);
  msiDataObjClose(*F_desc,*Status);

  # Read in tag template
  msiDataObjOpen(*Tag,*T_desc);
  msiDataObjRead(*T_desc, 10000, *Tag_buf);
  msiReadMDTemplateIntoTagStruct(*Tag_buf,*Tags);
  msiDataObjClose(*T_desc,*Status);

  # Extract metadata from file using tag template
  msiExtractTemplateMDFromBuf(*File_buf,*Tags,*Keyval);

  # Write result to stdout
  writeKeyValPairs("stdout", *Keyval," : ");

  # Add metadata to the file
  msiGetObjType(*Outfile,*Otype);
  msiAssociateKeyValuePairsToObj(*Keyval,*Outfile,*Otype);
}
INPUT *Tag="/$rodsZoneClient/home/$userNameClient/test/email.tag",
*Pathfile="/$rodsZoneClient/home/$userNameClient/test/sample.email",
*Outfile="/$rodsZoneClient/home/$userNameClient/test/sample.email", *Len=10000
OUTPUT ruleExecOut

4.195   Core :: Other User :: msiRegisterData

Example rule: iRODS/clients/icommands/test/rules4.0/acmsiRegisterData.r

msiRegisterData (   )

Parameters:
None

Description:
Register a new data object into the iRODS data grid.

Note:
Use this only within a core.re file as data object information has to be set in the rei structure. The rule example is in iRODS/clients/icommands/test/rules4.0/acmsiRegisterData.r.

Example Usage:

acRegisterData { msiRegisterData ::: misRollback; }

4.196   Core :: Other User :: msiStrToBytesBuf

Example rule: iRODS/clients/icommands/test/rules4.0/rulemsiStrToBytesBuf.r

msiStrToBytesBuf   (msParam_t *   str_msp,
                                         msParam_t *   buf_msp)

Parameters:
[in]   str_msp   - a STR_MS_T with the input string
[out]   buf_msp   - a BUF_LEN_MS_T with the string converted to binary.

Description:
Converts a string to a bytesBuf_t structure for use within microservices.

Note:
The example converts a string to a bytes-buffer, then writes the buffer into a file stored within iRODS.

Example Usage:

```
myTestRule {
# Input parameters are:
#  String
# Output parameter is:
#  Buffer

  # Convert string to bytes buffer
  msiStrToBytesBuf(*Str,*Buf);

  # Create a file and write buffer into the file
  msiDataObjCreate(*Path,*Flags,*F_desc);
  msiDataObjWrite(*F_desc,*Buf,*Len);
  msiDataObjClose(*F_desc,*Status);

  # Write the string to stdout
  writeLine("stdout","Wrote *Str into file *Path");
}
INPUT *Str="Test string for writing into a file",
*Path="/$rodsZoneClient/home/$userNameClient/sub1/foo2", *Flags="forceFlag="
OUTPUT ruleExecOut
```

4.197   Core :: Other User :: writeBytesBuf

Example rule: iRODS/clients/icommands/test/rules4.0/rulewriteBytesBuf.r

writeBytesBuf   (msParam_t *   where,
                               msParam_t *   inBuf   )

Parameters:
[in]   where   - a msParam of type STR_MS_T which is the buffer name in
                                    ruleExecOut. It can be "stdout" or "stderr".
[in]   inBuf   - a msParam of type STR_MS_T - related to the status output

Description:
This microservice writes the buffer in an inOutStruct to stdout or stderr.

Note:
none

Example Usage:

```
myTestRule {
# Input Parameters are:
#  Location for write (stdout, stderr)
#  String buffer

 # Make a query
 msiMakeGenQuery("DATA_ID, DATA_SIZE", *Condition,*GenQInp);

 # Issue the query and retrieve query result
 msiExecGenQuery(*GenQInp, *GenQOut);

 # Convert result to a buffer
 msiPrintGenQueryOutToBuffer(*GenQOut,*Form,*Buf);

 # write the result buffer
 writeBytesBuf("stdout", *Buf);
}
INPUT *Coll="/$rodsZoneClient/home/$userNameClient/sub1", *Condition="COLL_NAME like '*Coll'",
*Form="For data-ID %-6.6s the data size is %-8.8s"
OUTPUT ruleExecOut
```

4.198   Core :: Other User :: writePosInt

Example rule: iRODS/clients/icommands/test/rules4.0/writePosInt.r

writePosInt   (msParam_t *   where,
                          msParam_t *   inInt   )

Parameters:
[in]   where   - a msParam of type STR_MS_T which is the buffer name in ruleExecOut.
[in]   inInt   - the integer to write

Description:

This microservice writes a positive integer into a buffer.

Note:
To add an end of line, write a null after the positive integer using writeLine.

Example Usage:

```
myTestRule {
# Input parameters are:
#  Location (stdout, stderr)
#  Integer
 *A = 1;
 writeLine("stdout","Wrote an integer");
 writePosInt("stdout", *A);
 writeLine("stdout","");
}
INPUT null
OUTPUT ruleExecOut
```

4.199   Plugins :: msiobjget_http

msiobjget_http (msParam_t *   inRequestPath,
                             msParam_t *   inFileMode,
                             msParam_t *   inFileFlags,
                             msParam_t *   inCacheFilename **)**

Parameters:
[in]   inRequestPath   - a STR_MS_T containing the request sent to the external resource.
[in]   inFileMode   - a STR_MS_T containing the mode for the cache file creation.
[in]   inFileFlags   - a STR_MS_T containing access flags for cache file creation.
[in]   inCacheFilename   - a STR_MS_T containing the full path for the local cache filename.

Description:

This microservice gets a web object from a URL using microservice drivers. The object is stored in the cache file name on the local resource. The web object can be an http, https or ftp object.

Note:

The inFileMode argument specifies the permissions to use when creating the cache file:
      r or rb   Open file for reading.
      w or wb   Truncate to zero length or create file for writing.
      a or ab   Append; open or create file for writing at end-of-file.
      r+ or rb+ or r+b   Open file for update (reading and writing).
      w+ or wb+ or w+b   Truncate to zero length or create file for update.
      a+ or ab+ or a+b   Append; open or create file for update, writing at end-of-file.

The inFileFlags argument specifies the access mode for the cache file:
      O_RDONLY,

```
        O_WRONLY,
        O_RDWR
        O_TRUNC.
```

These can be combined by concatenation, e.g. O_WRONLYO_TRUNC

The inRequestPath starts with "http:", "https:", or "ftp:". The string after that is the iRODS logical path name. Examples are:
>   http://farm3.static.flickr.com/2254/5827459234_2fd1c55364_z.jpg
>   ftp://ftp.sdsc.edu/pub/outgoing/sekar/PPP.txt
>   https://wiki.irods.org/index.php

Example Usage:

```
myTestRule {
# Input parameters are:
#  inRequestPath - the string sent to the remote URL
#  inFileMode - the cache file creation mode
#  inFileFlags - the access modes for the cache file
#  inCacheFilename - the full path of the cache file on the local system
# No output parameters
# Output is the creation of a file in the vault
#  Wrote local file /home/reagan/Vaulttest/webfile from request
http://wiki.irods.org.pubs/iRODS_FACT_Sheet-0907c.pdf
  msiobjget_http(*Request, *Mode, *Flags, *Path);
  writeLine("stdout","Wrote local file *Path from request *Request");
}
INPUT *Request ="http://wiki.irods.org/pubs/iRODS_FACT_Sheet-0907c.pdf", *Mode = "w", *Flags =
"O_RDWR", *Path = "/home/reagan/Vaulttest/webfile"
OUTPUT ruleExecOut
```

4.200   Plugins :: msiobjget_irods

---

msiobjget_irods (	msParam_t *	inRequestPath,	
	msParam_t *	inFileMode,	
	msParam_t *	inFileFlags,	
	msParam_t *	inCacheFilename	**)**

Parameters:

[in]	inRequestPath	- a STR_MS_T containing the request sent to the external resource.
[in]	inFileMode	- a STR_MS_T containing the mode for the cache file creation.
[in]	inFileFlags	- a STR_MS_T containing access flags for cache file creation.
[in]	inCacheFilename	- a STR_MS_T containing the full path for the local cache filename.

Description:
This microservice gets an iRODS object from a remote iRODS data grid using microservice drivers. The object is stored in the local cache filename.

Note:
The inFileMode argument specifies the permissions to use when creating the cache file:

r or rb	Open file for reading.
w or wb	Truncate to zero length or create file for writing.

a or ab	Append; open or create file for writing at end-of-file.
r+ or rb+ or r+b	Open file for update (reading and writing).
w+ or wb+ or w+b	Truncate to zero length or create file for update.
a+ or ab+ or a+b	Append; open or create file for update, writing at end-of-file.

The inFileFlags argument specifies the access mode for the cache file:

O_RDONLY,
O_WRONLY,
O_RDWR
O_TRUNC.

These can be combined by concatenation, e.g. O_WRONLYO_TRUNC
The inRequestPath starts with "irods:" The string after that has three parts separated by a colon ":".

The first part is the iRODS host name.
The second part is the iRODS port number.
The third part consists of two sections,
a user name,
an iRODS logical pathname.

The user name can have a zone name delineated by @.
For LOCALZONE anonymous access:
irods:srbbrick14.sdsc.edu:2247:anonymous:$rodsZoneClient/home/$userNameClient/mytest/irm.c
For NON-FEDERATED REMOTE ZONE access:
irods:iren.renci.org:1247:anonymous@renci/renci/home/$userNameClient/README.txt

Example Usage:

myTestRule {
# Input parameters are:
# inRequestPath - the string sent to the remote iRODS data grid
# inFileMode - the cache file creation mode
# inFileFlags - the access modes for the cache file
# inCacheFilename - the full path of the cache file
# No output parameters
# Output is the creation of a file on the local vault
  msiobjget_irods(*Request, *Mode, *Flags, *Path);
}
INPUT *Request
="irods:iren.renci.org:1247:anonymous@renci/renci/home/$userNameClient/README.txt", *Mode = "w",
*Flags = "O_RDWR", *Path = "/home/reagan/Vaulttest/home/$userNameClient/sub1/rodsfile"
OUTPUT ruleExecOut

4.201   Plugins :: msiobjget_slink

msiobjget_slink (msParam_t *   inRequestPath,
                            msParam_t *   inFileMode,
                            msParam_t *   inFileFlags,
                            msParam_t *   inCacheFilename   )

Parameters:
[in]	inRequestPath	- a STR_MS_T containing the request sent to the external resource.
[in]	inFileMode	- a STR_MS_T containing the mode for the cache file creation.
[in]	inFileFlags	- a STR_MS_T containing access flags for cache file creation.
[in]	inCacheFilename	- a STR_MS_T containing the full path for the local cache filename.

Description:

This microservice gets an iRODS object from a soft link to another iRODS data grid using microservice drivers. The object is stored in the cache filename.

Note:

The inFileMode argument specifies the permissions to use when creating the cache file:

r or rb	Open file for reading.
w or wb	Truncate to zero length or create file for writing.
a or ab	Append; open or create file for writing at end-of-file.
r+ or rb+ or r+b	Open file for update (reading and writing).
w+ or wb+ or w+b	Truncate to zero length or create file for update.
a+ or ab+ or a+b	Append; open or create file for update, writing at end-of-file.

The inFileFlags argument specifies the access mode for the cache file:

O_RDONLY,
O_WRONLY,
O_RDWR
O_TRUNC.

These can be combined by concatenation, e.g. O_WRONLYO_TRUNC

The inRequestPath starts with "slink:". The string after that is the iRODS logical path name. An example is:

slink:/$rodsZoneClient/home/$userNameClient/mytest/iinit.c

Example Usage:

```
myTestRule {
# Input parameters are:
# inRequestPath - the string sent to the remote iRODS data grid
# inFileMode - the cache file creation mode
# inFileFlags - the access modes for the cache file
# inCacheFilename - the full path of the cache file
# No output parameters
# Output is the creation of a file on the local cache
  msiobjget_slink(*Request, *Mode, *Flags, *Path);
}
INPUT *Request ="slink:/renci/home/$userNameClient/README.txt", *Mode = "w", *Flags =
"O_RDWR", *Path = "/home/reagan/Vaulttest/home/$userNameClient/sub1/rodsfile"
OUTPUT ruleExecOut
```

4.202   Plugins :: msiobjput_http

---

msiobjput_http (msParam_t *   inMSOPath,
                           msParam_t *   inCacheFilename,
                           msParam_t *   inFileSize   )

Parameters:

[in]	inMSOPath	- a STR_MS_T containing the request sent to the external resource.
[in]	inCacheFilename	- a STR_MS_T containing the full path for the local cache filename to be written out.

[in]   inFileSize   - a STR_MS_T containing the size of the cache file.

Description:
This microservice puts an http object file using microservice drivers.
The object is written to the remote URL.

Note:
The inMSOPath starts with "http:", "https:", or "ftp:". The string after that is the iRODS logical path name.
Examples are:
        http://farm3.static.flickr.com/2254/5827459234_2fd1c55364_z.jpg
        ftp://ftp.sdsc.edu/pub/outgoing/sekar/PPP.txt
        https://wiki.irods.org/index.php

Example Usage:

```
myTestRule {
# Input parameters are:
#  inMSOPath - the string sent to the remote URL
#  inCacheFilename - the full path of the cache file
#  inFileSize - the size of the cache file, found from ls on the vault
# No output parameters
  msiobjput_http(*Request, *Path, *Size);
}
INPUT *Request ="http://farm3.static.flickr.com/2254/5827459234_2fd1c55364_z.jpg", *Path =
"/$rodsZoneClient/home/$userNameClient/sub1/rodsfile", *Size = "15"
OUTPUT ruleExecOut
```

4.203   Plugins :: msiobjput_irods

---

msiobjput_irods (msParam_t *   inMSOPath,
                        msParam_t *   inCacheFilename,
                        msParam_t *   inFileSize   )

Parameters:
[in]   inMSOPath   - a STR_MS_T containing the request sent to the external resource.
[in]   inCacheFilename   - a STR_MS_T containing the full path for the local cache filename
                                to be written out.
[in]   inFileSize   - a STR_MS_T containing the size of the cache file.

Description:
This microservice puts an iRODS object into a remote iRODS data grid using microservice drivers.
The object is written to the remote resource.

Note:
The inMSOPath starts with "irods:" The string after that has three parts separated by a colon ":".
        The first part is the iRODS host name.
        The second part is the iRODS port number.
        The third part consists of two sections,
                a user name,
                an iRODS logical pathname.
The user name can have a zone name delineated by @.
For LOCALZONE anonymous access:

irods:srbbrick14.sdsc.edu:2247:anonymous/$rodsZoneClient/home/$userNameClient/mytest/irm.c
For NON-FEDERATED REMOTE ZONE access:
    irods:iren.renci.org:1247:anonymous@renci/renci/home/$userNameClient/README.txt

Example Usage:

myTestRule {
# Input parameters are:
# inMSOPath - the string sent to the remote iRODS data grid
# inCacheFilename - the full path of the cache file
# inFileSize - the size of the cache file
# No output parameters
    msiobjput_irods(*Request, *Path, *Size);
}
INPUT *Request
="irods:iren.renci.org:1247:anonymous@renci/renci/home/$userNameClient/README.txt", *Path =
"/home/reagan/Vaulttest/home/$userNameClient/sub1/rodsfile", *Size = "15"
OUTPUT ruleExecOut

4.204   Plugins :: msiobjput_slink

---

msiobjput_slink (msParam_t *   inMSOPath,
                               msParam_t *   inCacheFilename,
                               msParam_t *   inFileSize   )

Parameters:
[in]   inMSOPath   - a STR_MS_T containing the request sent to the external resource.
[in]   inCacheFilename   - a STR_MS_T containing the full path for the local cache filename
                                to be written out.
[in]   inFileSize   - a STR_MS_T containing the size of the cache file.

Description:
This microservice puts an iRODS object into a remote iRODS data grid through a soft link using
microservice drivers. The object is written to the remote resource.

Note:
The inMSOPath starts with "slink:" The string after that is an iRODS logical path name. An example is:
    slink:/$rodsZoneClient/home/$userNameClient/mytest/iinit.c

Example Usage:

myTestRule {
# Input parameters are:
# inMSOPath - the string sent to the remote iRODS data grid
# inCacheFilename - the full path of the cache file
# inFileSize - the size of the cache file
# No output parameters
    msiobjput_slink(*Request, *Path, *Size);
}
INPUT *Request ="slink:/renci/home/$userNameClient/README.txt", *Path =
"/home/reagan/Vaulttest/home/$userNameClient/sub1/rodsfile", *Size = "15"
OUTPUT ruleExecOut

4.205   Rules :: rulegenerateBagIt.r

Description:
This rule generates a bag (tar file) containing a manifest, a list of checksums, and the files contained within a specified collection.

Note:
The generateBagIt rule creates the equivalent of a Submission Information Package. Extensions would be the inclusion of descriptive metadata, provenance metadata, and structural metadata.

Example Usage:

```
generateBagIt {
# ------------------------------------------------------
# generateBagIt
# ------------------------------------------------------
#
#  Terrell Russell
#  University of North Carolina at Chapel Hill
#  - August 2010
#  - Requires iRODS 2.4.1
#  - Conforms to BagIt Spec v0.96
#
# ------------------------------------------------------
#
### - creates NEWBAGITROOT
### - writes bagit.txt to NEWBAGITROOT/bagit.txt
### - rsyncs existing BAGITDATA to NEWBAGITROOT/data
### - generates payload manifest file of NEWBAGITROOT/data
### - writes payload manifest to NEWBAGITROOT/manifest-md5.txt
### - writes tagmanifest file to NEWBAGITROOT/tagmanifest-md5.txt
### - creates tarfile of new bag for faster download
### - gets filesize of new tarfile
### - outputs report and suggested download procedures
### - writes to rodsLog
#
# ------------------------------------------------------

  ### - creates NEWBAGITROOT
  msiCollCreate(*NEWBAGITROOT,"1",*Status);
  msiStrlen(*NEWBAGITROOT,*ROOTLENGTH);
  *OFFSET = int(*ROOTLENGTH) + 1;

  ### - writes bagit.txt to NEWBAGITROOT/bagit.txt
  writeLine("stdout","BagIt-Version: 0.96");
  writeLine("stdout","Tag-File-Character-Encoding: UTF-8");
  msiDataObjCreate("*NEWBAGITROOT" ++ "/bagit.txt","null",*FD);
  msiDataObjWrite(*FD,"stdout",*WLEN);
  msiDataObjClose(*FD,*Status);
  msiFreeBuffer("stdout");
```

193

```
### - rsyncs existing BAGITDATA to NEWBAGITROOT/data
msiCollRsync(*BAGITDATA,"*NEWBAGITROOT" ++ "/data","null","IRODS_TO_IRODS",*Status);

### - generates payload manifest file of NEWBAGITROOT/data
*NEWBAGITDATA = "*NEWBAGITROOT" ++ "/data";
*Query = select DATA_ID, DATA_NAME, COLL_NAME where COLL_NAME like
'*NEWBAGITDATA%%';
foreach(*Row in *Query) {
  *Object = *Row.DATA_NAME;
  *Coll = *Row.COLL_NAME;`
  *FULLPATH = "*Coll" ++ "/" ++ "*Object";
  msiDataObjChksum(*FULLPATH, "forceChksum=", *CHKSUM);
  msiSubstr(*FULLPATH,str(*OFFSET),"null",*RELATIVEPATH);
  writeString("stdout", *RELATIVEPATH);
  writeLine("stdout","   *CHKSUM")
}

### - writes payload manifest to NEWBAGITROOT/manifest-md5.txt
msiDataObjCreate("*NEWBAGITROOT" ++ "/manifest-md5.txt","null",*FD);
msiDataObjWrite(*FD,"stdout",*WLEN);
msiDataObjClose(*FD,*Status);
msiFreeBuffer("stdout");

### - writes tagmanifest file to NEWBAGITROOT/tagmanifest-md5.txt
writeString("stdout","bagit.txt    ");
msiDataObjChksum("*NEWBAGITROOT" ++ "/bagit.txt","forceChksum",*CHKSUM);
writeLine("stdout",*CHKSUM);
writeString("stdout","manifest-md5.txt    ");
msiDataObjChksum("*NEWBAGITROOT" ++ "/manifest-md5.txt","forceChksum",*CHKSUM);
writeLine("stdout",*CHKSUM);
msiDataObjCreate("*NEWBAGITROOT" ++ "/tagmanifest-md5.txt","null",*FD);
msiDataObjWrite(*FD,"stdout",*WLEN);
msiDataObjClose(*FD,*Status);
msiFreeBuffer("stdout");

### - creates tarfile of new bag for faster download
msiTarFileCreate("*NEWBAGITROOT" ++ ".tar",*NEWBAGITROOT,"null",*Status);

### - gets filesize of new tarfile
msiSplitPath("*NEWBAGITROOT" ++ ".tar",*Coll,*TARFILENAME);
*Query2 = select DATA_SIZE where COLL_NAME like '*Coll%%' AND DATA_NAME =
'*TARFILENAME';
foreach(*E in *Query2) {
  *FILESIZE = *E.DATA_SIZE;
  *Isize = int(*FILESIZE);
  if(*Isize > 1048576) {
    *PRINTSIZE = *Isize / 1048576;
    *PRINTUNIT = "MB";
  }
  else {
    if(*Isize > 1024) {
      *PRINTSIZE = *Isize / 1024;
      *PRINTUNIT = "KB";
    }
    else {
```

```
      *PRINTSIZE = *Isize;
      *PRINTUNIT = "B";
    }
  }
}

### - outputs report and suggested download procedures
writeLine("stdout","");
writeLine("stdout","Your BagIt bag has been created and tarred on the iRODS server:")
writeLine("stdout","  *NEWBAGITROOT.tar - *PRINTSIZE *PRINTUNIT");
writeLine("stdout","");
msiSplitPath("*NEWBAGITROOT" ++ ".tar",*COLL,*TARFILE);
writeLine("stdout","To copy it to your local computer, use:");
writeLine("stdout","  iget -Pf *NEWBAGITROOT.tar *TARFILE");
writeLine("stdout","");

### - writes to rodsLog
msiWriteRodsLog("BagIt bag created: *NEWBAGITROOT <- *BAGITDATA",*Status);
}
INPUT *BAGITDATA=$"/$rodsZoneClient/home/$userNameClient/sub1",
*NEWBAGITROOT=$"/$rodsZoneClient/home/$userNameClient/bagit"
OUTPUT ruleExecOut
```

APPENDIX A: POLICY ENFORCEMENT POINTS

A total of 70 policy enforcement points are in version 4.0.

1) acAclPolicy - This rule sets Access Control List policy. If not called or called with an argument other than STRICT, the STANDARD setting is in effect, which is fine for many sites. In the STANDARD setting, users are allowed to see certain metadata, for example the data-object and sub-collection names in each other's collections. When made STRICT by calling msiAclPolicy(STRICT), the General Query Access Control is applied on collections and data object metadata which means that ils, etc, will need 'read' access or better to the collection to return the collection contents (name of data-objects, sub-collections, etc). Formerly this was controlled at build-time via a GEN_QUERY_AC flag in config.mk. Default is the normal, non-strict level, allowing users to see other collections. In all cases, access control to the data-objects is enforced. Even with STRICT access control, the admin user is not restricted so various microservices and queries will still be able to evaluate system-wide information.

   Post irods 2.5, $userNameClient is available for use at this policy enforcement point, although this is only secure in a irods-password environment (not GSI), but you can then have rules for specific users:

   acAclPolicy {ON($userNameClient == "quickshare") { } }
   See rsGenQuery.c for more information on use of $userNameClient.

   acAclPolicy {msiAclPolicy("STRICT"); }
   Requested by Australian Research Collaboration Service. The typical use is to just set AclPolicy to strict or not for all users. When choosing a "STRICT" ACL policy you should consider setting the following permissions if you are using the PHP web browser:
   ichmod -M read public /ZONE_NAME
   ichmod -M read public /ZONE_NAME/home

   acAclPolicy { }

2) acBulkPutPostProcPolicy - This rule sets the policy for executing the post processing put rule (acPostProcForPut) for bulk put. Since the bulk put option is intended to improve the upload speed, executing the acPostProcForPut for every file rule will slow down the upload. This rule provides an option to turn the postprocessing off. Only one function can be called:
   msiSetBulkPutPostProcPolicy () - This microservice sets whether the acPostProcForPut rule will be run in bulk put. Valid values for the flag are:
   "on" - enable execution of acPostProcForPut.
   "off" - disable execution of acPostProcForPut (default).

   acBulkPutPostProcPolicy {msiSetBulkPutPostProcPolicy("on"); }

   acBulkPutPostProcPolicy {msiSetBulkPutPostProcPolicy("off"); }

3) acCheckPasswordStrength – This is a policy point for checking password strength (added after iRODS 3.2), called when the admin or user is setting a password. By default, this is a no-op but the simple rule example below can be used to enforce a minimal password length. Also, microservices could be developed to make other checks, such as requiring both upper and lower case, and/or special characters, etc.

   acCheckPasswordStrength(*password) {if(strlen(*password) <7) {msiDeleteDisallowed; }}

   acCheckPasswordStrength(*password) { }

4) acChkHostAccessControl - This rule checks the access control by host and user based on the policy given in the HostAccessControl file. The msi was developed by Jean-Yves Nief of IN2P3. Only one function can be called.
    msiCheckHostAccessControl() - checks the access control by host and user based on the policy given in the HostAccessControl file.

    acChkHostAccessControl {msiCheckHostAccessControl; }

    acChkHostAccessControl { }

5) acCreateDefaultCollections – control creation of standard collections for a new user.

    acCreateDefaultCollections { acCreateUserZoneCollections; }

    acCreateUserZoneCollections {
        acCreateCollByAdmin("/"++$rodsZoneProxy++"/home", $otherUserName);
        acCreateCollByAdmin("/"++$rodsZoneProxy++"/trash/home", $otherUserName);
    }

    acCreateCollByAdmin(*parColl, *childColl) {msiCreateCollByAdmin(*parColl,*childColl); }

6) acCreateUser – this rule enables pre-process and post-process for creation of a user.

    acCreateUser {
        acPreProcForCreateUser;
        acCreateUserF1;
        acPostProcForCreateUser; }

    acCreateUserF1 {
        ON($otherUserName == "anonymous") {
        msiCreateUser ::: msiRollback;
        msiCommit; } }

    acCreateUserF1 {
        msiCreateUser ::: msiRollback;
        acCreateDefaultCollections ::: msiRollback;
        msiAddUserToGroup("public") ::: msiRollback;
        msiCommit; }

7) acDataDeletePolicy - This rule sets the policy for deleting data objects. This is the PreProcessing rule for delete. Only one function can be called:
    msiDeleteDisallowed() - Disallow the deletion of the data object.

    acDataDeletePolicy {ON($objPath like "/foo/bar/*") {msiDeleteDisallowed; } }
            This rule prevents the deletion of any data objects or collections beneath the collection /foo/bar/
    acDataDeletePolicy {ON($rescName == "demoResc8") {msiDeleteDisallowed; } }
            This rule prevents the deletion of any data objects that are stored in the demoResc8 resource.

    acDataDeletePolicy {ON($objPath like "/$rodsZoneClient/home/$userNameClient/*") {msiDeleteDisallowed; } }

    acDataDeletePolicy { }

8) acDeleteUser – enable preprocess and postprocess for user deletion

```
            acDeleteUser {
                acPreProcForDeleteUser;
                acDeleteUserF1;
                acPostProcForDeleteUser; }

        acDeleteUserF1 {
            acDeleteDefaultCollections ::: msiRollback;
            msiDeleteUser ::: msiRollback;
            msiCommit; }

        acDeleteDefaultCollections { acDeleteUserZoneCollections; }
```

9) acDeleteUserZoneCollections – delete standard user collections within a zone

```
        acDeleteUserZoneCollections {
            acDeleteCollByAdmin("/"++$rodsZoneProxy++"/home", $otherUserName);
            acDeleteCollByAdmin("/"++$rodsZoneProxy++"/trash/home", $otherUserName); }

    acDeleteCollByAdmin(*parColl,*childColl) {msiDeleteCollByAdmin(*parColl,*childColl); }
```

10) acGetUserByDN - The acGetUserByDN by default is a no-op but can be configured to do some special handling of GSI DNs. See rsGsiAuthRequest.c.

```
        acGetUserByDN(*arg,*OUT) {msiExecCmd("t", "*arg", "null", "null", "null", *OUT); }

        acGetUserByDN(*arg,*OUT) { }
```

11) acPostProcForCollCreate - This rule sets the post-processing policy for creating a collection. Currently there is no function written specifically for this rule.

```
        acPostProcForCollCreate { }
```

12) acPostProcForCopy - Rule for post processing the copy operation.

```
        acPostProcForCopy { }
```

13) acPostProcForCreate - Rule for post processing of data object create.

```
        acPostProcForCreate { }
```

14) acPostProcForCreateResource - This rule sets the post-processing policy for creating a new resource.

```
        acPostProcForCreateResource(*RescName,*RescType,*RescClass,*RescLoc,
        *RescVaultPath, *RescZoneName) { }
```

15) acPostProcForCreateToken - This rule sets the post-processing policy for creating a new token.

```
        acPostProcForCreateToken(*TNameSpace,*TName,*ValueOne,*ValueTwo,*ValueThree,
        *TComment) { }
```

16) acPostProcForCreateUser - This rule sets the post-processing policy for creating a new user.

acPostProcForCreateUser {writeLine("serverLog", "TEST:acPostProcForCreateUser"); }

acPostProcForCreateUser { }

17) acPostProcForDataObjRead - Rule for post processing the read buffer. The argument passed is of type BUF_LEN_MS_T

acPostProcForDataObjRead(*ReadBuffer) {writeLine("serverLog", "TEST:acPostProcForDataObjRead"); }

acPostProcForDataObjRead(*ReadBuffer) { }

18) acPostProcForDataObjWrite - Rule for pre processing the write buffer. The argument passed is of type BUF_LEN_MS_T

acPostProcForDataObjWrite(*WriteBuffer) {writeLine("serverLog", "TEST:acPostProcForDataObjWrite"); }

acPostProcForDataObjWrite(*WriteBuffer) { }

19) acPostProcForDelete - This rule sets the post-processing policy for deleting data objects. Currently there is no function written specifically for this rule.

acPostProcForDelete { }

20) acPostProcForDeleteResource - This rule sets the post-processing policy for deleting an old resource.

acPostProcForDeleteResource(*RescName) { }

21) acPostProcForDeleteToken - This rule sets the post-processing policy for deleting an old token.

acPostProcForDeleteToken(*TNameSpace,*TName) { }

22) acPostProcForDeleteUser - This rule sets the post-processing policy for deleting an old user.

acPostProcForDeleteUser {writeLine("serverLog", "TEST:acPostProcForDeleteUser"); }

acPostProcForDeleteUser { }

23) acPostProcForFilePathReg - Rule for post processing the registration or a file path.

acPostProcForFilePathReg { }

24) acPostProcForGenQuery - This rule sets the post-processing policy for general query. The *genQueryInpStr is a pointer converted to a string and sent as a character string. You need to convert as follows:
    genQueryInp_t *genQueryInp;
    genQueryInp = (genQueryInp_t *) strtol((char *)genQueryInpStr->inOutStruct,
                    (char **) NULL,0);
The *genQueryOutStr is also a pointer sent out as a character string. You need to convert as follows:
    genQueryOut_t *genQueryOut;
    genQueryOut = (genQueryOut_t *) strtol((char *)genQueryOutStr->inOutStruct,
                    (char **) NULL,0);

The *genQueryStatusStr is an integer but sent as a character string. You need to convert as follows:
int genQueryStatus;
genQueryStatus = atoi((char *)genQueryStatusStr->inOutStruct);

acPostProcForGenQuery(*genQueryInpStr,*genQueryOutStr,*genQueryStatusStr)
{writeLine("serverLog", "TEST:acPostProcForGenQuery and Status = *genQueryStatusStr"); }

acPostProcForGenQuery(*genQueryInpStr,*genQueryOutStr,*genQueryStatusStr) { }

25) acPostProcForModifyAccessControl - This rule sets the post-processing policy for access control modification.

acPostProcForModifyAccessControl(*RecursiveFlag,*AccessLevel,*UserName,*Zone, *Path) {writeLine("serverLog", "TEST:acPostProcForModifyAccessControl: *RecursiveFlag,*AccessLevel,*UserName,*Zone,*Path"); }

acPostProcForModifyAccessControl(*RecursiveFlag,*AccessLevel,*UserName,*Zone, *Path) { }

26) acPostProcForModifyAVUmetadata - This rule sets the post-processing policy for adding/deleting and copying the AVUmetadata for data, collection, resources, and user.
option= add, adda, rm, rmw, rmi, cp
item type= -d,-D,-c,-C,-r,-R,-u,-U

acPostProcForModifyAVUMetadata(*Option,*ItemType,*ItemName,*AName,*AValue, *AUnit) {writeLine("serverLog", "TEST:acPostProcForModifyAVUMetadata:*Option,*ItemType, *ItemName"); }

acPostProcForModifyAVUMetadata(*Option,*ItemType,*ItemName,*AName,*AValue, *AUnit) { }

acPostProcForModifyAVUMetadata(*Option,*ItemType,*ItemName,*AName,*AValue) { }

27) acPostProcForModifyCollMeta - This rule sets the post-processing policy for modifying system metadata of a collection.

acPostProcForModifyCollMeta { }

28) acPostProcForModifyDataObjMeta - This rule sets the post-processing policy for modifying system metadata of a data object.

acPostProcForModifyDataObjMeta {writeLine("serverLog", "TEST:acPostProcForModifyDataObjMeta"); }

acPostProcForModifyDataObjMeta { }

29) acPostProcForModifyResource - This rule sets the post-processing policy for modifying the properties of a resource. Option specifies the modifying-action being performed by the administrator

acPostProcForModifyResource(*ResourceName,*Option,*NewValue) { }

30) acPostProcForModifyUser - This rule sets the post-processing policy for modifying the properties of a user. Option specifies the modifying-action being performed by the administrator

> acPostProcForModifyUser(*UserName,*Option,*NewValue) {writeLine("serverLog", "TEST:acPostProcForModifyUser: *UserName, *Option, *NewValue"); }

> acPostProcForModifyUser(*UserName,*Option,*NewValue) { }

31) acPostProcForModifyUserGroup - This rule sets the post-processing policy for modifying membership of a user group. Option specifies the modifying-action being performed by the administrator.

> acPostProcForModifyUserGroup(*GroupName,*Option,*UserName,*ZoneName) { }

32) acPostProcForObjRename - This rule sets the post-processing policy for renaming (logically moving) data and collections.

> acPostProcForObjRename(*sourceObject,*destObject) {writeLine("serverLog", "TEST:acPostProcForObjRename from *sourceObject to *destObject"); }

> acPostProcForObjRename(*sourceObject,*destObject) {applyAllRules(acPostProcForObjRenameALL(*sourceObject,*destObject),"0", "0"); }

> acPostProcForObjRenameALL(*AA,*BB) {writeLine("serverLog", "I was called! *AA *BB"); }

> acPostProcForObjRenameALL(*AA,*BB) {writeLine("serverLog", "DestObject: *AA"); }

> acPostProcForObjRename(*sourceObject,*destObject) { }

33) acPostProcForOpen - Rule for post processing of data object open.

> acPostProcForOpen {writeLine("serverLog", $objPath); }

> acPostProcForOpen { }

34) acPostProcForPhymv - Rule for post processing of data object move of a physical file path (e.g. - ireg command).

> acPostProcForPhymv {}

35) acPostProcForPut - Rule for post processing the put operation. Currently, three post processing functions can be used individually or in sequence by the rules for put, copy, filepathreg, create, open, phymv, and repl.
   1) msiExtractNaraMetadata - extract and register metadata from the just uploaded NARA files.
   2) msiSysReplDataObj(replResc, flag) - can be used to replicate a copy of the file just uploaded or a copied data object to the specified replResc . Valid values for the "flag" input are "all", "updateRepl" and "rbudpTransfer". More than one flag value can be set using the "%" character as separator. e.g., "all%updateRepl". "updateRepl" means update an existing stale copy to the latest copy. The "all" flag means replicate to all resources in a resource group or update all stale copies if the "updateRepl" flag is also set. "rbudpTransfer" means the RBUDP protocol will be used for the transfer. A "null" input means a single copy will be made in one of the resource in the resource group. It

may be desirable to do replication only if the data Object is stored in a resource group. For example, the following rule can be used:

```
acPostProcForPut {ON($rescGroupName != "")
{msiSysReplDataObj($rescGroupName,"all"); } }
```

3) msiSysChksumDataObj - checksum the just uploaded or copied data object.

```
acPostProcForPut {msiSysChksumDataObj; msiSysReplDataObj("demoResc8", "all"); }
```

```
acPostProcForPut {msiSysReplDataObj("demoResc8", "all"); }
```

```
acPostProcForPut {msiSysChksumDataObj; }
```

```
acPostProcForPut {delay("<A></A>") {msiSysReplDataObj('demoResc8', 'all'); } }
```

```
acPostProcForPut {delay("<PLUSET>1m</PLUSET>") {acWriteLine('serverLog',
'delayed by a minute message1'); acWriteLine('serverLog', 'delayed by a minute
message2'); } }
```

```
acWriteLine(*A,*B) {writeLine(*A,*B); }
```

```
acPostProcForPut {ON($objPath like "/$rodsZoneClient/home/$userNameClient/nvo/*")
{delay("<PLUSET>1m</PLUSET>") {msiSysReplDataObj('nvoReplResc', 'null'); } } }
```

```
acPostProcForPut {msiSysReplDataObj("demoResc8", "all"); }
```

```
acPostProcForPut {msiSetDataTypeFromExt; }
```

```
acPostProcForPut {ON($objPath like "/$rodsZoneClient/home/$userNameClient/tg/*")
{msiSysReplDataObj("nvoReplResc", "null"); } }
```

```
acPostProcForPut {ON($objPath like
"/$rodsZoneClient/home/$userNameClient/mytest/*") {writeLine("serverLog", "File Path
is "++$filePath); } }
```

```
acPostProcForPut {ON($objPath like
"/$rodsZoneClient/home/$userNameClient/mytest/*") {writeLine("serverLog", "File Path
is "++$filePath); msiSplitPath($filePath,*fileDir,*fileName); msiExecCmd("send.sh",
"*fileDir *fileName", "null", "null", "null", *Junk); writeLine("serverLog", "After File Path is
*fileDir *fileName"); } }
```

```
acPostProcForPut { ON($objPath like "\*txt") {writeLine("serverLog", "File $objPath"); } }
```

```
acPostProcForPut { }
```

36) acPostProcForRepl - Rule for post processing of data object replication.

```
acPostProcForRepl { }
```

37) acPostProcForRmColl - This rule sets the post-processing policy for removing a collection. Currently there is no function written specifically for this rule.

```
acPostProcForRmColl {msiGetSessionVarValue("all", "all"); }
```

```
acPostProcForRmColl { }
```

38) acPostProcForTarFileReg - Rule for post processing the registration of the extracted tar file (from ibun -x). There is no microservice associated with this rule.

    acPostProcForTarFileReg { }

39) acPreprocForCollCreate - This is the PreProcessing rule for creating a collection. Currently there is no function written specifically for this rule.

    acPreprocForCollCreate {writeLine("serverLog",
    "TEST:acPreprocForCollCreate:"++$collName); }

    acPreprocForCollCreate { }

40) acPreProcForCreateResource - This rule sets the pre-processing policy for creating a new resource.

    acPreProcForCreateResource(*RescName,*RescType,*RescClass,*RescLoc,*RescVault Path, *RescZoneName) { }

41) acPreProcForCreateToken - This rule sets the pre-processing policy for creating a new token.

    acPreProcForCreateToken(*TNameSpace,*TName,*ValueOne,*ValueTwo,*ValueThree, *TComment) { }

42) acPreProcForCreateUser - This rule sets the pre-processing policy for creating a new user.

    acPreProcForCreateUser {writeLine("serverLog", "TEST:acPreProcForCreateUser"); }

    acPreProcForCreateUser { }

43) acPreprocForDataObjOpen - Preprocess rule for opening an existing data object which is used by the get, copy and replicate operations. Currently, four preprocessing functions can be used individually or in sequence by this rule.
   1) msiSetDataObjPreferredResc(preferredRescList) - set the preferred resources of the opened object. The copy stored in this preferred resource will be picked if it exists. More than one resource can be input using the character "%" as separator. e.g., resc1%resc2%resc3. The most preferred resource should be at the top of the list.
   2) msiSetDataObjAvoidResc(avoidResc) - set the resource to avoid when opening an object. The copy stored in this resource will not be picked unless this is the only copy.
   3) msiSortDataObj(sortingScheme) - Sort the copies of the data object using this scheme. Currently, "random" and "byRescClass" sorting scheme are supported. If "byRescClass" is set, data objects in the "cache" resources will be placed ahead of of those in the "archive" resources. The sorting schemes can also be chained. e.g.,
      • msiSortDataObj(random); msiSortDataObj(byRescClass) means that the data objects will be sorted randomly first and then separated by class.
   4) msiStageDataObj(cacheResc) - stage a copy of the data object in the cacheResc before opening the data object.
The $writeFlag session variable has been created to be used as a condition for differentiating between open for read ($writeFlag == 0) and write ($writeFlag == 1).

    acPreprocForDataObjOpen {ON($writeFlag == "0") {msiStageDataObj("demoResc8"); } }

    acPreprocForDataObjOpen {ON($writeFlag == "0") {writeLine("serverLog", $objPath);} }

    acPreprocForDataObjOpen {ON($writeFlag == "1") { } }

acPreprocForDataObjOpen {msiSortDataObj("random");
msiSetDataObjPreferredResc("xyz%demoResc8%abc");
msiStageDataObj("demoResc8"); }

acPreprocForDataObjOpen {msiSetDataObjPreferredResc("demoResc7%demoResc8");
}

acPreprocForDataObjOpen {msiGetSessionVarValue("all", "all"); }

acPreprocForDataObjOpen { }

45) acPreProcForDeleteResource - This rule sets the pre-processing policy for deleting an old resource.

acPreProcForDeleteResource(*RescName) { }

46) acPreProcForDeleteToken - This rule sets the pre-processing policy for deleting an old token.

acPreProcForDeleteToken(*TNameSpace,*TName) { }

47) acPreProcForDeleteUser - This rule sets the pre-processing policy for deleting an old user.

acPreProcForDeleteUser {writeLine("serverLog", "TEST:acPreProcForDeleteUser"); }

acPreProcForDeleteUser { }

48) acPreProcForExecCmd - Rule for pre processing when remotely executing a command in server/bin/cmd
parameter contains the command to be executed

acPreProcForExecCmd(*cmd) { }

49) acPreProcForGenQuery - This rule sets the pre-processing policy for general query. The *genQueryInpStr is a pointer converted to a string and sent as a character string. You need to convert as follows:
genQueryInp = (genQueryInp_t *) strtol((char *)genQueryInpStr->inOutStruct, (char **)
NULL,0);

acPreProcForGenQuery(*genQueryInpStr) {writeLine("serverLog",
"TEST:acPreProcForGenQuery from"); }

acPreProcForGenQuery(*genQueryInpStr) {msiPrintGenQueryInp("serverLog",
*genQueryInpStr); }

acPreProcForGenQuery(*genQueryInpStr) { }

50) acPreProcForModifyAccessControl - This rule sets the pre-processing policy for access control modification.

acPreProcForModifyAccessControl(*RecursiveFlag,*AccessLevel,*UserName,*Zone,
*Path) {writeLine("serverLog", "TEST:acPreProcForModifyAccessControl:
*RecursiveFlag,*AccessLevel,*UserName,*Zone,*Path"); }

acPreProcForModifyAccessControl(*RecursiveFlag,*AccessLevel,*UserName,*Zone,
*Path) { }

51) acPreProcForModifyAVUmetadata - This rule sets the pre-processing policy for adding/deleting and copying the AVUmetadata for data, collection, resources, and user.
option= add, adda, rm, rmw, rmi, cp
item type= -d,-D,-c,-C,-r,-R,-u,-U

```
acPreProcForModifyAVUMetadata(*Option,*ItemType,*ItemName,*AName,*AValue,
*AUnit) {writeLine("serverLog",
"TEST:acPreProcForModifyAVUMetadata:*Option,*ItemType, *ItemName"); }

acPreProcForModifyAVUMetadata(*Option,*ItemType,*ItemName,*AName,*AValue,
*AUnit) { }

acPreProcForModifyAVUMetadata(*Option,*ItemType,*ItemName,*AName,*AValue) { }
```

52) acPreProcForModifyCollMeta - This rule sets the pre-processing policy for modifying system metadata of a collection.

```
acPreProcForModifyCollMeta { }
```

53) acPreProcForModifyDataObjMeta - This rule sets the pre-processing policy for modifying system metadata of a data object.

```
acPreProcForModifyDataObjMeta {writeLine("serverLog",
"TEST:acPreProcForModifyDataObjMeta"); }

acPreProcForModifyDataObjMeta { }
```

54) acPreProcForModifyResource - This rule sets the pre-processing policy for modifying the properties of a resource. Option specifies the modifying-action being performed by the administrator

```
acPreProcForModifyResource(*ResourceName,*Option,*NewValue) { }
```

55) acPreProcForModifyUser - This rule sets the pre-processing policy for modifying the properties of a user. Option specifies the modifying-action being performed by the administrator

```
acPreProcForModifyUser(*UserName,*Option,*NewValue) {writeLine("serverLog",
"TEST:acPreProcForModifyUser: *UserName,*Option,*NewValue"); }

acPreProcForModifyUser(*UserName,*Option,*NewValue) { }
```

56) acPreProcForModifyUserGroup - This rule sets the pre-processing policy for modifying membership of a user group. Option specifies the modifying-action being performed by the administrator

```
acPreProcForModifyUserGroup(*GroupName,*Option,*UserName,*ZoneName) { }
```

57) acPreProcForObjRename - This rule sets the pre-processing policy for renaming (logically moving) data and collections

```
acPreProcForObjRename(*sourceObject,*destObject) {writeLine("serverLog",
"TEST:acPreProcForObjRename from *sourceObject to *destObject"); }

acPreProcForObjRename(*sourceObject,*destObject) { }
```

58) acPreprocForRmColl - This is the PreProcessing rule for removing a collection. Currently there is no function written specifically for this rule.

    acPreprocForRmColl { }

59) acRenameLocalZone – rename zone and all collections within the zone.

    acRenameLocalZone(*oldZone,*newZone) {
            msiRenameCollection("/"++str(*oldZone)++"", *newZone) ::: msiRollback;
            msiRenameLocalZone(*oldZone,*newZone) ::: msiRollback;
            msiCommit; }

60) acRescQuotaPolicy - This rule sets the policy for the resource quota. Only one function can be called:
        msiSetRescQuotaPolicy( ) - This microservice sets whether the Resource Quota should be enforced. Valid values for the flag are:
            "on" - enable Resource Quota enforcement,
            "off" - disable Resource Quota enforcement (default).

    acRescQuotaPolicy {msiSetRescQuotaPolicy("off"); }

61) acSetChkFilePathPerm - This rule replaces acNoChkFilePathPerm. For now, the only safe setting is the default, msiSetChkFilePathPerm("disallowPathReg"), which prevents non-admin users from using imcoll and ireg. In the next release (after 3.1) we expect to be able to offer the other settings described below. You can experiment with the other settings, but we do not recommend them for production at this time. The rule sets the policy for checking the file path permission when registering a physical file path using commands such as ireg and imcoll. This rule also sets the policy for checking the file path when unregistering a data object without deleting the physical file. Normally, a normal user cannot unregister a data object if the physical file is located in a resource vault. Setting the chkType input of msiSetChkFilePathPerm to "noChkPathPerm" allows this check to be bypassed.   Only one function can be called:
        msiSetChkFilePathPerm(chkType) - Valid values for chkType are:
        o   "disallowPathReg" - Disallow registration of iRODS path using ireg and imcoll by a non-privileged user.
        o   "noChkPathPerm" - Do not check file path permission when registering a file. WARNING - This setting can create a security problem if used.
        o   "doChkPathPerm" - Check UNIX ownership of physical files before registering. Registration of a path inside an iRODS resource vault path is not allowed.
        o   "chkNonVaultPathPerm" - Check UNIX ownership of physical files before registering. Registration of a path inside an iRODS resource vault path is allowed if the vault path belongs to the user.

    acSetChkFilePathPerm {msiSetChkFilePathPerm("doChkPathPerm"); }

    acSetChkFilePathPerm {msiSetChkFilePathPerm("disallowPathReg"); }

62) acSetMultiReplPerResc - Preprocess rule for replicating an existing data object. Currently, one preprocessing function can be used by this rule.
        msiSetMultiReplPerResc - By default, the system allows one copy per resource. This microservice sets the number of copies per resource to unlimited.

    acSetMultiReplPerResc {msiSetMultiReplPerResc(); }

    acSetMultiReplPerResc { }

63) acSetNumThreads - Rule to set the number of threads for a data transfer. This rule supports a condition based on $rescName so that different policies can be set for different resources. Only one function can be used for this rule

msiSetNumThreads(sizePerThrInMb, maxNumThr, windowSize) - set the number of threads and the tcp window size. The number of threads is based on the two input parameters

sizePerThrInMb - The number of threads is computed using:

numThreads = fileSizeInMb / sizePerThrInMb + 1

where sizePerThrInMb is an integer value in MBytes. It also accepts the word "default" which sets sizePerThrInMb to a default value of 32

maxNumThr - The maximum number of threads to use. It accepts integer values up to 16. It also accepts the word "default" which sets maxNumThr to a default value of 4. A value of 0 means no parallel I/O. This can be helpful to get around firewall issues.

windowSize - the tcp window size in Bytes for the parallel transfer. A value of 0 or "default" means a default size of 1,048,576 Bytes.

The msiSetNumThreads function must be present or only one thread will be used for all transfers

acSetNumThreads {msiSetNumThreads("16", "4", "default"); }

acSetNumThreads {msiSetNumThreads("default", "16", "default"); }

acSetNumThreads {ON($rescName == "macResc") {msiSetNumThreads("default", "0", "default"); } }

acSetNumThreads {msiSetNumThreads("default", "16", "default"); }

64) acSetPublicUserPolicy - This rule sets the policy for the set of operations that are allowable for the user "public" Only one function can be called.

msiSetPublicUserOpr(oprList) - Sets a list of operations that can be performed by the user "public". Only 2 operations are allowed - "read" - read files; "query" - browse some system level metadata. More than one operation can be input using the character "%" as separator. e.g., read%query.

acSetPublicUserPolicy {msiSetPublicUserOpr("read%query"); }

acSetPublicUserPolicy { }

65) acSetRescSchemeForCreate - This is the preprocessing rule for creating a data object. It can be used for setting the resource selection scheme when creating a data object which is used by the put, copy and replicate operations. Currently, three preprocessing functions can be used by this rule:

1) msiSetNoDirectRescInp(rescList) - sets a list of resources that cannot be used by a normal user directly. More than one resources can be input using the character "%" as separator. e.g., resc1%resc2%resc3. This function is optional, but if used, should be the first function to execute because it screens the resource input.

2) msiSetDefaultResc(defaultRescList, optionStr) - sets the default resource. From version 2.3 onward, this function is no longer mandatory, but if it is used, if should be executed right after the screening function msiSetNoDirectRescInp.

o defaultResc - the resource to use if no resource is input. A "null" means there is no defaultResc. More than one resource can be input using the character "%" as separator.

- optionStr - Can be "forced", "preferred" or "null". A "forced" input means the defaultResc will be used regardless of the user input. The forced action only applies to users with normal privilege.
3) msiSetRescSortScheme(sortScheme) - set the scheme for selecting the best resource to use when creating a data object.
    - sortScheme - The sorting scheme. Valid schemes are "default", "random", "byLoad" and "byRescClass". The "byRescClass" scheme will put the cache class of resource on the top of the list. The "byLoad" scheme will put the least loaded resource on the top of the list: in order to work properly, the RMS system must be switched on in order to pick up the load information for each server in the resource group list.

The scheme "random" and "byRescClass" can be applied in sequence. e.g.,
    msiSetRescSortScheme(random);
    msiSetRescSortScheme(byRescClass);
will select randomly a cache class resource and put it on the top of the list. Note that the msiOprDisallowed microservice can be used by all of the data object operation rules to disallow the execution of certain actions.

    acSetRescSchemeForCreate {msiSetNoDirectRescInp("xyz%demoResc8%abc");
    msiSetDefaultResc("demoResc8", "noForce"); msiSetRescSortScheme("default"); }

    acSetRescSchemeForCreate {msiSetDefaultResc("demoResc", "null");
    msiSetRescSortScheme("random"); msiSetRescSortScheme("byRescClass"); }

    acSetRescSchemeForCreate {msiSetDefaultResc("demoResc7%demoResc8",
    "preferred"); }

    acSetRescSchemeForCreate {ON($objPath like
    "/$rodsZoneClient/home/$userNameClient/protected/*") {msiOprDisallowed;} }

    acSetRescSchemeForCreate {msiSetDefaultResc("demoResc", "null"); }

    acSetRescSchemeForCreate {msiGetSessionVarValue("all", "all");
    msiSetDefaultResc("demoResc", "null"); }

    acSetRescSchemeForCreate {msiSetDefaultResc("demoResc", "forced");
    msiSetRescSortScheme("random"); msiSetRescSortScheme("byRescClass"); }

66) acSetRescSchemeForRepl - This is the preprocessing rule for replicating a data object. This rule is similar to acSetRescSchemeForCreate except it applies to replication. All the microservices for acSetRescSchemeForCreate also apply to acSetRescSchemeForRepl.

    acSetRescSchemeForRepl {msiSetDefaultResc("demoResc", "null"); }

67) acSetReServerNumProc - This rule sets the policy for the number of processes to use when running jobs in the irodsReServer. The irodsReServer can now multi-task such that one or two long running jobs cannot block the execution of other jobs. One function can be called: msiSetReServerNumProc(numProc) - numProc can be "default" or a number in the range 0-4. A value of 0 means no forking. numProc will be set to 1 if "default" is the input.

acSetReServerNumProc {msiSetReServerNumProc("default"); }

68) acSetVaultPathPolicy - This rule sets the policy for creating the physical path in the iRODS resource vault. Two functions can be called:
    1) msiSetGraftPathScheme(addUserName, trimDirCnt) - Set the VaultPath scheme to GRAFT_PATH - graft (add) the logical path to the vault path of the resource when

generating the physical path for a data object. The first argument (addUserName) specifies whether the userName should be added to the physical path. e.g. $vaultPath/$userName/$logicalPath. "addUserName" can have two values - yes or no. The second argument (trimDirCnt) specifies the number of leading directory elements of the logical path to trim. A value of 0 or 1 is allowable. The default value is 1.

2) msiSetRandomScheme() - Set the VaultPath scheme to RANDOM meaning a randomly generated path is appended to the vaultPath when generating the physical path. e.g., $vaultPath/$userName/$randomPath. The advantage with the RANDOM scheme is renaming operations (imv, irm) are much faster because there is no need to rename the corresponding physical path.

    acSetVaultPathPolicy {msiSetRandomScheme; }

    acSetVaultPathPolicy {msiSetGraftPathScheme("yes", "1"); }
        This default is GRAFT_PATH scheme with addUserName == yes and trimDirCnt == 1. Note : if trimDirCnt is greater than 1, the home or trash entry will be taken out.

69) acTicketPolicy - This is a policy point for ticket-based access (added in iRODS 3.1), where the administrator can allow ticket use by all users, no users, only certain users, or not certain users. The rule is executed when the server receives a ticket for use for access and if the rule fails (none found to apply), the ticket is not used. The default policy is to allow all users. To disallow for all users, comment out acTicketPolicy { }.

    acTicketPolicy {ON($userNameClient != "anonymous") { } }
        This disallows ticket usage for user anonymous (passwordless logins).

    acTicketPolicy { }

70) acTrashPolicy - This rule sets the policy for whether the trash can should be used. The default policy is the trash can will be used. Only one function can be called.
    msiNoTrashCan() - Set the policy to no trash can.

    acTrashPolicy {msiNoTrashCan; }

    acTrashPolicy { }

71) acVacuum – optimize database indices.

    acVacuum(*arg1) { delay(*arg1) { msiVacuum;} }

72) Helper rules: These are actions for getting iCAT results for performing iRODS operations. These rules generate the genQueryOut_ structure for each action for the given condition

    acGetIcatResults(*Action,*Condition,*GenQOut) {ON((*Action == "replicate") %% (*Action == "trim") %% (*Action == "chksum") %% (*Action == "copy") %% (*Action == "remove")) {msiMakeQuery("DATA_NAME, COLL_NAME", *Condition,*Query); msiExecStrCondQuery(*Query, *GenQOut); cut; } }

    acGetIcatResults(*Action,*Condition,*GenQOut) {ON(*Action == "chksumRescLoc") {msiMakeQuery("DATA_NAME, COLL_NAME, RESC_LOC", *Condition,*Query); msiExecStrCondQuery(*Query, *GenQOut); cut; } }

    acGetIcatResults(*Action,*Condition,*GenQOut) {ON(*Action == "list") {msiMakeQuery("DATA_NAME, COLL_NAME, DATA_RESC_NAME,

```
DATA_REPL_NUM, DATA_SIZE", *Condition,*Query); msiExecStrCondQuery(*Query,
*GenQOut); cut; } }
```

Rules for purging expired files

```
acPurgeFiles(*Condition) {ON((*Condition == "null") %% (*Condition == ""))
{msiGetIcatTime(*Time, "unix"); acGetIcatResults("remove", "DATA_EXPIRY < '*Time'",
*List); foreach(*List) {msiDataObjUnlink(*List,*Status); msiGetValByKey(*List,
"DATA_NAME", *D); msiGetValByKey(*List, "COLL_NAME", *E);
writeLine("stdout","Purged File *E/*D at *Time"); } } }
```

```
acPurgeFiles(*Condition) {msiGetIcatTime(*Time, "unix"); acGetIcatResults("remove",
"DATA_EXPIRY < '*Time' AND *Condition", *List); foreach(*List)
{msiDataObjUnlink(*List,*Status); msiGetValByKey(*List, "DATA_NAME", *D);
msiGetValByKey(*List, "COLL_NAME", *E); writeLine("stdout","Purged File *E/*D at
*Time"); } }
```

Additional helper rules.

```
acConvertToInt(*R) {assign(*A,$sysUidClient); assign($sysUidClient,*R); assign(*K,
$sysUidClient); assign(*R,*K); assign($sysUidClient,*A); }
```

```
printHello { print_hello; }
```

APPENDIX B: LIST OF PERSISTENT STATE VARIABLES

Persistent State Attribute	Explanation
AUDIT_ACTION_ID	Internal identifier for type of action that is audited
AUDIT_COMMENT	Comment on audit action for this instance
AUDIT_CREATE_TIME	Creation timestamp for audit action
AUDIT_MODIFY_TIME	Modification timestamp for audit action
AUDIT_OBJ_ID	Internal Identifier of the object (data, collection, user, etc.) on which the audit action was performed
AUDIT_USER_ID	Internal Identity of user whose action was audited
COLL_ACCESS_COLL_ID	Aliased Collection identifier used for access control
COLL_ACCESS_NAME	Access string for collection (cf. DATA_ACCESS_NAME)
COLL_ACCESS_TYPE	Internal identifier for access name
COLL_ACCESS_USER_ID	Internal identifier of the user whose action is audited.
COLL_COMMENTS	Comments about the collection
COLL_CREATE_TIME	Collection creation timestamp
COLL_FILEMETA_CREATE_TIME	When a Unix directory is imported into iRODS from client-side, the directory metadata in the file system is captured in the iCAT under COLL_FILEMETA. This is useful when getting the directory back into the client as the "original" metadata can be re-created. The COLL_FILEMETA_CREATE_TIME variable holds the value when the directory metadata was inserted into iCAT
COLL_FILEMETA_CTIME	Original Unix directory create time at the client-side.
COLL_FILEMETA_GID	Original Unix Group-id for the directory (used for ACLs) at the client-side.
COLL_FILEMETA_GROUP	Original Unix Group name for the directory (used for ACLs) at the client-side.
COLL_FILEMETA_MODE	Original Unix ACL for the directory at the client-side.
COLL_FILEMETA_MODIFY_TIME	Value when the directory metadata was modified in iCAT
COLL_FILEMETA_MTIME	Original Unix timestamp for last modification at the client-side
COLL_FILEMETA_OBJ_ID	Original Unix object_id for the director at the client-side.
COLL_FILEMETA_OWNER	Original Unix owner for the directory at the client-side.
COLL_FILEMETA_SOURCE_PATH	Original Unix path for the directory at the client-side.
COLL_FILEMETA_UID	Original Unix user-id of owner for the directory at the client-side.
COLL_ID	Collection internal identifier
COLL_INHERITANCE	Attributes inherited by sub-collections from parent-collection: ACL, metadata, pins, locks
COLL_MAP_ID	Internal identifier denoting the type of collection.
COLL_MODIFY_TIME	Last modification timestamp for collection
COLL_NAME	Logical collection name
COLL_OWNER_NAME	Collection owner
COLL_OWNER_ZONE	Home zone of the collection owner
COLL_PARENT_NAME	Parent collection name
COLL_TOKEN_NAMESPACE	See TOKEN_NAMESPACE (also DATA_TOKEN_NAMESPACE), not used
DATA_ACCESS_DATA_ID	Internal identifier of the digital object for which access is defined
DATA_ACCESS_NAME	Access string in iCAT used for data, collections, etc. (e. g. read object) iquest "SELECT TOKEN_NAME WHERE TOKEN_NAMESPACE ='access_type'"
DATA_ACCESS_TYPE	Internal ICAT identifier
DATA_ACCESS_USER_ID	User or group (name) for which the access is defined on digital object
DATA_CHECKSUM	Checksum stored as tagged list: <BINHEX>12344</BINHEX> <MD5>22234422</MD5>
DATA_COLL_ID	Collection internal identifier
DATA_COMMENTS	Comments about the digital object
DATA_CREATE_TIME	Creation timestamp for the digital object
DATA_EXPIRY	Expiration date for the digital object
DATA_FILEMETA_CREATE_TIME	When a Unix file is imported into iRODS from client-side, the file metadata in the file system is captured in the iCAT under DATA_FILEMETA. This is useful when getting the file back into the client as the "original" metadata can be re-created. The DATA_FILEMETA_CREATE_TIME variable holds the value when the file metadata was inserted into iCAT
DATA_FILEMETA_CTIME	Original Unix file create time at the client-side.
DATA_FILEMETA_GID	Original Unix Group-id for the file (used for ACLs) at the client-side.
DATA_FILEMETA_GROUP	Original Unix Group name for the directory file (used for ACLs) at the client-side.
DATA_FILEMETA_MODE	Original Unix ACL for the file at the client-side.
DATA_FILEMETA_MODIFY_TIME	Value when the file metadata was modified in iCAT
DATA_FILEMETA_MTIME	Original Unix timestamp for last modification at the client-side
DATA_FILEMETA_OBJ_ID	Original Unix object_id for the file at the client-side.
DATA_FILEMETA_OWNER	Original Unix owner for the file at the client-side.
DATA_FILEMETA_SOURCE_PATH	Original Unix path for the file at the client-side.

DATA_FILEMETA_UID	Original Unix user-id of owner for the file at the client-side.
DATA_ID	Unique Data internal identifier. A digital object is identified by (zone, collection, data name, replica, version). The identifier is same across replicas and versions.
DATA_MAP_ID	Internal identifier denoting the type of data
DATA_MODIFY_TIME	Last modification timestamp for the digital object
DATA_NAME	Logical name of the digital object
DATA_OWNER_NAME	User who created the object
DATA_OWNER_ZONE	Home zone of the user who created the object
DATA_PATH	Physical path name for digital object in resource
DATA_REPL_NUM	Replica number starting with "1"
DATA_REPL_STATUS	Replica status: locked, is-deleted, pinned, hide
DATA_RESC_GROUP_NAME	Name of resource group in which data is stored
DATA_RESC_NAME	Logical name of storage resource
DATA_SIZE	Size of the digital object in bytes
DATA_STATUS	Digital object status: locked, is-deleted, pinned, hide
DATA_TOKEN_NAMESPACE	Namespace of the data token: e.g. data type, not used
DATA_TYPE_NAME	Type of data: jpeg image, PDF document
DATA_VERSION	Version string assigned to the digital object. Older versions of replicas have a negative replica number
DVM_BASE_MAP_BASE_NAME	Name for the Data Base of Data Variable Set of Maps (e. g. "core" in core.dvm)
DVM_BASE_MAP_COMMENT	Comments for DVM_BASE_MAP
DVM_BASE_MAP_CREATE_TIME	Creation time for DVM_BASE_MAP
DVM_BASE_MAP_MODIFY_TIME	Last Modification time for DVM_BASE_MAP
DVM_BASE_MAP_OWNER_NAME	Owner's name of the DVM_BASE_MAP
DVM_BASE_MAP_OWNER_ZONE	Owner's zone name of the DVM_BASE_MAP
DVM_BASE_MAP_VERSION	Version of the DVM_BASE_MAP (empty or 0 means current)
DVM_BASE_NAME	Foreign key reference to DVM_BASE_MAP_BASE_NAME
DVM_COMMENT	Comment for the DVM
DVM_CONDITION	Condition for applying the DVM Mapping corresponding to DVM_EXT_VAR_NAME
DVM_CREATE_TIME	Creation time of the DVM Mapping
DVM_EXT_VAR_NAME	External name for the Map (the actual $-variable)
DVM_ID	An internal identifier for DVM Mapping
DVM_INT_MAP_PATH	Internal Structure path in REI corresponding to DVM_EXT_VAR_NAME
DVM_MODIFY_TIME	Last modification time for the DVM Mapping
DVM_OWNER_NAME	Owner's name of the DVM_Mapping
DVM_OWNER_ZONE	Owner's zone name of the DVM Mapping
DVM_STATUS	Status of the DVM_Mapping (empty is valid)
DVM_VERSION	Version for the DVM_Mapping (empty or 0 means current)
FNM_BASE_MAP_BASE_NAME	Name for the Data Base of Function Name Set of Maps (e. g. "core" in core.fnm). This can be used for giving virtual names for microservices and rules and for versioning names for the same.
FNM_BASE_MAP_COMMENT	Comments for FNM_BASE_MAP
FNM_BASE_MAP_CREATE_TIME	Creation time for FNM_BASE_MAP
FNM_BASE_MAP_MODIFY_TIME	Last Modification time for FNM_BASE_MAP
FNM_BASE_MAP_OWNER_NAME	Owner's name of the FNM_BASE_MAP
FNM_BASE_MAP_OWNER_ZONE	Owner's zone name of the FNM_BASE_MAP
FNM_BASE_MAP_VERSION	Version of the FNM_BASE_MAP (empty or 0 means current)
FNM_BASE_NAME	Foreign key reference to FNM_BASE_MAP_BASE_NAME
FNM_COMMENT	Comment for the FNM Mapping
FNM_CREATE_TIME	Creation time of the FNM Mapping
FNM_EXT_FUNC_NAME	External name for the FNM Mapping
FNM_ID	An internal identifier for FNM Mapping
FNM_INT_FUNC_NAME	Internal Structure path in REI corresponding to FNM_EXT_FUNC_NAME
FNM_MODIFY_TIME	Last modification time for the FNM Mapping
FNM_OWNER_NAME	Owner's name of the FNM_Mapping
FNM_OWNER_ZONE	Owner's zone name of the FNM Mapping
FNM_STATUS	Status of the FNM_Mapping (empty is valid)
FNM_VERSION	Version for the FNM_Mapping (empty or 0 means current)
META_ACCESS_META_ID	Internal identifier of the (AVU) metadata for which access is defined
META_ACCESS_NAME	See DATA_ACCESS_NAME
META_ACCESS_TYPE	Internal ICAT identifier
META_ACCESS_USER_ID	User or group (name) for which the access is defined on metadata
META_COLL_ATTR_ID	Internal identifier for metadata attribute for collection
META_COLL_ATTR_NAME	Metadata attribute name for collection
META_COLL_ATTR_UNITS	Metadata attribute units for collection
META_COLL_ATTR_VALUE	Metadata attribute value for collection

META_COLL_CREATE_TIME	Creation time for the metadata for collections
META_COLL_MODIFY_TIME	Last modification time for the metadata for collections
META_DATA_ATTR_ID	Internal identifier for metadata attribute for digital object
META_DATA_ATTR_NAME	Metadata attribute name for digital object
META_DATA_ATTR_UNITS	Metadata attribute units for digital object
META_DATA_ATTR_VALUE	Metadata attribute value for digital object
META_DATA_CREATE_TIME	Time stamp when metadata was created
META_DATA_MODIFY_TIME	Time stamp when metadata was modified
META_MET2_ATTR_ID	Internal identifier for metadata attribute for metadata
META_MET2_ATTR_NAME	Metadata attribute name for metadata
META_MET2_ATTR_UNITS	Metadata attribute units for metadata
META_MET2_ATTR_VALUE	Metadata attribute value for metadata
META_MET2_CREATE_TIME	Creation time for the metadata for metadata
META_MET2_MODIFY_TIME	Last modification time for the metadata for metadata
META_MSRVC_ATTR_ID	Internal identifier for metadata attribute for microservice
META_MSRVC_ATTR_NAME	Metadata attribute name for microservice
META_MSRVC_ATTR_UNITS	Metadata attribute units for microservice
META_MSRVC_ATTR_VALUE	Metadata attribute value for microservice
META_MSRVC_CREATE_TIME	Creation time for the metadata for microservice
META_MSRVC_MODIFY_TIME	Last modification time for the metadata for microservice
META_NAMESPACE_COLL	Namespace of collection AVU-triplet attribute
META_NAMESPACE_DATA	Namespace of digital object AVU-triplet attribute
META_NAMESPACE_MET2	Namespace of metadata AVU-triplet attribute
META_NAMESPACE_MSRVC	Namespace of microservice AVU-triplet attribute
META_NAMESPACE_RESC	Namespace of resource AVU-triplet attribute
META_NAMESPACE_RULE	Namespace of rule AVU-triplet attribute
META_NAMESPACE_USER	Namespace of user AVU-triplet attribute
META_RESC_ATTR_ID	Internal identifier for metadata attribute for resource
META_RESC_ATTR_NAME	Metadata attribute name for resource
META_RESC_ATTR_UNITS	Metadata attribute units for resource
META_RESC_ATTR_VALUE	Metadata attribute value for resource
META_RESC_CREATE_TIME	Creation time for the metadata for resource
META_RESC_MODIFY_TIME	Last modification time for the metadata for resource
META_RULE_ATTR_ID	Internal identifier for metadata attribute for a rule
META_RULE_ATTR_NAME	Metadata attribute name for a rule
META_RULE_ATTR_UNITS	Metadata attribute units for a rule
META_RULE_ATTR_VALUE	Metadata attribute value for a rule
META_RULE_CREATE_TIME	Creation time for the metadata entry for a rule
META_RULE_MODIFY_TIME	Last modification time for the metadata for a rule
META_TOKEN_NAMESPACE	See TOKEN_NAMESPACE
META_USER_ATTR_ID	Internal identifier for metadata attribute for user
META_USER_ATTR_NAME	Metadata attribute name for user
META_USER_ATTR_UNITS	Metadata attribute units for user
META_USER_ATTR_VALUE	Metadata attribute value for user
META_USER_CREATE_TIME	Internal identifier of the (AVU) metadata for which access is defined
META_USER_MODIFY_TIME	See DATA_ACCESS_NAME
MSRVC_ACCESS_MSRVC_ID	Internal ICAT identifier
MSRVC_ACCESS_NAME	User or group (name) for which the access is defined on metadata
MSRVC_ACCESS_TYPE	Internal ICAT identifier
MSRVC_ACCESS_USER_ID	User or group (name) for which the access is defined on the microservice
MSRVC_COMMENT	Comments for microservice
MSRVC_CREATE_TIME	Creation time for the microservice
MSRVC_DOXYGEN	Doxygen documentation for the microservice
MSRVC_HOST	Host types at which the microservice can be executed
MSRVC_ID	Internal Id for the microservice
MSRVC_LANGUAGE	Language in which the microservice is written
MSRVC_LOCATION	The Location of the microservice executable
MSRVC_MODIFY_TIME	Last Modification time for the microservice
MSRVC_MODULE_NAME	Module name for the microservice
MSRVC_NAME	Name of the microservice
MSRVC_OWNER_NAME	Owner name of the microservice
MSRVC_OWNER_ZONE	Owner's zone name of the microservice
MSRVC_SIGNATURE	Digital signature (checksum) for the microservice
MSRVC_STATUS	Status of the microservice
MSRVC_TOKEN_NAMESPACE	See TOKEN_NAMESPACE
MSRVC_TYPE_NAME	Type of the microservice

MSRVC_VARIATIONS	Variations (or forms) of the microservice
MSRVC_VER_COMMENT	Comments on the microservice
MSRVC_VER_CREATE_TIME	Creation time of version of the microservice
MSRVC_VER_MODIFY_TIME	Last modification time of version of the microservice
MSRVC_VER_OWNER_NAME	Owner name of the version of the microservice
MSRVC_VER_OWNER_ZONE	Owner zone name of the version of the microservice
MSRVC_VERSION	Version of the microservice
QUOTA_LIMIT	High limit for quota for resource in QUOTA_RESC_ID for QUOTA_USER_ID
QUOTA_MODIFY_TIME	Last modification time of quota
QUOTA_OVER	Flag if quota is exceeded
QUOTA_RESC_ID	Internal Resource ID for quota
QUOTA_RESC_NAME	Resource Name for quota
QUOTA_USAGE	Name of Usage for quota (normally write)
QUOTA_USAGE_MODIFY_TIME	Last modification time of quota usage
QUOTA_USAGE_RESC_ID	Internal Resource ID for quota usage
QUOTA_USAGE_USER_ID	Internal User ID for quota usage
QUOTA_USER_ID	Internal User ID for quota
QUOTA_USER_NAME	User Name for Quota
QUOTA_USER_TYPE	User type name for quota
QUOTA_USER_ZONE	User zone name for quota
RESC_ACCESS_NAME	See DATA_ACCESS_NAME
RESC_ACCESS_RESC_ID	Internal identifier of the resource for which access is defined
RESC_ACCESS_TYPE	Internal ICAT identifier
RESC_ACCESS_USER_ID	User or group (name) for which the access is defined on resource
RESC_CLASS_NAME	Resource class: primary, secondary, archival
RESC_COMMENT	Comment about resource
RESC_CREATE_TIME	Creation timestamp of resource
RESC_FREE_SPACE	Free space available on resource
RESC_FREE_SPACE_TIME	Time at which free space was computed
RESC_ID	Internal resource identifier for resource in the group
RESC_INFO	Tagged information list: <MAX_OBJ_SIZE>2GBB</MAX_OBJ_SIZE> <MIN_LATENCY>1msec</MIIN_LATENCY>
RESC_LOC	Resource IP address
RESC_MODIFY_TIME	Last modification timestamp for resource
RESC_NAME	Logical name of the resource
RESC_STATUS	Operational status of resource
RESC_TOKEN_NAMESPACE	See TOKEN_NAMESPACE
RESC_TYPE_NAME	Resource type: HPSS, SamFS, database, orb
RESC_VAULT_PATH	Resource path for storing files
RESC_ZONE_NAME	Name of the iCAT, unique globally
RULE_ACCESS_NAME	Internal identifier of the iRODS rule for which access is defined
RULE_ACCESS_RULE_ID	See DATA_ACCESS_NAME
RULE_ACCESS_TYPE	Internal ICAT identifier
RULE_ACCESS_USER_ID	User or group (name) for which the access is defined on iRODS rule
RULE_BASE_MAP_BASE_NAME	Name for the Data Base of Rule Set of Maps (e. g. "core" in core.re).
RULE_BASE_MAP_COMMENT	Comments for RULE_BASE_MAP
RULE_BASE_MAP_CREATE_TIME	Creation time for RULE_BASE_MAP
RULE_BASE_MAP_MODIFY_TIME	Last Modification time for RULE_BASE_MAP
RULE_BASE_MAP_OWNER_NAME	Owner's name of the RULE_BASE_MAP
RULE_BASE_MAP_OWNER_ZONE	Owner's zone name of the RULE_BASE_MAP
RULE_BASE_MAP_PRIORITY	Prioritization of the RULE_BASE_MAP (empty or 0 means current). This tells which map has priority over other maps. This can define a tree/forest.
RULE_BASE_MAP_VERSION	Version of the RULE_BASE_MAP (empty or 0 means current)
RULE_BASE_NAME	Rule base to which the rule is a member
RULE_BODY	Body of the rule
RULE_COMMENT	Comments on the rule
RULE_CONDITION	Condition of the rule
RULE_CREATE_TIME	Creation time of the rule
RULE_DESCR_1	Description of rule (1)
RULE_DESCR_2	Description of rule (2)
RULE_DOLLAR_VARS	Session variables used in the rule
RULE_EVENT	Event name of the rule (can be viewed as rule name)
RULE_EXEC_ADDRESS	Host name where the delayed Rule will be executed
RULE_EXEC_ESTIMATED_EXE_TIME	Estimated execution time for the delayed Rule
RULE_EXEC_FREQUENCY	Delayed Rule execution frequency
RULE_EXEC_ID	Internal identifier for a delayed Rule execution request

RULE_EXEC_LAST_EXE_TIME	Previous execution time for the delayed Rule
RULE_EXEC_NAME	Logical name for a delayed Rule execution request
RULE_EXEC_NOTIFICATION_ADDR	Notification address for delayed Rule completion
RULE_EXEC_PRIORITY	Delayed Rule execution priority
RULE_EXEC_REI_FILE_PATH	Path of the file where the context (REI) of the delayed Rule is stored
RULE_EXEC_STATUS	Current status of the delayed Rule
RULE_EXEC_TIME	Time when the delayed Rule will be executed
RULE_EXEC_USER_NAME	User requesting a delayed Rule execution
RULE_ICAT_ELEMENTS	Permanent (#-variables) affected by the rule
RULE_ID	Internal identifier for the rule
RULE_INPUT_PARAMS	Parameters used as input when invoking the rule
RULE_MODIFY_TIME	Last modification time of the rule
RULE_NAME	Name of the rule (can be different from RULE_EVENT
RULE_OUTPUT_PARAMS	Output parameters set by the rule invocation
RULE_OWNER_NAME	Owner name of the rule
RULE_OWNER_ZONE	Owner's zone name of the rule
RULE_RECOVERY	Recovery part of the rule
RULE_SIDEEFFECTS	Side effects (%-variables) – used as a semantic of what the rule does
RULE_STATUS	Status of the rule (valid/active or otherwise)
RULE_TOKEN_NAMESPACE	See TOKEN_NAMESPACE
RULE_VERSION	Version of the rule
SL_CPU_USED	Server load information: cpu used. Server load information is computed periodically for all servers in the grid, if enabled by the administrator.
SL_CREATE_TIME	Server load information: creation time of the entry
SL_DISK_SPACE	Server load information: disk space used
SL_HOST_NAME	Server load information: host name of the server
SL_MEM_USED	Server load information: memory used
SL_NET_INPUT	Server load information: network input load
SL_NET_OUTPUT	Server load information: network output load
SL_RESC_NAME	Server load information: resource for which disk space is provided
SL_RUNQ_LOAD	Server load information: run queue load
SL_SWAP_USED	Server load information: swap space used
SLD_CREATE_TIME	Server load digest information: digest creation time
SLD_LOAD_FACTOR	Server load information: load factor computed rom server load information
SLD_RESC_NAME	Server load information: resource name for which the load factor is computed
TICKET_ALLOWED_GROUP_NAME	User group to which the ticket (TICKET_ALLOWED_GROUP_TICKET_ID) is valid
TICKET_ALLOWED_GROUP_TICKET_ID	Identifier for the ticket
TICKET_ALLOWED_HOST	Host for which the ticket (TICKET_ALLOWED_HOST_TICKET_ID) is valid Allows invocation of the ticket-based access only from this host. Useful for scheduled jobs
TICKET_ALLOWED_HOST_TICKET_ID	Identifier for the ticket
TICKET_ALLOWED_USER_NAME	User to which the ticket (TICKET_ALLOWED_GROUP_TICKET_ID) is valid
TICKET_ALLOWED_USER_TICKET_ID	Identifier for the ticket
TICKET_COLL_NAME	Collection name on which the ticket is issued
TICKET_CREATE_TIME	Ticket creation time
TICKET_DATA_COLL_NAME	Collection name of the object on which the ticket is issued
TICKET_DATA_NAME	Data name of the object on which the ticket is issued
TICKET_EXPIRY	Expiration date for a ticket
TICKET_ID	Identifier for the ticket
TICKET_MODIFY_TIME	Last modification time for the ticket
TICKET_OBJECT_ID	(Internal) Object Id for the object on which the ticket is issued
TICKET_OBJECT_TYPE	Ticket may be for data, resource, user, rule, metadata, zone, collection, token
TICKET_OWNER_NAME	Name of the person who created the ticket
TICKET_OWNER_ZONE	Home zone of the person who created the ticket
TICKET_STRING	Human readable name for the ticket
TICKET_TYPE	Type of ticket, either "read" or "write"
TICKET_USER_ID	Identifier of the person who is using the ticket
TICKET_USES_COUNT	Number of times a ticket has been used
TICKET_USES_LIMIT	Maximum number of times a ticket may be used
TICKET_WRITE_BYTE_COUNT	Number of bytes written for accesses through a given ticket
TICKET_WRITE_BYTE_LIMIT	Maximum number of bytes that may be written using a given ticket
TICKET_WRITE_FILE_COUNT	Number of files written for accesses through a given ticket
TICKET_WRITE_FILE_LIMIT	Maximum number of files that can be written using a given ticket
TOKEN_COMMENT	Comment on token
TOKEN_ID	Internal identifier for token name

TOKEN_NAME	A value in the token namespace; e.g. "jpg image"
TOKEN_NAMESPACE	Namespace for tokens; e.g. data type, resource_type, rule_type,...
TOKEN_VALUE	Additional token information string (e. g. dot extensions for jpg: jpg, .jpg2, jg)
TOKEN_VALUE2	Additional token information string
TOKEN_VALUE3	Additional token information string
USER_COMMENT	Comment about the user
USER_CREATE_TIME	Creation timestamp
USER_DN	Distinguished name in tagged list: <authType>distinguishedName</authType>
USER_GROUP_ID	Internal identifier for the user group
USER_GROUP_NAME	Logical name for the user group
USER_ID	User internal identifier
USER_INFO	Tagged information: <EMAIL>user@unc.edu</EMAIL> <PHONE>5555555555</PHONE>
USER_MODIFY_TIME	Last modification timestamp
USER_NAME	User name
USER_TYPE	User role (rodsgroup, rodsadmin, rodsuser, domainadmin, groupadmin, storageadmin, rodscurators)
USER_ZONE	Home Data Grid or user
ZONE_COMMENT	Comment about the zone
ZONE_CONNECTION	Connection information in tagged list; <PASSWORD>RPS1</PASSWORD> <GSI>DISTNAME</GSI>
ZONE_CREATE_TIME	Date and time stamp for creation of a data grid
ZONE_ID	Data Grid or zone identifier
ZONE_MODIFY_TIME	Date and time stamp for modification of a data grid
ZONE_NAME	Data Grid or zone name, name of the iCAT
ZONE_TYPE	Type of zone: local/remote/other

APPENDIX C: SESSION VARIABLES

When a policy enforcement point is reached within the iRODS framework, associated Session Variables will be available. The Session Variables may be used within a Rule to decide between options and control the execution of the Rule. Not all Session Variables are available at each policy enforcement point. In particular, note that a limited set of Session Variables are available when Rules are executed interactively.

The available Session Variables can be grouped into seven sets: 1) *SuserAndConn*, 2) *SdataObj1*, 3) *SdataObj2*, 4) *SrescInfo*, 5) *Scollection*, 6) *SuserAdmin1*, 7) and *SuserAdmin2*.

1. The *SuserAndConn (S1)* set contains Session Variables relating to information about the client user and the current client/server connection. This set of Session Variables should be available in all Rules.

2. The *SdataObj1 (S2)* set contains just one Session Variable, objPath. It is available in pre-processing Rules before a data object is created.

3. The *SdataObj2 ((S3)* set contains Session Variables relating to information on a data object.

4. The *SrescInfo (S4)* set contains Session Variables relating to information on an iRODS data storage resource.

5. The *Scollection (S5)* set contains Session Variables relating to information on a Collection.

6. The *SuserAdmin1 (S6)* set contains Session Variables relating to information on users for administration purposes.

7. The *SuserAdmin2 (S7)* set contains Session Variables for information on new users.

The Session Variables available within each set are listed in Table 6.

Table 6. Session Variables Available for Use Within Rules

$ Session State Set	Available $ Session Variables	$ Session State Set	Available $ Session Variables	$ Session State Set	Available $ Session Variables
S1	authStrClient	S3	backupRescName	S4	freeSpace
S1	authStrProxy	S3	chksum	S4	freeSpaceTimeStamp
S1	connectApiTnx	S3	collId	S4	rescClass
S1	connectCnt	S3	dataAccess	S4	rescClassInx
S1	connectOption	S3	dataAccessInx	S4	rescComments
S1	connectSock	S3	dataComments	S4	rescGroupName
S1	connectStatus	S3	dataId	S4	rescId
S1	otherUser	S3	dataOwner	S4	rescInfo
S1	privClient	S3	dataOwnerZone	S4	rescLoc
S1	privProxy	S3	dataSize	S4	rescMaxObjSize
S1	rodsZoneClient	S3	dataType	S4	rescName
S1	rodsZoneProxy	S3	destRescName	S4	rescType
S1	userAuthSchemeClient	S3	filePath	S4	rescTypeInx
S1	userAuthSchemeProxy	S3	objPath	S4	rescVaultPath
S1	userNameClient	S3	replNum	S4	zoneName
S1	userNameProxy	S3	replStatus		
		S3	statusString	S5	collName

S2	objPath	S3	version	S5	collParentName
		S3	writeFlag		
				S6	otherUserName
				S6	otherUserZone
				S6	otherUserType
				S7	otherUserName
				S7	otherUserZone

When Microservices are executed using the irule command, only the S1 set will be available for the referenced Microservices. Table 6 lists which Session Variable sets are available for use with each of the default iRODS Rules.

Default Rules in core.re	Description	Session Variable Sets
acAclPolicy		none
acBullkPutPostProcPolicy		
acCheckPasswordStrength	Check password strength	
acChkHostAccessControl	Set policy for host access control	
acCreateDefaultCollections	Create default collections (home, trash)	S1, S6
acCreateUser	Create a new user	S1,(S7 or S6?)
acDataDeletePolicy	Pre-process for file delete	S1, S3, S4
acDeleteUser	Delete user	S1, S7
acDeleteUserZoneCollections	Delete collections in a Data Grid Zone	S1
acGetUserByDN	Used for special handling of GSI distinguished names	S1
acPostProcForCollCreate	Post-process for collection create	S1, S5
acPostProcForCopy	Apply processing to file on copy	S1, S3, S4
acPostProcForCreate	Post-process on file create	S1, S3, S4
acPostProcForCreateResource	Post-process on resource creation	S1
acPostProcForCreateToken	Post-process on token creation	S1
acPostProcForCreateUser	Post-process for user create	S1
acPostProcForDataObjRead		
acPostProcForDataObjWrite		
acPostProcForDelete	Post-process for file delete	S1, S3, S4
acPostProcForDeleteResource	Post-process on resource deletion	S1
acPostProcForDeleteToken	Post-process on token deletion	S1
acPostProcForDeleteUser	Post-process for user delete	S1
acPostProcForFilePathReg	Post-process for registering a file path	S1, S3, S4
acPostProcForGenQuery		S1

acPostProcForModifyAccessControl	Post-process for modification of ACLs on data or collection	S1
acPostProcForModifyAVUMetadata	Post-process for modification of AVU metadata for data/collection/resource/user	S1
acPostProcForModifyCollMeta	Post-process on modification of collection metadata	S1, S5
acPostProcForModifyDataObjMeta	Post-process on modification of data metadata	S1, S2
acPostProcForModifyResource	Post-process on resource modification	S1
acPostProcForModifyUser	Post-process for user modify	S1
acPostProcForModifyUserGroup	Post-process for user group modify	S1
acPostProcForObjRename	Post-process for object move	S1, S2
acPostProcForOpen	Post-process for file read or file read. $writeFlag == 0 for open for read, == 1 for open for write	S1, S3, S4
acPostProcForPhymv		
acPostProcForPut	Apply processing to file on put	S1, S3, S4
acPostProcForRepl		
acPostProcForRmColl	Post-process for collection delete	S1, S5
acPostProcForTarFileReg		
acPreprocForCollCreate	Pre-process for collection create	S1, S5
acPreProcForCreateResource	Pre-process for resource creation	S1
acPreProcForCreateToken	Pre-process on token creation	S1
acPreProcForCreateUser	Pre-process for user create	S1
acPreprocForDataObjOpen	Pre-process for file open or read, select which copy of a file to open. $writeFlag == 0 for open for read, == 1 for open for write	S1, S3, S4
acPreProcForDeleteResource	Pre-process on resource deletion	S1
acPreProcForDeleteToken	Pre-process on token deletion	S1
acPreProcForDeleteUser	Pre-process for user delete	S1
acPreProcForGenQuery		S1
acPreProcForModifyAccessControl	Pre-process for modification of ACLs on data or collection	S1
acPreProcForModifyAVUMetadata	Pre-process for modification of AVU metadata for data/collection/resource/user	S1
acPreProcForModifyCollMeta	Pre-process on modification of collection metadata	S1, S5
acPreProcForModifyDataObjMeta	Pre-process on modification of data metadata	S1, S2
acPreProcForModifyResource	Pre-process on resource modification	S1
acPreProcForModifyUser	Pre-process for user modify	S1
acPreProcForModifyUserGroup	Pre-process for user Group modify	S1
acPreProcForObjRename	Pre-process for moving a file	S1, S2
acPreprocForRmColl	Pre-process for collection delete	S1, S5
acRenameLocalZone	Rename the Data Grid Zone from the name "oldZone" to the name "newZone"	S1
acRescQuotaPolicy		

acSetChkFilePathPerm		S1,S3,S4
acSetMultiReplPerResc	Specify number of copies per resource	S1
acSetNumThreads	Set the default number of threads for data transfers	S1
acSetPublicUserPolicy	Set policy for allowed operations by public	S1
acSetRescSchemeForCreate	Pre-process on file create, define selection scheme for default resource	S1, S2
acSetRescSchemeForRepl		
acSetReServerNumProc		S1
acSetVaultPathPolicy	Set policy for assigning physical path name	S1, S3, S4
acTicketPolicy		
acTrashPolicy	Set policy for using trash can	S1, S2
acVacuum	Optimize the Postgresql database after waiting "arg1" specified time. See delay Microservice	S1

APPENDIX D: Persistent State Variable Sets for Each Microservice

Microservice		Persistent State Set
-	Negation operator for arithmetic	0
!	Negation operator for boolean variables	0
!=	Negation operation for conditional test	0
.	Structure operator for extracting variables from structure	0
*	Workflow variable	0
/	Division operator for arithmetic	0
&&	And operator for query	0
%	Module operator for arithmetic	0
%%	Or operator for query	0
^	Exponentiation operator for arithmetic	0
^^	Calculate nth root for arithmetic	0
+	Addition operator for arithmetic	0
++	Addition operator for strings	0
<	Less than operator for conditional tests	0
<=	less than or equal operator for conditional tests	0
=	Assignment operator for variables	0
==	Equal operator for conditional tests	0
>	Greater than operator for conditional tests	0
>=	Greater than or equal operator for conditional tests	0
||	Or operator for query	0
abs	Absolute value operator for arithmetic	0
applyAllRules	Apply all rules	0
average	Average operator for arithmetic	0
bool	Boolean type operator	0
break	Break loop execution operator for workflow	0
ceiling	Calculate closest larger integer for arithmetic	0
cons	List definition operator	0
cut	No retry operator on failure for workflow	0
datetime	Date-time converter for workflow	0
datetimef	Data-time formatted converter for workflow	0
delay	Delay execution of a rule	60
double	Double type operator	0
elem	List element operator	0
errorcode	Trap error code operator for workflow	0
errormsg	Trap error message operator for workflow	0
Eval	Evaluate code	0
exp	Exponentiation operator for arithmetic	0
Fail	Fail operator for workflow	0
floor	Calculate closest lower integer for arithmetic	0
for	For loop operator for workflow	0
foreach	For each loop operator for workflow list	0
hd	Calculate the head of a list	0
if	Conditional test for workflow	0
int	Integer type operator	0
let	Define function variables in an expression	0
like	Similarity operator for query	0
like regex	Similarity operator for query	0
list	List structure type	0
log	Logarithm operator for arithmetic	0
match	Matches a string against a regular expression	0
max	Maximum operator for arithmetic	0
min	Minimum operator for arithmetic	0
msiAclPolicy	Set access control policy	0
msiAddConditionToGenQuery	Add condition to a general query	0
msiAddKeyVal	Add key-value pair to an in-memory structure	0
msiAddKeyValToMspStr	Add key-value pair to an in-memory structure for concatenating command arguments	0
msiAddSelectFieldToGenQuery	Add select field to a general query	0

msiAddUserToGroup	Admin - add a user to a group	66
msiAdmAddAppRuleStruct	Admin - add rules to an in-memory structure	0
msiAdmClearAppRuleStruct	Admin - clear rules from the in-memory structure	0
msiAdmShowCoreRE	Admin - list rules from rule base (core.re file)	0
msiAdmShowDVM	Admin - list persistent state names	0
msiAdmShowFNM	Admin - list function names (microservices)	0
msiAssociateKeyValuePairsToObj	Add attribute-value-units to a digital object, specified as key-value pairs	7
msiBytesBufToStr	Format a buffer into a string	0
msiCheckAccess	Check access control	28
msiCheckHostAccessControl	Check host access control	65
msiCheckOwner	Check owner of a digital object	0
msiCheckPermission	Check access permissions	0
msiCloseGenQuery	Close the memory structure for a general query	0
msiCollCreate	Create a collection	24
msiCollectionSpider	Apply workflow to digital objects in a collection	15
msiCollRepl	Replicate a collection	18
msiCollRsync	Recursively synchronize a source collection with a target collection	14
msiCommit	Commit a change to the metadata catalog	0
msiCopyAVUMetadata	Copy attribute-value-units between digital objects	27
msiCreateCollByAdmin	Admin - create a collection	2
msiCreateUser	Admin - create a user	63
msiCreateUserAccountsFromDataObj	Create user accounts specified in a list in a digital object	20
msiCutBufferInHalf	Decrease size of an in-memory buffer	0
msiDataObjAutoMove	Move a file into a destination collection	13
msiDataObjChksum	Checksum a digital object	15
msiDataObjClose	Close a digital object	47
msiDataObjCopy	Copy a digital object	16
msiDataObjCreate	Create a digital object	13
msiDataObjGet	Get a digital object	13
msiDataObjLseek	Seek to a location in a digital object	0
msiDataObjOpen	Open a digital object	20
msiDataObjPhymv	Physically move a digital object	22
msiDataObjPut	Put a digital object into the data grid	0
msiDataObjRead	Read a digital object	0
msiDataObjRename	Rename a digital object	13
msiDataObjRepl	Replicate a digital object	13
msiDataObjRsync	Synchronize a digital object with an iRODS collection	15
msiDataObjTrim	Delete selected replicas of a digital object	13
msiDataObjUnlink	Delete a digital object	20
msiDataObjWrite	Write a digital object	0
msiDeleteCollByAdmin	Admin- delete a collection	36
msiDeleteDisallowed	Turn off deletion for a digital object	0
msiDeleteUnusedAVUs	Delete unused attribute-value-unit triplets	52
msiDeleteUser	Delete a user	67
msiDeleteUsersFromDataObj	Delete users specified in a list in a digital object	20
msiDigestMonStat	Generate and store load factors for monitoring resources	61
msiDoSomething	Template for constructing a new microservice	0
msiExecCmd	Execute a remote command	0
msiExecGenQuery	Execute general query	user defined
msiExecStrCondQuery	Convert a string to a query and execute	user defined
msiExit	Add a user explanation to the error stack	0
msiExportRecursiveCollMeta	Recursively export collection metadata into a buffer using pipe-delimited format	33
msiExtractTemplateMDFromBuf	Use a template to apply pattern matching to a buffer and extract key-value pairs	0
msiFlagDataObjwithAVU	Add an attribute-value-unit to a digital object	27
msiFlagInfectedObjs	Parse the output from clamscan and flag infected objects	20
msiFloatToString	Convert a binary variable to a string	0
msiFlushMonStat	Delete old usage monitoring statistics	0
msiFreeBuffer	Free space allocated to an in-memory buffer	0
msiGetCollectionACL	Get access controls for a collection	6

msiGetCollectionContentsReport	Generate a report of collection contents	34
msiGetCollectionPSmeta	Get attribute-value-units from a collection in pipe-delimited format	38
msiGetCollectionSize	Get the size of a collection	35
msiGetContInxFromGenQueryOut	Get continuation index for whether additional rows are available for a query result	0
msiGetDataObjACL	Get access control list for a digital object	19
msiGetDataObjAIP	Create XML file containing system and descriptive metadata	12
msiGetDataObjAVUs	Get attribute-value-units from a digital object	32
msiGetDataObjPSmeta	Get attribute-value-units from a digital object in pipe-delimited format	32
msiGetDiffTime	Get the difference between two system times	0
msiGetIcatTime	Get the system time from the metadata catalog	0
msiGetMoreRows	Get more query results	0
msiGetObjectPath	Convert from in-memory structure to string for printing	0
msiGetObjType	Get the type of digital object (file, collection, user, resource)	31
msiGetQuote	Get stock quotation by accessing external web service	0
msiGetRescAddr	Get the IP address of a storage resource	0
msiGetSessionVarValue	Get value of a session variable from in-memory structure	0
msiGetStderrInExecCmdOut	Retrieve standard error from remote command execution	0
msiGetStdoutInExecCmdOut	Retrieve standard out from remote command execution	0
msiGetSystemTime	Get the system time from the iRODS server	0
msiGetTaggedValueFromString	Use pattern-based extraction to retrieve a value for a tag from a string	0
msiGetUserACL	Get access control list for a user	30
msiGetUserInfo	Get information about a user	64
msiGetValByKey	Extract a value from in-memory structure that holds result of a query	0
msiGoodFailure	Force failure in a workflow without initiating recovery procedures	0
msiHumanToSystemTime	Convert human time format to system time format	0
msiListEnabledMS	List enabled microservices	0
msiMakeGenQuery	Make a general query	0
msiMakeQuery	Construct a query	0
msiMergeDataCopies	Merge multiple collections to create an authoritative version	17
msiNoChkFilePathPerm	Set policy for checking the file path permission when registering a physical file path	0
msiNoTrashCan	Set policy for use of trash can	0
msiobjget_http	Get an http page from a registered web site	0
msiobjget_irods	Get a file from a registered iRODS path name	0
msiobjget_slink	Get a digital object referenced by a soft link to an iRODS data grid	20
msiobjput_http	Write a registered http page	0
msiobjput_irods	Write a registered iRODS digital object	0
msiobjput_slink	Write a registered iRODS digital object in a remote iRODS data grid	0
msiObjStat	Get status of digital object for workflow	21
msiOprDisallowed	Disallow an operation	0
msiPhyBundleColl	Physically bundle a collection	23
msiPhyPathReg	Register a physical path	0
msiPrintGenQueryInp	Print a general query	0
msiPrintGenQueryOutToBuffer	Write contents of output results from a general query into a buffer	0
msiPrintKeyValPair	Print a key value pair returned from a query	0
msiQuota	Admin - calculate storage usage and check storage quotas	46
msiReadMDTemplateIntoTagStruct	Parse a buffer holding a tag template and store the tags in an in-memory tag structure	0
msiRecursiveCollCopy	Recursively copy a collection	5
msiRemoveKeyValuePairsFromObj	Remove attribute-value-unit from digital object, specified as key-value pair	28
msiRenameCollection	Rename a collection	8
msiRenameLocalZone	Admin - Rename the local zone (data grid)	40
msiRmColl	Remove a collection	39
msiRollback	Roll back a database transaction	0
msiSendMail	Send e-mail message	0
msiSendStdoutAsEmail	Send standard output as an e-mail message	0
msiServerBackup	Backup an iRODS server to a local vault	3
msiServerMonPerf	Monitor server performance	57
msiSetACL	Set an access control	4
msiSetBulkPutPostProcPolicy	Control acPostProcForPut policy when using a bulk put operation	0
msiSetChkFilePathPerm	Disallow non-admin user from registering files	0

msiSetDataObjAvoidResc	Disallow use of a storage resource	0
msiSetDataObjPreferredResc	Set the preferred storage resource	0
msiSetDataType	Set the type of digital object (file, collection, user, resource)	41
msiSetDataTypeFromExt	Set a recognized data type for a digital object based on its extension	42
msiSetDefaultResc	Set the default storage resource	0
msiSetGraftPathScheme	Define the physical path name for storing files	0
msiSetMultiReplPerResc	Allow multiple replicas to exist on the same storage resource	0
msiSetNoDirectRescInp	Define a list of resources that cannot be used by a normal user	0
msiSetNumThreads	Set the number of threads used for parallel I/O	0
msiSetPublicUserOpr	Set a list of operations that can be performed by the user "public"	0
msiSetQuota	Set resource usage quota	55
msiSetRandomScheme	Set the physical path name based on a randomly generated path	0
msiSetReplComment	Set data object comment field	29
msiSetRescQuotaPolicy	Turn resource quotas on or off	0
msiSetRescSortScheme	Set the scheme used for selecting a storage resource	0
msiSetReServerNumProc	Set the number of execution threads for processing rules	0
msiSetResource	Set the resource to use within a workflow	0
msiSleep	Sleep for a specified interval	0
msiSortDataObj	Sort the order in which resources will be accessed to retrieve a replicated digital object	0
msiSplitPath	Split a path into a collection and file name	0
msiStageDataObj	Stage a digital object to a specified resource	0
msiStrArray2String	Convert an array of strings to a list of strings separated by "%"	0
msiStrCat	Concatenate a string to a target string	0
msiStrchop	Remove the last character of a string	0
msiString2KeyValPair	Convert a string to a key-value pair in memory structure	0
msiString2StrArray	Convert a list of strings separated by "%" to an in-memory array of strings	0
msiStripAVUs	Remove attribute-value-units from a digital object	28
msiStrlen	Get the length of a string	0
msiStrToBytesBuf	Load a string into an in-memory buffer	0
msiStructFileBundle	Create a bundle of files in a collection for export as a tar file	13
msiSysChksumDataObj	Checksum a digital object	45
msiSysMetaModify	Modify system metadata attributes	43
msiSysReplDataObj	Admin - replicate a digital object	18
msiTarFileCreate	Create a tar file	47
msiTarFileExtract	Extract files from a tar file	20
msiVacuum	Optimize indices in the metadata catalog	0
msiWriteRodsLog	Write a string into iRODS/server/log/rodsLog	0
nop	Null operation	0
not like	Not like operator for query	0
not like regex	Not like operator for query using regular expression	0
remote	Execute rule at a remote site	0
setelem	Set an element in a list	0
size	Return the number of elements in a list	0
split	Split a string	0
str	Convert a variable to a string	0
strlen	Return the length of a string	0
substr	Create a specified sub-string	0
succeed	Cause a workflow to immediately succeed (workflow operator)	0
time	Get the current time	0
timestr	Convert a datetime variable to a string	0
timestrf	Convert a datetime variable to a string using a format	0
tl	Calculate the tail of a list	0
triml	Trim a prefix of a string	0
trimr	Trim a suffix of a string	0
while	While loop (workflow operator)	0
writeLine	Write a line to standard output or standard error	0
writePosInt	Write a positive integer to standard output or standard error	0
writeString	Write a string to standard output or standard error	0
writeBytesBuf	Write a buffer to standard output or standard error	0
writeKeyValPairs	Write key-value pairs to standard output or standard error from an in-memory structure	0
writeString	Write a string to standard output or standard error	0

APPENDIX E. Persistent State Variable Sets

The sets of persistent state information are listed in table in this appendix. Each persistent state information set identifies whether a persistent state:

- 1 – attribute is read
- 2 – attribute is modified
- 3 – attribute is both read and modified.

Persistent State Variable Sets	2	3	4	5	6	7	8	9	10	11	12	13	14	15	16	17	18	19	20	21	22	23
Number of microservices	1	1	1	1	1	1	1	1	1	1	1	10	1	3	1	1	2	1	1	1	1	1
COLL_ACCESS_COLL_ID	2	3	3	1	1	1	1	1	1													
COLL_ACCESS_TYPE	2	3	3	1	1	1	1	1	1													
COLL_ACCESS_USER_ID	2	3	3	1	1	1	1	1	1													
COLL_CREATE_TIME	2	3	1	1				1	1	1	1	1	1	1	1	1	1	1	1	1	1	1
COLL_ID	3	3	1	1	1	1	1	3	1	1	1	1	1	1	1	1	1	1	1	1	1	1
COLL_INHERITANCE		1							1	1												
COLL_MODIFY_TIME	2	3	1	1			2	1	1	1	1	1	1	1	1	3	1	1	1	1	1	1
COLL_NAME	3	3	1	1	1	1	1	3	1	1	1	1	1	1	1	1	1	1	1	1	1	1
COLL_OWNER_NAME	2	3	1	1				1	1	1	1	1	1	1	1	1	1	1	1	1	1	1
COLL_OWNER_ZONE	2	3	1	1				1	1	1	1	1	1	1	1	1	1	1	1	1	1	1
COLL_PARENT_NAME	2	2					3						1									
DATA_ACCESS_DATA_ID		3	1	1	1	1	1		1	1	1	1	1	1	1	1	1	1				
DATA_ACCESS_TYPE		3	1	1	1	1	1		1	1	1	1	1	1	1	1	1	1				
DATA_ACCESS_USER_ID		3	1	1	1	1	1		1	1	1	1	1	1	1	1	1	1				
DATA_CHECKSUM				1				3	2	1	1	1	3	3	3	1	3	1	1	1	2	
DATA_COLL_ID		1	1	1	1	1	1		1	2	1	1	1	1	1	1	3	3	1	1	1	
DATA_COMMENTS				1						1	1	1	1	1	1	1	3		1			
DATA_CREATE_TIME				1				3	2	1	1	1	1	1	1	1	3	1	1	1		
DATA_EXPIRY				1						1	1	1	1	1	1	1	3		1			
DATA_ID		1	1	1	1	1	1	3	2	1	1	1	1	1	1	1	3	1	1	1		
DATA_MAP_ID				1						1	1	1	1	1	1	1	3		1			
DATA_MODIFY_TIME				1				3	2	1	1	1	1	3	3	3	1	1	1			
DATA_NAME		1	1	1	1	1	1	3	2	1	1	1	1	1	1	1	3	1	1	1		
DATA_OWNER_NAME				1				3	2	1	1	1	1	1	1	1	3	1	1	1		
DATA_OWNER_ZONE				1				3	2	1	1	1	1	1	1	1	3	1	1	1		
DATA_PATH				1				3	2	1	1	1	1	1	1	1	3		1		2	
DATA_REPL_NUM				1				3	2	1	1	1	1	1	1	1	3		1			
DATA_RESC_GROUP_NAME				1				2	2	1	1	1	1	1	1	1	3		1		2	
DATA_RESC_NAME				1				3	2	1	1	1	1	1	1	1	3		1		2	
DATA_SIZE				1				3	2	1	1	1	1	1	1	1	3	1	1	1		2
DATA_STATUS				1						1	1	1	1	1	1	1	3		1			
DATA_TYPE_NAME				1				2	2	1	1	1	1	1	1	1	3		1			
DATA_VERSION				1				2	2	1	1	1	1	1	1	1	3		1			
META_COLL_ATTR_ID			2			3																
META_COLL_ATTR_NAME			2			3																
META_COLL_ATTR_UNITS			2			3																
META_COLL_ATTR_VALUE			2			3																
META_COLL_CREATE_TIME			2			3																
META_COLL_MODIFY_TIME			2			3																
META_DATA_ATTR_ID			2			3				3												
META_DATA_ATTR_NAME			2			3				1	1											
META_DATA_ATTR_UNITS			2			3				1	1											
META_DATA_ATTR_VALUE			2			3				1	1											
META_DATA_CREATE_TIME			2			3				2												
META_DATA_MODIFY_TIME			2			3				2												
TOKEN_ID	1	1	1	1	1	1	1	1	1	1	1	1	1	1	1	1	1	1				
TOKEN_NAME	1	1	1	1	1	1	1	1	1	1	1	1	1	1	1	1	1	1				
TOKEN_NAMESPACE	1	1	1	1	1	1	1	1	1	1	1	1	1	1	1	1	1	1				

Persistent State Variable Sets	2	3	4	5	6	7	8	9	10	11	12	13	14	15	16	17	18	19	20	21	22	23
USER_GROUP_ID		1	1	1	1	1	1	1		1		1	1	1	1	1						
USER_ID	1	1	1	1	1	1	1	1	1	1	1	1	1	1	1	1	1	1				
USER_NAME	1	1	1	1	1	1	1	1	1	1	1	1	1	1	1	1	1	1				
USER_TYPE		1	1		1	1	1	1	1			1	1	1	1	1						
USER_ZONE	1		1	1	1	1	1	1	1			1	1	1	1	1						
ZONE_NAME			1																			
ZONE_TYPE			1																			

Additional persistent state attribute sets for operations on files and collections.

Persistent State Variable Sets	24	25	26	27	28	29	30	31	32	33	34	35	36	37	38	39	40	41	42	43	44	45	46	47
Number of microservices	1	1	1	3	3	1	1	2	2	1	1	1	1	1	1	1	1	1	1	1	1	1	1	2
COLL_CREATE_TIME	1																							
COLL_ID	1	1	1	1	1	1	1	1	1	1	1	1	1	1	1	1								
COLL_MODIFY_TIME	1																	2	2					
COLL_NAME	1	1	1	1	1	1	1	1	1	1	1	1	1	1	1	2								
COLL_OWNER_NAME	1																							
COLL_OWNER_ZONE	1																	2							
COLL_PARENT_NAME												1						2						
DATA_ACCESS_DATA_ID		1	1	1	1	1	1											1	1	1	1	1		
DATA_ACCESS_TYPE		1	1	1	1	1	1											1	1	1	1			
DATA_ACCESS_USER_ID		1	1	1	1	1	1											1	1	1	1			
DATA_CHECKSUM		1	3																				2	
DATA_COLL_ID		1	1	1	1	1	1	1	1	1	1	1	1											
DATA_COMMENTS		1	1		2															2				
DATA_CREATE_TIME		1	1																					
DATA_EXPIRY		1	1																	2				
DATA_ID		1	1	1	1	1	1	1	1	1	1							1	1	1	1	1		
DATA_MAP_ID		1	1																					
DATA_MODIFY_TIME		1	1															2			2			
DATA_NAME		1	1	1	1	1	1	1	1	1														
DATA_OWNER_NAME		1	1																				1	
DATA_OWNER_ZONE		1	1															2					1	
DATA_PATH		1	1							1														
DATA_REPL_NUM		1	1								1								1	1	1	1		
DATA_RESC_GROUP_NAME		1	1																				1	
DATA_RESC_NAME		1	1																					
DATA_SIZE		1	1								1												1	2
DATA_STATUS		1	1																					
DATA_TYPE_NAME		1	1							1								2	2	2				
DATA_VERSION		1	1																					
META_COLL_ATTR_ID									1					1										
META_COLL_ATTR_NAME									1					1										
META_COLL_ATTR_UNITS									1					1										
META_COLL_ATTR_VALUE									1					1										
META_DATA_ATTR_ID				2				1	1															
META_DATA_ATTR_NAME				2				1	1															
META_DATA_ATTR_UNITS				2				1	1															
META_DATA_ATTR_VALUE				2				1	1															
META_DATA_CREATE_TIME				2																				
META_DATA_MODIFY_TIME				2																				
QUOTA_LIMIT																							1	
QUOTA_MODIFY_TIME																							2	
QUOTA_OVER																							2	
QUOTA_RESC_ID																							3	
QUOTA_USAGE																							3	
QUOTA_USAGE_RESC_ID																							1	
QUOTA_USAGE_USER_ID																							1	
QUOTA_USER_ID																							3	

Persistent State Variable Sets	24	25	26	27	28	29	30	31	32	33	34	35	36	37	38	39	40	41	42	43	44	45	46	47
RESC_ID																							1	
RESC_MODIFY_TIME																	2							
RESC_NAME			1																				1	
RESC_ZONE_NAME																	2							
RESC_VAULT_PATH			1																					
RULE_MODIFY_TIME																	2							
RULE_OWNER_ZONE																	2							
TOKEN_ID		1	1	1	1	1												1	1	1	1			
TOKEN_NAME		1	1	1	1	1												1	1	1	1			
TOKEN_NAMESPACE		1	1	1	1	1												1	1	1	1			
USER_GROUP_ID		1	1	1	1	1												1	1	1	1	1	1	
USER_ID		1	1	1	1	1	1											1	1	1	1	1	1	
USER_MODIFY_TIME																	2							
USER_NAME		1	1	1	1	1	1											1	1	1	1	1	1	
USER_TYPE		1	1	1	1	1												1	1	1	1		1	
USER_ZONE		1	1	1	1	1											2	1	1	1	1		1	
ZONE_ID																	1							
ZONE_MODIFY_TIME																	2							
ZONE_NAME																	3							

Persistent state attributes modified by microservices for audit trails, rules, and users

Persistent State Variable Sets	1	48	49	50	51	52	53	54	55	56	57	58	59	60	61	62	63	64	65	66	67
Number of microservices	5	1	1	1	1	1	1	1	1	3	1	1	2	1	1	1	1	1	1	1	1
AUDIT_ACTION_ID	1																				
AUDIT_COMMENT	1																				
AUDIT_CREATE_TIME	1																				
AUDIT_MODIFY_TIME	1																				
AUDIT_OBJ_ID	1																				
AUDIT_USER_ID	1																				
DVM_BASE_MAP_BASE_NAME		3	1																		
DVM_BASE_MAP_CREATE_TIME		2																			
DVM_BASE_MAP_MODIFY_TIME		2																			
DVM_BASE_MAP_OWNER_NAME		2																			
DVM_BASE_MAP_OWNER_ZONE		2																			
DVM_BASE_MAP_VERSION		3	1																		
DVM_BASE_NAME		3																			
DVM_CONDITION		3	1																		
DVM_CREATE_TIME		2																			
DVM_EXT_VAR_NAME		3	1																		
DVM_ID		3	1																		
DVM_INT_MAP_PATH		3	1																		
DVM_MODIFY_TIME		2																			
DVM_OWNER_NAME		2																			
DVM_OWNER_ZONE		2																			
DVM_VERSION		2																			
FNM_BASE_MAP_BASE_NAME				1	2																
FNM_BASE_MAP_CREATE_TIME					2																
FNM_BASE_MAP_MODIFY_TIME					2																
FNM_BASE_MAP_OWNER_NAME					2																
FNM_BASE_MAP_OWNER_ZONE					2																
FNM_BASE_MAP_VERSION				1	2																
FNM_BASE_NAME					3																
FNM_CREATE_TIME					2																
FNM_EXT_FUNC_NAME				1	3																
FNM_ID				1	3																

Persistent State Variable Sets	1	48	49	50	51	52	53	54	55	56	57	58	59	60	61	62	63	64	65	66	67
FNM_INT_FUNC_NAME				1	3																
FNM_MODIFY_TIME					2																
FNM_OWNER_NAME					2																
FNM_OWNER_ZONE					2																
META_COLL_ATTR_ID						2															
META_DATA_ATTR_ID						2															
MSRVC_MODULE_NAME							1	2													
MSRVC_NAME							1	2													
MSRVC_SIGNATURE							1	2													
MSRVC_VERSION							1	2													
MSVRC_HOST							1	2													
MSVRC_ID							1	2													
MSVRC_LANGUAGE							1	2													
MSVRC_LOCATION							1	2													
MSVRC_STATUS							1	2													
MSVRC_TYPE_NAME							1	2													
QUOTA_LIMIT									3												
QUOTA_MODIFY_TIME									2												
QUOTA_OVER									2												
QUOTA_RESC_ID									3												
QUOTA_USAGE									1												
QUOTA_USAGE_RESC_ID									1												
QUOTA_USAGE_USER_ID									1												
QUOTA_USER_ID									3												
RESC_GROUP_RESC_ID										1											
RESC_GROUP_NAME										1											
RESC_ID									1	1											
RESC_NAME									1	1	1										
RESC_ZONE_NAME									1												
RESC_VAULT_PATH											1										
RULE_BASE_MAP_BASE_NAME												3	1								
RULE_BASE_MAP_CREATE_TIME												2									
RULE_BASE_MAP_MODIFY_TIME												2									
RULE_BASE_MAP_OWNER_NAME												2									
RULE_BASE_MAP_OWNER_ZONE												2									
RULE_BASE_MAP_PRIORITY												2	1								
RULE_BASE_MAP_VERSION												3	1								
RULE_BASE_NAME												1									
RULE_BODY												1	1								
RULE_CONDITION												1	1								
RULE_EVENT												1	1								
RULE_EXEC_ADDRESS														2							
RULE_EXEC_ESTIMATED_EXE_TIME														2							
RULE_EXEC_FREQUENCY														2							
RULE_EXEC_ID														2							
RULE_EXEC_NAME														2							
RULE_EXEC_NOTIFICATION_ADDR														2							
RULE_EXEC_PRIORITY														2							
RULE_EXEC_REI_FILE_PATH														2							
RULE_EXEC_TIME														2							
RULE_EXEC_USER_NAME														2							
RULE_ID												3	1	1							
RULE_NAME												1	1								
RULE_RECOVERY												1	1								
SLD_RESC_NAME															1						
SLD_CREATE_TIME															1						
TOKEN_ID															1						
TOKEN_NAME															1	1					
TOKEN_NAMESPACE																1					
TOKEN_VALUE2															1						
USER_COMMENT																		1			

Persistent State Variable Sets	1	48	49	50	51	52	53	54	55	56	57	58	59	60	61	62	63	64	65	66	67
USER_CREATE_TIME																	2	1			
USER_GROUP_ID									1								2		1	2	
USER_ID									1								2	1	1	1	1
USER_INFO																		1			
USER_MODIFY_TIME																	2	1			
USER_NAME									1								2	1	1	1	1
USER_TYPE									1								2	1		1	
USER_ZONE									1								2	1		1	1
ZONE_NAME									1		1										
ZONE_TYPE									1		1										

AUTHOR BIOGRAPHIES

Chen, Sheau-Yen
Sheau-Yen Chen is a staff member at the University of California, San Diego and a long-term member of the DICE group. She has administered both Storage Resource Broker and iRODS data grids.

Conway, Mike
Mike Conway is a staff member of the Data Intensive Cyber Environments Center at the University of North Carolina at Chapel Hill. He leads the development of the Java client interface to iRODS. Mike has a B.S.B.A in Information Systems from Appalachian State University and an M.S.I.S. in Information and Library Science from the University of North Carolina at Chapel Hill.

Coposky, Jason
Jason Coposky is Chief Technologist of the iRODS Consortium. Jason has been at the Renaissance Computing Institute since 2006 and heading iRODS development since 2010. Jason has a B.S. in Computer Science from the University of Pittsburgh.

Moore, Reagan W.
Reagan Moore is a professor in the School of Information and Library Science at the University of North Carolina, Chapel Hill, chief scientist for Data Intensive Cyber Environments at the Renaissance Computing Institute, and director of the Data Intensive Cyber Environments Center at University of North Carolina. He coordinates research efforts in development of data grids, digital libraries, and preservation environments. Developed software systems include the Storage Resource Broker data grid and the integrated Rule-Oriented Data System. Supported projects include the National Archives and Records Administration Transcontinental Persistent Archive Prototype, and science data grids for seismology, oceanography, climate, high-energy physics, astronomy, and bioinformatics. An ongoing research interest is use of data grid technology to automate execution of management policies and validate trustworthiness of repositories. Dr. Moore's previous roles include the following: director of the DICE group at the San Diego Supercomputer Center, and Manager of production services at SDSC. He previously worked as a computational plasma physicist at General Atomics on equilibrium and stability of toroidal fusion devices. He has a Ph.D. in plasma physics from the University of California, San Diego (1978), and a B.S. in physics from the California Institute of Technology (1967).

Rajasekar, Arcot
Arcot Rajasekar is a professor in the School of Library and Information Science at the University of North Carolina, Chapel Hill, and a chief scientist at the Renaissance Computing Institute (RENCI). Previously, he was at the San Diego Supercomputer Center at the University of California, San Diego, leading the Data Grids Technology Group. He has been involved in research and development of data grid middleware systems for over a decade and is a lead originator behind the concepts in the Storage Resource Broker (SRB) and the integrated Rule Oriented Data Systems (iRODS), two premier data grid middleware developed by the Data Intensive Cyber Environments Group. Dr. Rajasekar has a Ph.D. in computer science from the University of Maryland at College Park and has more than 100 publications in the areas of data grids, logic programming, deductive databases, digital library, and persistent archives.

Russell, Terrell
Terrell Russell has been working on iRODS since 2008 when the DICE group first came to Chapel Hill. Terrell is now a Senior Data Management Research Scientist at the Renaissance Computing Institute (RENCI) and part of the iRODS Development Team. Terrell has B.S. and M.S. degrees from North Carolina State University in Computer Engineering, Information Technology and Service Organizations, and Computer Networking and a PhD in Information and Library Science from the University of North Carolina at Chapel Hill.

Schroeder, Wayne
Wayne Schroeder led the DICE (Data Intensive Cyber Environment) group of INC (Institute of Neural Science) at the University of California San Diego, was a senior software engineer with the iRODS team. He has over 35 years of experience in software engineering, with expertise in data management, computer security, networking, scientific applications, high performance computing, and system support/administration. Besides iRODS, career highlights include six years at LLNL (the Lawrence Livermore National Laboratory) - primarily at the NMFECC (National Magnetic Fusion Energy Computer Center), many years at SDSC (the San Diego Supercomputer Center) where he contributed to its successful launch, managed the SDSC Central Systems Software group, and developed computer security software, and 2 years at a start-up (Entropia) helping to develop a cycle harvesting system. He earned a B.S. in computer science in 1976, magna cum laude, with a minor in psychology.

de Torcy, Antoine
Antoine de Torcy began working the DICE group in 2003, first at the University of California, San Diego, and since 2008, at the University of North Carolina, Chapel Hill. He is now part of the iRODS Development Team at the Renaissance Computing Institute (RENCI). His technical expertise has helped various groups build preservation environments based on iRODS and focused on data and metadata. Antoine holds an engineering degree in applied mathematics and computer science from the University of Paris–Dauphine.

Wan, Michael
Michael Wan led the DICE (Data Intensive Cyber Environment) group of the INC (Institute of Neural Science) at the University of California, San Diego. He was the chief software architect of the integrated Rule-Oriented Data System (iRODS) through 3.3 and the Storage Resource Broker (SRB). Before SRB, Michael spent 10 years developing operating systems and archival storage systems at SDSC. Michael received his B.S. degree from Illinois State University and M.S. from Georgia Institute of Technology.

Ward, Jewel H.
Jewel Ward has been working with iRODS since 2007 and has been a part of the DICE group since 2009. Jewel received her PhD in Library and Information Science from the University of North Carolina at Chapel Hill. Prior to beginning the doctoral program, she was a Program Manager for the Digital Archive at the University of Southern California and a Post-master's Research Assistant in the Research Library at Los Alamos National Laboratory.

Xu, Hao
Hao Xu is a Research Scientist in the Data Intensive Cyber Environments group at the University of North Carolina at Chapel Hill. He has been working on improving the rule engine and the rule language of iRODS since 2010. His research interests include automatic theorem proving, programming languages, distributed data systems, and formal methods in software development. He graduated from Beihang University with a B.E. in Computer Science and Engineering and a B.S. minor in Applied Mathematics and has a PhD in Computer Science from the University of North Carolina at Chapel Hill.

INDEX OF MICROSERVICES